HIDDEN GOD

WORKS OF THE AUTHOR IN ENGLISH

Epistemology. New York, Wagner, 1949.

Ontology. New York, Wagner, 1952.

Aristotle in the West. Louvain, Nauwelaerts, 1955.

The Philosophical Movement in the Thirteenth Century. Edin-

burgh, Nelson, 1955.

FERNAND VAN STEENBERGHEN
PROFESSOR AT THE UNIVERSITY OF LOUVAIN

HIDDEN GOD

HOW DO WE KNOW
THAT GOD EXISTS ?

*Vere tu es Deus absconditus,
Deus Israel Salvator!*
(Isaias, XLV, 15)

TRANSLATED BY
THEODORE CROWLEY, O.F.M.

READER IN SCHOLASTIC PHILOSOPHY AT
THE QUEEN'S UNIVERSITY, BELFAST

PUBLICATIONS
UNIVERSITAIRES DE LOUVAIN
2, PLACE CARDINAL MERCIER
LOUVAIN

B. HERDER BOOK CO.
314 NORTH JEFFERSON
SAINT LOUIS
MISSOURI 63103

1966

IMPRIMATUR

Lovanii, die 8 Septembris 1965.

† Albertus DESCAMPS,
Ep. Tuneten., Rect. Univ.

69713

CONTENTS

PREFACE

In hope that this little book will answer an appeal that is often heard and that is becoming more insistent from day to day.

On the one hand, intellectual confusion has never been so profound. As a result of the upheavals due to two world wars, all traditional values are called in question and men are groping for a way out in an atmosphere saturated with scepticism. Many go so far as to ask if life has meaning. Under various influences, which we shall have to diagnose, the old religious beliefs are, in many circles, going through an acute crisis and the number of atheists or agnostics shows an alarming increase.

On the other hand, many well-meaning people complain that religious literature provides no satisfactory answer to their problem. They are disappointed with works written to defend the main theistic positions: the arguments proposed are not entirely satisfactory; they are surprisingly confused on many points and they offend against logical cogency. Some difficulties are passed over and consequently remain unanswered.

In Great Britain, the controversies recently stirred up by the work of Dr. Robinson, *Honest to God*, show the interest taken in religious questions and the extreme confusion that surrounds ideas concerning the problem of God (his existence and nature) and the correlative problem of the appropriate human religious attitudes.

The issues at stake in the controversy dividing theists and atheists are so essential, so vital for each one of us, that no effort can be spared to ensure the triumph of truth. Now, I believe that defenders of the theistic thesis are often victims of a slavish attachment to certain scholastic traditions which are an embarrassment and prevent them from adopting a critical attitude towards positions now out of date.

Provided we rid ourselves of these shackles, I believe that the exposition and solution of this important problem can be considerably improved. That is the purpose of this essay. Its aim is to bring order and clarity into our ideas by putting the problem in its proper setting, by clearing up misunderstandings and by ruling out positions deemed untenable. It is for the reader to judge how success-fully this has been achieved.

It would be well, however, not to lose sight of the nature and level of this work. It is not an advanced scientific treatise aiming at an exhaustive study of a very limited theme. It is addressed to a wide public of educated readers and the problem it studies is one with innumerable conn-exions. The inevitable result is that certain aspects of this vast problem are barely outlined and that criticism of cer-tain positions deemed indefensible may appear rather hurried. That is why it is indispensable to note the panoramic nature of this exposition. If, at times, the reader cannot find here a satisfactory answer to all his questions, let him keep in mind our aim in this essay: it is not an exhaustive examination, but an introduction and general survey meant to guide and stimulate the educated man in his personal reflections, with the help of suitable reading.

The English translation is the work of my colleague and friend, Rev. Fr. Theodore Crowley, O.F.M., Reader in Scholastic Philosophy at The Queen's University, Belfast. I have the impression (in so far as I am able to judge) that he has done his work well. I have great pleasure in expressing my deep gratitude to him for his generous collaboration. The translator has adapted, for the benefit of English-speaking readers, the select bibliography given at the end of the volume.

Louvain, 7th of October, 1965.

CHAPTER I

THE PROBLEM

Is there a "problem" of the existence of God? In some Christian circles it is not rare to find people who are timorous and who grow angry and protest at the mere mention of the "problem" of the existence of God. They are not prepared to admit that the existence of God can be treated "problematically", as if it belonged to the category of debatable, and, to that extent, uncertain, opinions. They assert with a vehemence not always free from passion that the existence of God is a truth universally admitted by all who are in good faith and whose minds are not overcast by adverse prejudices or by looseness of morals. They conclude that there are no bona fide atheists, except, perhaps, in cases where normal thinking processes are disturbed by intellectual deformation.

In the eyes of these people a "proof" of God's existence presents no difficulty and is almost superfluous. At best it can only serve to confirm, by formal reasoning, the conviction reached by spontaneous reflection on the human situation. And if a Christian intellectual talks to an ecclesiastic to tell him about his difficulties regarding the existence of God or of Providence, the only answer he may get is the trite advice: "Don't worry; they are only temptations. Get rid of them by prayer and don't allow your thoughts to dwell on them".

This attitude corresponds to that of the theologians who hold that there can be no convinced atheists. So natural to man is knowledge of the supreme Being that only bad faith, intellectual deformation or moral perversity could explain the position of those who deny the existence of God.

Without going into the question of atheism *in extenso*, we shall make a few observations in order to dispel various misunderstandings.

Atheism

It is possible that there are no *atheists properly so called* or *positive atheists*, if we understand by that men who are sincerely convinced of the non-existence of God as a result of having demonstrated to themselves the *impossibility* of his existence. To show that a hypothesis is absurd, it is necessary to show either that it is self-contradictory or that it contradicts something known to be true. Demonstrations of this kind occur frequently in the rational sciences — in mathematics, for example. In experimental and observational sciences one could conceive the rejection of some hypothesis touching the *nature* or *properties* of a body if it contradicted some duly established scientific law. But it is not easy to see how one could prove scientifically the *non-existence* of anything whatever. How could the zoologist demonstrate the *impossibility* of an animal species mentioned in Assyrian or Greek mythology? All that can be expected from the scientist is the statement that no traces have ever been discovered of dragons or unicorns — either as actually existing animal species or as vanished species of which fossils have been unearthed.

How metaphysics could positively eliminate the "God" hypothesis is just as difficult to estimate. Though it relies to some extent on experience, metaphysics is *par excellence* a rational science and consequently can and, in fact, does contain demonstrations *ab absurdo*. But how could the absurdity of the hypothesis "God" be demonstrated? Suppose that there is no way of proving satisfactorily that the world of experience is caused: the conclusion would be agnosticism and the hypothesis "God" would be *gratuitous*; but it would not be *absurd*. To show that the hypothesis is absurd, it would be necessary to show that the theistic explanation is self-contradictory or that it contradicts some metaphysical law that we know is true. There is nothing to suggest that any metaphysician has ever succeeded in doing this. There seems even to be no way of setting about such a demonstration. By hypothesis God is transcendent and His mysterious reality cannot be expressed, positively and properly (*proprie*), in human concepts. Such a being is in no way open to a demonstration of non-existence *ab absurdo*.

Agnosticism

Though it is impossible in practice to demonstrate the non-existence of something, there are cases where it is possible to show that the existence of something is *unlikely* or *improbable*. It is improbable that dragons ever existed: they left no remains and their appearance in mythology can be easily explained by the fable-making proclivity of the human imagination. In like manner it is conceivable that some people might think that the hypothesis "God" is unlikely and that they would then be led to doubt seriously about his existence. When St. Thomas, at the beginning of the *Summa theologiae*, asks whether God exists (*Utrum Deus sit*), he begins (as is customary in the scholastic method of discussion) by giving two reasons against the existence of God. His choice of reasons is noteworthy.

The first concerns the existence of evil in the world: the existence of an infinitely good Being would seem to exclude the existence of his "contrary", i.e. of evil; but evil exists; it seems improbable therefore that an infinitely good Being exists.

The second reason is no less noteworthy: there is no need to appeal to causes that are superfluous; now, everything that happens in the world can be explained without recourse to the hypothesis "God", for all events are explained either by the laws of nature or by the action of human liberty; it seems therefore useless to bring in a transcendent Cause.

Unless we claim that the existence of God is self-evident — St. Thomas always denied this categorically — it is obvious that objections of this kind can give rise to grave doubts and serious wavering in regard to God's existence. Insofar as these doubts are not dispelled by a satisfactory and, therefore, convincing demonstration, it is only natural that people should adopt a waiting attitude or one of ignorance. It has a well-known name: *agnosticism*. There may be no true atheists, but there can be no doubt that there are agnostics and that their number has increased alarmingly since the beginning of the twentieth century.

Marxist Propaganda

Clear confirmation of what we have been saying about atheism and agnosticism is to be found in the anti-religious propaganda generously distributed by communist agencies. I have before me a series of pamphlets published in East Berlin(¹). Their object is to prove that, for the dialectical materialist, "eternal and infinite" matter is self-sufficient; that science can explain all phenomena, including the origin of life and man's appearance on the earth; that none of the classical proofs of God's existence can withstand criticism; and, finally, that nature's disorders seem to conflict with the hypothesis of an omnipotent and all-wise Creator. But even if one were to subscribe to all these statements, the non-existence of

(¹) The titles of these pamphlets are eloquent: Olof KLOHR, *Naturwissenschaft, Religion und Kirche* (1958); Herbert GUTE, *Glauben oder Wissen* (1958); G.A. GURJEW, *Wissenschaftliche Voraussicht-religiöses Vorurteil* (1958); Herbert PFAFFE, Karl-Heinz NEUMANN, *Kein Platz für Gott im Weltall* (1958); Rudolf ROCHHAUSEN, *Der Sputnik und der liebe Gott* (1958); Jacob SEGAL, *Wie das Leben auf der Erde entstand* (1958); Günter OSTMANN, Harald WESSEL, *Ist der Mensch von Gott erschaffen?* (1958).

God has not yet been demonstrated. The very most one could say is that His existence is not proved or that it seems unlikely. If they were logical, Marxists would profess that they were agnostics. Their atheism is a "dogma", a gratuitous and indemonstrable postulate. That they attach such great importance to it is due to the fact that religion, which is for them the opium of the people, seems to present a serious obstacle to man's emancipation. It must be said immediately, so as to avoid misunderstanding, that their criticisms are perfectly justified when they are directed against some puerile conceptions of God's omnipotence or providence, against the heavy-handed tactics defenders of orthodoxy sometimes employ when dealing with scientists (Marxists exploit incidents like the condemnation of Galileo very cleverly), and against the unholy alliance of some ecclesiastics with the upholders of antiquated social privileges.

Belief in God

The phenomenon of agnosticism is not perhaps as disturbing as superficial observation of contemporary society might lead one to believe. A Gallup inquiry into belief in God was carried out in the United States in 1954. Those interviewed were asked did they believe in God and, if so, what proof they found most convincing. It is surprising and consoling to observe that 96 % of Americans interviewed said that they were theists. As regards the proof they found most convincing, the answers can be classified in order of decreasing frequency as follows:

1. The order and beauty of the universe.

2. The need to find an explanation for the origin af man and of the world.
3. The teaching of the Bible (or of some ecclesiastical authority).
4. Experience of life.
5. Men find belief in God very consoling.

In its commentary on the results of this inquiry, the American weekly, *Time*, quotes Étienne Gilson, who remarked that the choice made by the Americans was not bad and that the primacy given to the proof from the order of the Cosmos could claim the authority of St. Paul (*Rom.* I, 20) [2].

The Gallup poll corroborates the opinion of many observers that, in spite of the practical materialism displayed in many fields in the United States, the Americans are, in the vast majority, a religious people. The same could be said for Canada, Latin America, Spain, Ireland, Greece, the Muslim world, and perhaps also for Italy, Portugal and Switzerland. Belief in an impersonal Absolute of a pantheistic kind would more likely be found among Buddhists and Hindus. Little is known about the state of affairs behind the Iron Curtain, but there are indications that the Slavs have not given up their belief in God despite the atheistic propaganda of militant communism.

An inquiry carried out recently among the youth of France led to surprising discoveries. Not only were 85% of them baptized, but 86% believed in the existence of God. Of the 14% who said they were atheists, 5%

[2] Cf. *Time*, January 10, 1955, p. 31.

admitted that they were not at all certain that God did not exist and they were, consequently, agnostics and not atheists (³). On the other hand, in the *Grandes Écoles* of Paris, 60% of the pupils are practising Catholics and 96% are theists.

These figures may appear reassuring and may indicate a welcome revival of religion in the rising generation, at least in France. But what would be the outcome of a survey taken in Germany, England, the Scandinavian countries, in some industrial regions of Belgium and France, in some university circles in Western Europe? There can be little doubt that agnosticism has many adepts in these areas and is rapidly gaining ground. This is a fact that it would be childish to deny. It has to be faced, firstly to explain it and subsequently to react against it by assisting those who genuinely seek truth.

The Causes of Agnosticism

How are we to account for the advance of agnosticism? We might spend a considerable length of time over superficial and secondary causes, i.e. causes pertaining to social factors: the practical materialism of a pleasure-seeking world, its forgetfulness of spiritual values, the contagiousness of religious indifference, especially in the

(³) The originator of this inquiry was M.G. Hourdin. Note also the following figures: 14% of young people believe that religion is opposed to science; 12% are of opinion that it might disappear one day and 7% feel that it takes from man's happiness. Cf. G. HOURDIN, *La nouvelle vague croit-elle en Dieu?* (Collection «*Tout le monde en parle*», 10), Paris, 1960.

lower social classes, the propaganda of militant atheism, particularly Marxist atheism. But beneath the surface, if you try to analyse the state of mind of an agnostic who thinks for himself, you will find to your astonishment that his agnosticism is due to one or other of the objections mentioned by St. Thomas — the scandal of evil and the uselessness of the theistic explanation.

Firstly, the *scandal of evil*. Contemporary literature is very revealing in this respect. In the XIXth century, the Romantics (Hugo, Lamartine, Musset, Vigny, especially Nerval, Baudelaire and Rimbaud) insisted on the miserable and "unbearable" condition of man on this earth. But the existentialists introduced descriptions that shocked people, accents of cruel realism, to express the tragic and "absurd" destiny of the human race. Albert Camus makes a diagnosis of "man in rebellion": "Metaphysical rebellion is the movement by which man rebels against his situation and against all creation. It is metaphysical because it contests the ends of man and of creation... The rebel contrasts the principle of justice which is in himself with the principle of injustice he sees at work in the world"[4]. Gabriel Marcel, for his part, considers "the pessimism more closely associated with those who sneer and those who swear rather than with those who sigh and those who weep" as one of the peculiarities of modern man[5]".

Here, as ever, literature is the reflection, the echo and the expression of life itself. Who has not heard, during

[4] A. CAMUS, *L'homme révolté*, Paris, 1951, pp. 39-40.

[5] In a collective work *Le mal est parmi nous*, Paris, 1951, p. 37.

the darkest hours of the war, the thoughts of people upset by the spectacle of unpunished monstrosities, of so much undeserved suffering, of the apparent triumph of violence and crime? In a great many cases, it is not the agnostic's belief in a transcendent Absolute that is shaken but his faith in Providence: he is not prepared to admit that the world as he sees it is governed by a wise, good and all-powerful Being. On the contrary, he has the impression of being delivered up without protection to the blind laws of nature and the wickedness of men.

In the world of scientists — physicists, chemists, biologists, doctors, etc. — it is rather the *superfluous character of the theist explanation* (the second objection of St. Thomas) which fosters agnosticism. The general development of learning from the middle ages to our own time seems to confirm the accuracy of the "law of the three states" first formulated by Auguste Comte: the theological or fictitious state (from fetichism to monotheism by way of polytheism), the metaphysical or abstract state, the scientific or positive state. Theological yielded to metaphysical explanation and the latter in turn to positive explanation. Science is continually advancing. What primitive peoples of all ages attributed to the gods or to good or evil spirits, what scholastics explained by means of metaphysical entities, scientists now explain by the laws of nature, known and verified by experimental methods. Unless he is on his guard, if he lets himself be hypnotized by the wonderful achievements of contemporary science, if he lets himself be imprisoned within the limits of the problematic and methods of positive science, the scientist runs the risk of no longer perceiving its limits, nor the important problems that, of their nature, remain beyond its reach. This intellectual myopia, very common in scientific circles, inevitably leads the scientist to agnosticism when he finds himself confronted with the problem of God.

Anti-religious Marxist literature constantly extols the advances of reason and science in the service of human and social progress. Marxism contrasts this with religious belief which, in the course of history and still in our own time, never ceases to impede the advance of learning by forcing people to believe in fables and legends ([6]).

Errors regarding God's Nature

The problem of God is one that regards not only agnostics, i.e. those who say they are unable to pierce the mystery of an eventual beyond-the-empirical world. Many, who admit the existence of an Absolute, go astray when it comes to determining its *essential attributes*. Some say it is an impersonal Being, a kind of reification of Destiny, or Nature, or Cosmic Law. Others admit that the Absolute is a personal, intelligent Being, but do not allow that He is creative Cause: he may be the Intelligence who brings order into the original chaos (Anaxa-

([6]) Some examples of this Marxist popular anti-religious literature have been mentioned above. Over against these the following may be mentioned: J. NACHTERGAELE, *Est-il vrai que... le spoutnik a tué Dieu?* (Collection «*Est-il vrai que?...*», 19), Brussels, no date, 16 pp.; J. DE VRIES, *Gibt es einen Gottesbeweis? Wissenschaft und Gottesglaube* (Collection *Entscheidung*, 19), Kevelaer, 1959, 32 pp.

goras) or who explains the evolution of the cosmos (Aristotle). There are others who think the Absolute a creative Spirit to whom the universe owes its existence but who has no interest in the evolution of the world and the fate of humanity (Averroes). Others, finally, think the Absolute is a Principle immanent in the world, the secret and ever-active source of cosmic energies: here we come across the various forms of pantheism: for some the immanent Principle is an Intelligence (Spinoza), for others an instinctive Force (Maeterlinck), for others a purely material Energy (Stoics, Marx etc.).

It is clear that these deviations have to be criticized and set right if we are to defend the proper notion of the Absolute as a personal, creative and provident being.

Believers and the Problem of God

That is not all. The problem is not devoid of meaning or of interest even in the case of those who have solid religious convictions. *Living personal conviction* must not be confused with *scientific demonstration*(7). Many people have deep personal convictions concerning morality and religion and these are fully justified by a complex of reflections and experiences which vary more or less from

(7) So as to avoid all ambiguity, remark once for all that unless otherwise stated, the term *science* (and the adjective *scientific*) is used here in its widest sense and means *knowledge that is methodical and critical* as opposed to spontaneous or pre-scientific knowledge. Understood in this way, science comprises, not only the positive sciences, but also the philosophical and theological sciences. These categories of science employ vastly different methods.

one person to another. When it comes to turning this living conviction, based on reasons dimly perceived, into a scientific certitude, i.e. when it comes to making these reasons explicit, systematic and critical, a very real problem arises immediately and one that we cannot afford to pass over. It is lawful and laudable to examine these living convictions critically with a view to rendering their foundations secure.

The history of religious thougt fully confirms the distinction we have made between personal conviction and scientific demonstration. Many thinkers have had solid and objectively based convictions regarding the existence of God, but they never succeeded in making explicit really satisfactorily, on the plane of scientific demonstration, their deep and living thought. As historians we are able to see in their writings both the accuracy of their implicit thought and the shortcomings of their explicit thought, and the reasons for the relative failure of their scientific essay.

Two Difficulties

Our reflections up to the present all point to an affirmative answer to the question raised at the very beginning of this chapter. There is a problem of the existence of God: the existence of *atheists* properly so called may be questioned, but there exist many *agnostics*, who really doubt about God's existence and confess that they are unable to resolve their doubt. In addition, many people have wrong ideas about the nature of the Absolute.

Lastly, even believers are faced with the problem of proving God's existence *scientifically*.

Two difficulties may arise in connexion with this conclusion and we must examine them briefly.

The first would come from those who believe that the existence of God is immediately evident; in their eyes it would be superfluous to examine the "problem" of God's existence for the problem is a false one. The reader may be surprised to learn that some thinkers held this opinion, but there can be no doubt about the fact: some very lofty minds, by temperament given to religious and even mystical contemplation, admitted *the immediate and perceptible presence of God in human consciousness* (St. Bonaventure, for example); others said that the proposition "God exists" is analytical (St. Anselm). But, if we look at the matter more closely, even these thinkers do not suppress every problem of God's existence. Those who claim that God is immediately and perceptibly present still insist that He is not an object of experience in the same way as the self or the corporeal world; His presence in the depths of conscience is perceived only under favourable circumstances, but not always nor in all cases. To perceive this divine presence a "method" of recollection and religious attention is necessary, and this method is not immediately attainable by all. As for the analytical nature of the proposition "God exists", those who hold this admit that it is only as the result of a reflection on the term "God" that it becomes evident. The following question, therefore, has a meaning and object that all agree to: "*How can man get to know with certainty that God exists?*".

The second difficulty is of an entirely different nature: it might arise in the case of a Christian who was worried whether the examination of the problem of God's existence was compatible with the firmness demanded for the assent of supernatural faith. Indeed, the Christian's situation may appear paradoxical, faced as he apparently is by two irreducible duties: that of firmly believing what God revealed, without ever suspending his assent, and, on the other hand, that of making sure that he has good reasons for believing, which means critically examining these reasons and, especially, the reasons for believing in God's existence. It is easy to answer this difficulty. In the first place, the act of supernatural faith does not have for direct object the existence of God, but revealed truths which we firmly believe on the *authority* of God who speaks. As regards "motives of credibility" or reasons for believing, they are examined at the scientific level and in answer to a *methodic* doubt which is perfectly compatible with the assent of faith. Besides, the assent of faith is also compatible with *psychological* doubt regarding the reasons for believing, provided it is not voluntarily accepted as entailing real suspension of the assent of faith([8]).

Having answered the preliminary question forming the object of this chapter in the affirmative, the ground is now clear for new problems.

([8]) It is perhaps well to note that, though the assent of faith supposes personal reasons for believing, it by no means entails that the believer should be able to give, before making an act of faith, a philosophical demonstration of the existence of God.

CHAPTER II

PRECISE OBJECT OF INQUIRY

Nominal Definition of God

There is then a "problem" of the existence of God which
we have formulated in these terms: "How can we know
with certainty that God exists?". No sooner is it formulated than it gives rise to a second: what are we to understand by the word "God"? what does it denote? Or, in
scholastic terms, how should the word be *nominally
defined* at the outset of this inquiry and where does the
definition come from? The question is obviously fundamental and unavoidable, for to try to prove that something
exists, without knowing what it is the existence of which
one is trying to prove, is senseless. Every proof of existence
presupposes a nominal definition of what it is that is
supposed to exist. We must agree about what we mean
by the term "God" when we set about proving that God
exists.

Before we do this it will not be out of place to dispel
a misunderstanding. Here is what a professor of religious
doctrine wrote to me when he had read the article here
substantially reprinted([1]):

([1]) *Le problème philosophique de l'existence de Dieu*, pre-

What struck me most forcibly about your manner of stating the problem of God was its profoundly "essentialist" character. The very idea of beginning with a nominal definition is significant in this respect. If I understand you properly you try to prove that our idea of God exists in reality, though you are prepared to correct, if need be, this very summary definition. You start from the essence to prove its existence. I have nothing to say against this procedure other than that it is not the only one. My experience of teaching apologetics has led me to adopt a different one. Without troubling to define "God" even nominally, I examine existing realities—man, the world, the human situation—and I try to understand. I do not start from a notion, nor from a system, nor even from some social or religious standpoint that I seek to justify. I start from existing realities and all I ask is to understand them. The problem is then, not to determine to what extent it is possible with scientific certainty to know that a Creator of the universe exists, but to establish with scientific certainty the meaning of this universe. God is the solution. Nevertheless, I do not first propose God as a hypothesis to be demonstrated. Analysis of existing being gradually reveals the elements of the solution. This, I think, indicates more than a difference in method: there is a difference in philosophical outlook, a more existential bent.

Is Science not more likely to keep on the right track if it follows as closely as possible the twists and turns of experience? To start from the idea of God and then ask if there is any reality corresponding to it, is that not like putting the cart before the horse?

The "difference of philosophical outlook" to which the writer of the letter refers (the "essentialist" as opposed to the "existentialist" attitude) is purely apparent.

There is no question of starting from a mere idea,

mière partie, in *Revue philosophique de Louvain*, février 1947, pp. 5-20.

from a mere mental figment, and asking whether or not something corresponds to it in reality. We have to start from the real, from experience. The writer of the letter starts from a global consideration of the real world: "man, the world, the human situation". We start from the religious fact, one element in the human situation. Belief in God is very widespread and there are a great many religions, all implying a belief in God. Noting this fact, we ask ourselves whether this belief is solidly grounded or not and whether we can know with certitude the existence of the superior being called God. Logically, to answer this question, we must state what we mean by the term "God"; we must, in other words, begin with a nominal definition. This is the method that has to be followed in every demonstration of existence, as Aristotle already remarked in the *Posterior Analytics*. Our correspondent, too, in the course of his inquiry, will be forced to define, at least implicitly, what he means by the term "God" before proving that God exists. Suppose that his reflections on the world lead him to the conclusion that it is constituted by contingent beings, i.e. non-necessary beings. To infer from this that there exists a Being superior to this world, he has to appeal to one of the forms of the principle of causality, and this will be the argument:

Major premiss: Every contingent being is caused by a necessary Being.

Minor premiss: But the beings of my experience are contingent.

Conclusion: Therefore, they are caused by a necessary Being.

It is easy to see that the major premiss, i.e., the principle of causality, contains a nominal definition of God: "God is the necessary Being, cause of contingent beings".

Briefly, to start from the religious fact and from an idea of God taken from man's beliefs is at least as "existential" and realistic as to act as if the religious fact were inexistent. And is it not a more natural, not to say more honest, attitude of mind on the part of a professor of religious knowledge?

Aspects of the Problem of God

We need then a nominal definition of the term "God", and not an aprioristic, fanciful definition, but one drawn from the fact of belief in God — a fact the nature, origin and value of which we shall have to examine. How are we to set about getting this nominal definition? At first sight it might seem as if the simplest solution would be just to take the accepted meaning of the term "God". Of course the meaning of words is a matter of convention, but that does not mean that it is arbitrary and a matter of individual taste. To depart from the accepted meaning of words for no good reason would give rise to needless complications and endless ambiguities. There is therefore something to be said for starting by taking the term "God" in its accepted sense and finding out whether it has to be refined or modified.

But it is not quite as simple as that. When we try to define the accepted meaning of the term "God", we find that the term is more or less equivocal, that its meaning is vague. This is due to the fact that the problem of God can be considered from so many different points of view: it is at one and the same time a human, a religious and a scientific problem.

In the first place, it is a *human problem*. Part of the material universe in virtue of his bodily organism, but conscious of his freedom and personality, man finds himself engaged in the struggle for existence on the physical plane and, on the moral plane, responsible for directing his life. By the mystery that encompasses him on all sides he is inevitably led to ask a series of questions like the following: What is the origin and destiny of the universe? What is the origin and destiny of man? What is the nature of duty? His conscious life raises him above the material universe, but, nevertheless, he is acutely aware of his insecurity and unhappiness. Suffering, sin and death are a ceaseless reminder of his lowly condition. On the other hand, the countless marvels revealed by the study of nature and the order that presides over universal evolution cause admiration and sometimes even stupefaction. And thus, by various converging paths, man is led to acknowledge the existence of a personal Being who is the ultimate explanation of all things, in the speculative as well as in the moral order. This transcending Personality is source of all being and his providence governs the world. He is the author of the natural as well as of the moral law. This sovereign being is denoted by the name "God". Looked at from this first point of view, the problem of God should be formulated as follows: "*Is it possible to prove scientifically that a personal, transcendent being exists and that this being is the ultimate explanation of all else, in the theoretical order of reasons of things as well as in the practical order of personal destiny, the meaning of life and foundation of moral obligation?"*

There is nothing artificial about these reflections and they are not the invention of some philosopher's fertile brain. They are the genuine expression of a historical state of affairs. History shows that all the peoples of the world, the primitive as well as the civilized, have come up against this problem of God. Here is how M. Rabeau describes the idea that primitive peoples form of God: "It is the idea of a spiritual, omnipotent, omniscient, Being, without defect, perfectly good, Providence, author of the moral order, who made all things simply by thinking and willing them"(²).

Next, it is a *religious problem.* History shows that a great many people give an affirmative answer to the human problem which has just been described. They may differ in their ideas of the divine attributes, but they admit the existence of a personal supreme Being. A remarkably large proportion of the human race professes strict monotheism. Now belief in God involves "organized" religion (a new historical phenomenon), the regulation of divine worship. And since man is a social animal, religion everywhere assumed social and traditional forms. There exist consequently "positive religions", i.e. religions

(²) G. RABEAU, *Dieu, son existence et sa providence* (Bibliothèque catholique des sciences religieuses), Paris, 1933, pp. 61-62.

based on and organized around a certain number of human conventions. They determine certain patterns of behaviour, both individual and collective, that express what men feel about God and the acts of adoration, submission, praise and reparation that he feels it is his duty to perform. Under these conditions, as a member of a social community, (family, clan, nation), the individual is incorporated from birth into a religious fellowship.

In a religious society of this kind the problem of God's existence appears in an appreciably different light from the purely human problem referred to above. On the one hand, the problem is solved beforehand by the very existence of the religious institution, which is based on the affirmation of God's existence as a personal Being having certain definite attributes. On the other hand, confronted with this "*fait accompli*", reason cannot renounce either its rights or its obligations. But the problem is posed in different terms. It is no longer a question of examining the claims of the more or less vague aspirations of the human spirit in quest of an ultimate explanation of reality, but one of examining the grounds of the fundamental postulate on which the whole religious edifice is built. In other words, the problem of the existence of God becomes part of the *rational justification* of religion, a problem of *apologetics* or of *fundamental theology*.

The situation is still more complicated in the case of those positive religions that claim to be of divine origin or by divine right. Christianity makes this claim, and especially the Catholic Church, which claims to be the depositary of a divine message, of a divine "revelation" guaranteed by divine signs and proposed to man for his belief. Here once again the existence of God seems to be a foundation and its solidity will have to be tested. This is a particularly delicate task, at least at first sight, because of the nature of the supernatural act of faith(³).

In brief, the problem of God considered as a religious problem or one of apologetics has for object to study the idea of God as it occurs in any particular religious society, and to examine the reasons that can be adduced in favour of the existence of a Being answering to this idea. It should therefore be put in this way: "*Is it possible to prove scientifically the existence of a being possessing the attributes of God as he is conceived in Judaism, Christianity or Mohammedanism?*"(⁴).

It is clear that the nominal definition of God is furnished, in this case, by the religious society whose credentials have to be examined.

It is superfluous to insist on the real and vital character of the problem defined in this way. And we find that, in the history of the Christian Church especially, the rational

(³) This difficulty was referred to before and the principle of the solution indicated: cf. p. 23.

(⁴) It is not evident that an affirmative answer should be given to this question, at least in every case, even supposing that these religions acknowledge and worship the true God. For it is conceivable that the existence of God is beyond scientific research and can be known only in some other way. It is also conceivable that some divine attributes are beyond the reach of rational inquiry and that, consequently, the "God of Jesus Christ", for example, is not altogether identical with the "God of the philosophers".

demonstration of the existence of God and the deduction of the divine attributes are themes for reflection and discussion that never fail to excite interest and that have preoccupied all great Christian thinkers.

In the third place, it is a *scientific problem*. The development of human civilizations involves among other things progress of knowledge, the creation of scientific life and the organization of different orders of knowledge. Science reconsiders critically and systematizes the data of spontaneous knowledge. In the pursuit of this task, it comes up against the problem of God both as a human and as a religious problem.

It comes up against it as a *human problem* at the very heart of philosophy, where philosophy sets itself to discover the hidden origins of universal order: metaphysical problems of the one and the many, of coming to be, of contingency and of evil; cosmological problems concerning nature and its profound laws; psychological and moral problems regarding the origin and destiny of man. The problem of God here becomes a *philosophical* one, and the term "God" will be more accurately defined in the light of the fundamental metaphysical problems. For one philosopher God will be the "Absolute Being", First Principle of all relative beings. For another, God will be defined as the "Unique and Infinite Substance". For yet another, God will be "Pure and Unchangeable Act", or the "Supreme Good", source of every participated good, etc.

Science comes up against the *religious or apologetic problem* at various levels. At the level of *positive* science, it deals with the religious fact under all its aspects (history of religions, ethnography, religious sociology, psychology of religion etc.). At the *philosophical* level, philosophy of religion tries to determine the nature and value of man's religious behaviour and to give a critical estimate of the various historical religions of humanity. Finally, on the *theological* plane, Fundamental Theology treats the problem of God as an introduction to Faith and Theology, or as a "theological epistemology". Apologetics treats of the problem of God with a view to defending the Faith and providing a rational justification of it. To sum up, scientific effort, no matter in what field it may be applied, has always for object to determine to what extent common-sense solutions can be integrated into a critical and systematic synthesis of human knowledge. If we are to treat the problem of God scientifically, it will therefore be necessary to reconsider what was said about it from the human and religious points of view. The statements that were made will have to be critically re-examined and given scientific rigour so as to give the problem its proper setting in this or that scientific discipline and to give the nominal definition of God, adopted on the threshold of the inquiry, the most accurate meaning.

There are thus several points of view. At first sight this seems to make things more difficult as it entails several nominal definitions. This in its turn seems to imply that the term "God" is to some extent ambiguous. Is it not necessary to distinguish several accepted meanings of the term? And does this not imply that we have to choose between them?

The difficulty seems to be confirmed by the article *Dieu* (*God*) in the *Vocabulaire technique et critique de la philosophie* published by André Lalande([5]). It distinguishes two basic meanings of the word "God": it is sometimes used to denote the *highest principle of explanation* of the universe, sometimes to denote an *active, personal being*, transcending man, immanent by its providence and ultimate guardian of the moral order. Lalande gives several sub-divisions of each of these fundamental meanings.

In reality, the ambiguity is more apparent than real. Lalande, in his commentary, points out how closely connected are the different meanings. Briefly, the two basic meanings correspond to the two points of view referred to in connexion with the *human problem* of the existence of God. There God appears as the ultimate explanation both in the *speculative* order (the principle of cosmic order) and in the *practical* order (principle of moral order). It suffices to remark that these are but partial aspects of one order, the order of natures (essences), to see that the principle that is first in one can, and probably ought to, coincide with the first principle in the other. As for the idea of God that occurs in the great *positive religions* and, in particular, in Christianity, it is easy to see that it is in no way incompatible with the purely human idea of the first principle of the cosmic and moral orders; it is a refinement and enrichment of it, giving a more detailed description of the divine attributes, especially those that are commonly called, though

([5]) 5th ed., Paris, 1947, pp. 219-224.

inaccurately, God's "moral perfections". This substantial agreement of the human and religious senses of the word is not surprising since, as we have seen, the genesis of the religious sense and the creation of religious societies follow the discovery of the human problem of the existence of God. Finally, the *scientific problem* of the existence of God involves no new object compared with the two preceding problems; it merely reconsiders and develops them on the plane of systematic and critical reflection.

To sum up, the word "God" is currently used in senses that seem appreciably different at first sight. On reflection, however, they appear rather to be different nuances or complementary aspects of one fundamental meaning. It is better, therefore, to speak of analogy rather than of ambiguity or equivocity. The different nominal definitions we have come accross can easily be reduced to one, provided the connexions between the different aspects of the problem of God are not lost to view. Clearly the *scientific* problem dominates the other two; it is a more advanced and methodical study of the same problem. On the other hand, even though the human and religious problems are expressed in different terms and in different contexts, their solutions must agree. If it should happen to be impossible to prove the existence of a First Cause of the universe, it would be equally impossible to vindicate the fundamental presuppositions of religion. On the contrary, if reason can vindicate the existence of this First Cause, the basic pre-requisite of religion is also established. The religious problem does not therefore differ essentially from the human problem, but by introducing it into the framework of a positive religion it does no more than help to formulate it more accurately.

The Provident Creator of the Universe

After what has been said, let us try to find the basic notion hidden under the different nuances of meaning of the term "God" and see if it provides us with a satisfactory nominal definition. Open any Larousse dictionary at the word "God" and you will find the following definition: "Supreme Being, creator and preserver of the universe". That would seem to be, then, the most general current meaning of the word. Is it a good definition to start with? Is it satisfactory? Does it correspond to what we have in mind when we discuss the problem of God?

Supreme Being. Unquestionably this idea forms part of what "God" usually stands for, but it is too vague, since it tells us nothing about the *nature* of God nor about his *relations* with other beings. It attributes to him merely a supremacy of dignity or perfection.

Creator of the universe. Here is an idea that is incomparably richer than the previous one. "Creator" means cause of existence and therefore cause of the whole of its effect or total cause. The "creator of the universe" means the sole cause of everything else that exists. This idea, too, is undoubtedly part of the current idea of God which is far removed from the idea of an immanent and impersonal Absolute to be found in pantheism. Besides, an Absolute of this kind is of no interest from a religious point of view and, obviously, is not what we have in mind when we discuss the problem of God.

Preserver of the universe. This third part of the definition given in Larousse appears subordinate and is simply a corollary of the preceding one, since only the cause that brings a thing into existence can preserve it in existence. As against this, an essential part of the current meaning of the word is missing, unless the author meant, clumsily enough, to express it by the term "Preserver": it is the *personal and provident* character of God. This is indeed an essential part of the definition for, when we seek God, it is of paramount importance for us to know whether our acts of religion, our worship, are directed to *somebody*. And not only to somebody, but to somebody *interested in us*, somebody whose providence watches over our destiny. It would be better therefore to replace the word "Preserver" by the word "Provident".

The term "God" connotes then a "*Provident Creator of the universe*". This nominal definition seems satisfactory, as it corresponds to the idea commonly held in all human societies that have come under the influence of the great monotheistic religions and it is sufficiently significant for our purpose. It refers to both the *human* and the *religious* problems that have been mentioned previously and it can also serve to define the problem of God at the *scientific* level, as all its three constituents (creator, provident, universe) can be accurately and scientifically defined [6].

[6] St.Thomas proposes practically the same nominal definition: see *Philosophical Studies* (Maynooth), XII (1963), p. 146.

To dispel any uneasiness or misunderstanding in the reader's mind, it is as well to remark that a nominal definition in no way prejudices the solution to be given to the problem that it helps to formulate. Not only could the answer be *negative* ("It is impossible to know with scientific certainty that a Provident Creator of the universe exists"), but it could be partly negative and partly affirmative (e.g. "The existence of a Creator can be scientifically proved, but not that of Providence"), in which case the resultant definition of God would *not be as rich* as the nominal definition from which one started. The solution might also lead to a *fuller definition* by bringing to light new attributes of God not included in the original nominal definition.

To sum up, the nominal definition of God given at the beginning helps to guide the inquiry and to stimulate reflection. It expresses a human and religious preoccupation whose real significance needs to be examined. It is a working hypothesis and, on this count, subject to revision. It has therefore only provisional value, which the solution of the problem can either confirm or reject. From now on the problem will be formulated in the following manner: *"To what extent can we know with scientific certainty that a Provident Creator of the universe exists?"*

CHAPTER III

SURVEY OF METHODS

Now that the problem has been clearly and accurately formulated, questions concerning method immediately arise. Had nobody ever attempted to solve the problem before, these questions could be very troublesome. We would be in the position of pioneers, clearing a way through new and unexplored regions, instead of being able to profit from the lessons of history and from the mistakes of those that had gone before. Though this is not our plight, it is strangely enough no less awkward, so numerous have been the attempts made in the past, so many and so divergent are the tracks of those who have attacked the problem at one time or another.

The extreme diversity in the methods employed in the course of history to solve the problem of God can be explained by differences in intellectual climate, in scientific or philosophical formation, in temperament and interests, that exist between thinkers. Strangely enough, it often goes hand in hand with convergence in the fundamental thought and in the solutions put forward. This being the case, our first task must be to sort out the principal methods used in the numerous attempts made to prove the existence of God and so bring some order into this strange mixture.

Prolegomena of the Proof

In the first place a distinction ought to be made between *proofs properly so called* and arguments that are really no more than *preliminary* considerations or *prolegomena*, the object of which is to draw attention to the problem, to excite the curiosity and the sympathy that the search for God demands, to remove prejudice, to underline the importance of the question, in fine, to induce the psychological predispositions most favourable to the effort demanded by the examination of the problem of God. These "psychological preparations" will be discussed later on.

Among proofs properly so called, we can distinguish two principal groups of methods: *empirical methods* and *rational methods*.

Empirical Methods

The *empirical methods* aim at discovering, in the domain of human experience, some *experience of the divine*, i.e. some direct manifestation of God's presence or of his action. And here, too, two orientations are possible:

1) The *historical method* is used to prove the historical fact of a divine manifestation to men, of a divine intervention in the world, of a divine revelation, guaranteed by "objective signs" (miracles, prophecies, surpassing holiness of the divine messenger, etc.). This method is used to prove the existence of God from an examination

of the person, teaching and miracles of Christ as they are related in the Gospels. The point would be to prove that Christ is the living manifestation of God in human form, a genuine "theophany". The same method is used in arguing to the existence of God from facts of a miraculous nature, like those of Lourdes, Lisieux or other places of pilgrimage. In all these cases the proof boils down to this: "God exists, since He showed himself unquestionably in such and such circumstances".

2) The *psychological method* is used to prove the existence of God by arguing from some inner religious experience. This experience can be either *common*, accessible to all (it is alleged that when a man enters into himself and reflects, he will find deep down in his own conscience the ineffable but incontrovertible presence of the sovereign Master), or *privileged* (e.g. one possible only for mystics, who will then make God known to their fellow-men). It would not be difficult to illustrate this method of proof from the history of religious belief. Examples can be found in passages in the writings of St. Augustine and, perhaps, even still more marked, in the writings of St. Bonaventure. The ontologism of Malebranche, and especially that of Gioberti, implies that there is in the human mind a certain intuition of God, a certain experience of the divine, accessible to all men. As for the proof of the existence of God from the religious experience of mystics, it is well known that it has been fully developed by Henri Bergson in *Les deux sources de la morale et de la religion*.

Rational Methods

Rational methods aim at proving the existence of God by *reasoning* from facts. Taking as their starting point the natural order, reality as given in our experience, they aim at showing that reality, in whole or in part, implies, as a condition of intelligibility, the existence of a transcendent being. God is discovered, not as a *fact* whose existence is known because it enters the series of events forming the stuff of our experience, but as the supreme *principle* of reality, the original *necessity* without which the universe would remain unintelligible.

Rational methods are in turn distinguished according to the nature of the object from which reflection takes its start and according to the nature of this reflection.

1) *Scientific* or *positive method* starts from facts and laws taken from the positive sciences such as physics, astronomy, biology and geology. The idea is to prove, for example, that, to account for the origin of matter, movement, energy, light, life, instinct, — all these data being considered at the positive level — it is necessary to admit the existence of God.

History presents us with many examples of this kind of reasoning. A little book of apologetics, very popular in its day, contains proofs for the existence of God drawn from the origin of the light of the sun and the stars, the loss of energy, the existence of matter, the origin of life and of plant and animal species[1]. Later on we shall

[1] J. JOOSSENS, *Les questions actuelles*, nouv. éd., Paris-Bruxelles, 1913.

examine more recent attempts to use science to prove the existence of God.

2) The *philosophical method*, on the contrary, sets the proof of God's existence on the plane of philosophical reflection and criticism. It can take three different forms according to its starting point (²):

— the *cosmological* form: the existence of God is proved from a critical analysis of motion in the material order, or of cosmic becoming, or of the order in nature (for example, the Five Ways of St. Thomas in the *Summa theologiae*, with the exception of the Fourth);

— the *psychological* form: the existence of God is proved by a critique of human activity, either in the order of thought (for example, the Augustinian proof, the ontological argument of St. Anselm, Descartes's proof, that of P. Maréchal), or in the order of will (for example, Kant's proof by the postulates of practical reason, Blondel's proof);

— the *metaphysical* form: the existence of God is proved by the metaphysical critique of finite being as such (for example, the Avicennian proof, adopted by William of Auvergne and by St. Thomas in the *De ente et essentia*, and the Fourth Way).

A proper study of these different methods would need a volume to itself. But our present purpose does not demand this. In the criticisms that we shall offer of the principal inadequate solutions of the problem of God's

(²) Considering the nature of the reflection involved, all philosophical proofs are on the *metaphysical* plane.

existence, we shall have an opportunity to indicate the weaknesses inseparable from certain methods, methods which must in consequence either be abandoned altogether or at least be completed by others. In this way the ground will be sufficiently cleared to allow us to proceed in our quest for a satisfactory solution to our problem.

Chapter IV

PSYCHOLOGICAL PREPARATIONS

In the last chapter we made a distinction between *proofs properly so called* and *psychological preparations* to the proof.

Les us call *psychological preparations* all those considerations and arguments which, while not sufficient of themselves to prove the existence of the Creator, nevertheless dispose the mind to seek Him, either by ridding it of unfavourable prejudices, or by awakening in it a certain wonder and restlessness, or by implanting seeds of reflections apt to turn the mind towards God, by rousing from their lethargy and indifference superficial and smug minds conscious of no problem. These *preliminaries* or *prolegomena* are logically prior to and extrinsic to the proof of God's existence. What value have they?

It would be wrong to condemn them off-hand in deference to the demands of "impartial" and "objective" inquiry. Of course, as in all scientific research, so too in the search for God, the legitimate demands of philosophical criticism must be respected and a scrupulous regard shown for truth. Neither fear of failure, nor impatience to succeed, nor over-anxiety to reach an affirmative answer, must be allowed to thwart the calm work of reflection. On the other hand, we must not lose sight of the fact that scaling the heights of metaphysics is an arduous undertaking and the human eye is dazzled by the vision of the highest truths (as the bat, said Aristotle, by the sun). It is a good thing to encourage the seeker in his efforts, to stimulate his love of the true by bringing before his mind the magnificence and vital importance of the issues at stake in his inquiry. The highest truths deliver themselves up only to those who hunger and thirst after justice.

Let us now have a closer look at the more important of these psychological preparations.

Arguments from authority

All forms of *argument from authority* — universal consent of mankind, agreement of great thinkers, the testimony of men of God — may be treated under one heading.

And, in the first place, what can we infer from the *universal consent of mankind* in its belief in the existence of a supreme personal Being? It goes without saying that the first thing that we must do is prove the existence of unanimous, or at least morally unanimous, consent. The second step must be to prove that this unanimous consent is not mistaken but implies the existence of its object.

Rationalists and positivists have been eager to exploit the history of religions to the advantage of atheism. Primitive man, they hold, knew no form of religion other than magic. This gave rise to polytheism, and belief in one God, Creator of the universe, appears only at the end of a long evolution and under the influence of psychological factors.

The investigations of the historico-cultural school founded by P.W. Schmidt have completely upset this hypothesis by showing that existing primitive religions are basically monotheistic and that the further back we push our inquiry in an effort to discover the religious beliefs of primitive man, the more we find monotheism the prevailing religion. In view of these discoveries, the religious history of the race appears in a new light. Worship of the one, supreme God came first. Although constantly threatened in the course of time by countless deviations of the religious sense, it survived, nevertheless, and periodically re-asserted itself and, finally, took permanent form in the great monotheistic religions: Judaism, Christianity, Islam. Consequently, taking into account the secondary and derivative character of magic, fetishism and polytheism, it can be said that belief in God is morally universal.

Protagonists of the argument have put forward two explanations of this remarkable universality going back to the origins of the race. One is that if, in spite of the great diversity of peoples, cultures, civilizations, superstitions and rites, this belief should have proved so persistent, it can be due only to the fact that it is the normal and natural result of the mind's search for truth and reveals an underlying harmony between the human mind and monotheism. In other words, the question of the nature and origin of the universe necessarily leads to knowledge of God. The other consists in pointing out the contrast between belief in monotheism and the very limited intellectual possibilities open to primitive man. From this it is inferred that this belief in monotheism is the trace of a divine revelation made to the first men. In any event, the history of religions leads to belief in God's existence. "The study of the most ancient 'cultural cycles', taken alone, is sufficient to prove the existence of God" ([1]).

This second explanation has few adepts nowadays and it is commonly held that it is not possible to prove that these early religions contain traces of a primitive *revelation*. Partisans of the argument from universal consent stress rather the *rational* nature of monotheistic belief: man is led to acknowledge God as principle of the order in the universe, cosmic and moral, by natural reflection and, consequently, the monotheism found in all pagan religions, latent or explicit, implies God's existence. But the idea of God we find there is, owing to various factors, often distorted. The principal forms of distortion we find are polytheism, pantheism, and dualism ([2]). All things considered, it can be said that the religious soul of the pagan "bears valid and impressive witness to the truth of God"([3]).

Considerations of this nature, suggested by religious

([1]) G. RABEAU, *Dieu, son existence et sa providence*, p. 65. Paris, 1933. Read the whole of chapter II: L'origine de l'idée de Dieu. La sociologie et l'existence de Dieu (pp. 32-65).

([2]) J. DANIÉLOU, *Dieu et nous*, pp. 41-52. Paris, 1956.

([3]) *Ibidem*, p. 52. Read the whole first chapter: Le Dieu des religions (pp. 13-53).

sociology and history of religions, call for a few critical remarks. These have no ambition to bring down the imposing edifice of proof raised on universal consent, but are intended to determine its nature and significance.

In the first place, there is no reason for thinking that because a belief is unanimous, it is therefore solidly established. Geocentrism was believed unanimously until the sixteenth century, but it proved to be only a mistaken idea commonly entertained. It might perhaps be thought that a common mistake touching a vital problem concerning man's destiny (this is true of the problem of God), is difficult to conceive; still it would be necessary to justify this opinion.

In the second place, how is the conclusion that belief in God is morally universal arrived at? Only by including religious beliefs far removed from genuine monotheism, such as polytheism (provided it admits the existence of a sovereign God), pantheism and dualism. This obviously detracts from the argument. At the present time, though the majority of men worship one, personal God, Creator of the universe (this is the common teaching of the three great monotheistic religions), Hinduism and Buddhism are inspired by a pantheistic metaphysics, whilst communist countries parade their atheistic ideology, the creed no doubt of a substantial minority.

Finally, it is not easy to prove that God's existence is the sole possible explanation of the belief of mankind. If the common mistake of geocentrism can be explained by the seeming movement of the sun round the earth, can we not look on belief in God as the easy way out, the lazy man's solution of the enigma of nature? Could it not be the result of certain psychological tendencies natural to man: an anthropomorphic interpretation of the forces of nature, the need for justice, protection etc.? To refute these suggested explanations, it is necessary to demonstrate that belief in God rests on objectively valid reasons and that it implies, so to speak, a vague perception of a direct proof of the existence of God. This means that the argument from universal consent is no more than an *introduction* to the real proof, a manner of calling attention to the profoundly human character of the problem of God and of suggesting that an affirmative solution is probable. This explains why, all things considered, it seems preferable to put this argument among the psychological preparations for the real proof.

Another argument that, on examination, leads to a similar conclusion is the one from the *convergence of great thinkers* in admitting the existence of a transcendent Absolute. Though not unanimous, the agreement is nevertheless remarkable — even when the more or less serious divergences that make their appearance once it comes to determining the nature or attributes of the Absolute are taken into account.

It remains that this argument like the previous one, taken in itself, is an *indirect* one, resting as it does on the testimony and intellectual authority of these thinkers. Unless the value of their authority and testimony is scientifically established, the argument will not carry conviction. This means that the nature and object of the agreement appealed to has to be studied, i.e. the basic common conviction of these thinkers has to be brought out. Once again, the need to formulate a direct proof for God's existence is obvious and the argument from authority has been no more than a prolegomenon, of psychological interest only.

* * *

The most interesting form of the argument from authority seems to be that based on the *evidence of privileged persons* who, in a special way, appear to be *God's witnesses*: the prophets, the apostles, the great mystics. It is a most suggestive line of argument and many find it more convincing than the soundest reasoning. It should therefore be ranked among the most important psychological preparations.

But in reality it is more than a psychological preparation because it appeals to religious experience properly so called, to the experience of the divine. In so far as it can be shown that this experience is genuine, then it constitutes a proof for the existence of God by the empirical method and will be considered in a later chapter where the proofs from religious experience will be dealt with.

Presumptions

Presumptions in favour of God's existence form a second group of psychological preparations. What is one to think, for example, of considerations tending to prove that without God the *moral order* has no secure foundation or that the *social order* must sink into anarchy?

Consequences of atheism such as these should make every thinking man reflect and convince him that the existence of a supreme Lawgiver and supreme Rewarder is both *likely* and *desirable*. But, unless it can be shown to begin with that social order is absolutely necessary, that the sense of moral obligation cannot be sufficiently explained by certain traits inherent in human nature or by the influence of tradition, that morality and law are not the outcome of a tacit contract between men for the purpose of making life on earth possible, — and before the existence of God has been proved, demonstrations of this kind are rather problematical —, these considerations do not apodictically *demonstrate* God's existence.

The same objections could be urged against the argument from *man's desire* for happiness, justice, immortality, or from the *absurdity of a human existence* having no other horizon than this life here below with all its crimes and scandals, where the innocent suffer and the wicked prosper. Should human desires be gratified, or can they be? Is there room for justice in the universe? Is not the destiny of man absurd? It is just this scandal of disorder, the absence of moral order and justice here below, that furnishes the atheist with his principal objection to God's existence. St. Thomas does not underestimate the difficulty. In the *Summa theologiae*, as we have seen, he mentions two principal reasons against God's existence and the presence of evil in the world is one of them (4).

---

4) Videtur quod Deus non sit, quia si unum contrariorum

To prove that order has to exist, that the universe must be intelligible, that life must have a meaning, recourse has to be had to metaphysics. The proof for God's existence really forms one with the whole metaphysical dialectic as we shall show later on. Once again, presumptions in favour of God's existence have proved to be no more than a psychological approach to the real proof.

Approaches

There is a third category of psychological preparations which can be called *approaches towards the proof* of God's existence. It embraces all those considerations that tend to bring out either the signs of creatural indigence or the reflections of God's wisdom, power and goodness in creation. The "arguments from authority" had recourse to extrinsic evidence and were therefore *indirect proofs*; the "presumptions" in favour of the existence of God appealed to a moral sense present in man in order to emphasize the *likelihood* of the theistic thesis; the arguments we are now about to consider go further: they go to the *heart of the problem*, for their object is to lay bare the conditions of creatural existence and discover in them traces of dependence on God. Many well-known

fuerit infinitum, totaliter destruetur aliud. Sed hoc intelligitur in hoc nomine Deus, quod sit quoddam bonum infinitum. Si ergo Deus esset, nullum malum inveniretur. Invenitur autem malum in mundo. Ergo Deus non est (It seems that God dose not exist, because if one of two contraries be infinite, the

apologetical or oratorical developments that aim at exalt-
ing the role of divine Providence in the world can be
classed under this heading.

In one case it is the manifest contingency ([5]) of certain
classes of beings as, for example, of living things that
are born and die, that is stressed. In another, consideration of the instability and frailty of human nature leads
to the conclusion that it is basically dependent. The
solidarity, too, of beings is used to prove that none of
them can lay claim to the characters of an absolute or
unconditioned reality. In all these cases the *imperfection*
and *emptiness* of the things of experience is used as a
springboard to rise above this visible world in quest of a
more substantial and stable reality.

We can also rely on the *perfections* of beings within
our experience and endeavour to discover in them
manifestations of the wisdom, power and goodness of a
higher being, fount of these perfections. This method, of
course, implies that the dependence of these beings has
been previously established: if they were self-sufficient
and self-explanatory, there would be no need to refer
their perfections to an extrinsic cause. The point is to

other would be altogether destroyed. But the name God
means that He is infinite goodness. If, therefore, God existed, there would be no evil discoverable. But there is evil
in the world. Therefore God does not exist. *Summa theologiae*, I[a], q. 2, a. 3, *Utrum Deus sit*). Cf. above p. 12.

([5]) *Contingency*: property of being able to be or not be.
Contingency is opposed to necessity. A being that begins or
ceases to exist does not necessarily exist, for, if its existence
were necessary, if it could not not be, it would always exist.

find positive traces of divine action in the marvellous, natural order that pervades all nature from nuclear physics, through all grades of living things, to the movements of the heavenly bodies.

What are we to think of these attempts?

There can be no doubt about their psychological interest in that they stimulate reflection, nor about their value as first steps in the search for God. By drawing attention to the very obvious frailty of man and of all living things they raise the mind to the consideration of more enduring realities and, in the long run, to the consideration of an Absolute transcending the material universe. By pointing out the prodigious finality manifest everywhere in nature, the hypothesis of an Intelligence presiding over the destiny of the cosmos is rendered more probable. But, taken by themselves, considerations such as these are not sufficient to lead the mind to the knowledge of the true God whom we are seeking, that is to say, to the provident Creator of the universe. For, in order to be able to say legitimately that a universal creative Cause exists, it is not enough to go beyond the material universe nor to affirm the existence of some kind of Demiurge, source of order in the cosmos. We must resolutely press beyond these preliminary considerations and raise our minds to metaphysical reflection on the relativity of finite being as such: nothing short of reflection of this kind (as we shall see) can reveal the existence of one, infinite Being, cause of finite beings.

Chapter V

INEFFECTUAL ATTEMPTS

Let us leave the consideration of psychological preparations and turn our attention to proofs properly so called. The first thing we have to do is to clear the ground, as many of the proofs that have appeared in the course of history are radically defective and basically unacceptable despite the praiseworthy intentions of their authors. To go through them all would take us too far afield; it will suffice to examine the most typical.

Ordinary Religious Experience

All appeals to *ordinary religious experience* seem to belong to this category, i.e. every recourse to an *empirical method of a psychological kind*, mystical experience excluded. The peace enjoyed by the religious man, the sweetness and rest he finds in prayer, the deep joy that accompanies trust in God or loyalty in His service, are all manifestations of the religious aspirations of the human heart and can form the basis of a *presumption* in favour of the existence of the transcendent object towards which they are directed. But this ordinary religious experience is not a rigorous proof of God's existence. In the first place, there is nothing to show that these religious experiences are a genuine *experience of the divine* in itself. In the natural order, there is nothing to account for such an experience; in the supernatural order, theologians agree that the action of grace is imperceptible, at least ordinarily. Furthermore, even if such an experience were given us, it would be *incommunicable* and consequently would have no scientific significance. Finally, it isn't hard to see the *danger of illusion* involved in the use of this method: pious and fervent souls are only too prone to confuse the products of imagination and sensibility with an authentic Presence.

Why have the religious aspirations of humanity the value of *presumptions* in favour of God's existence? Because they are deeply ingrained in human nature and because it is not easy to explain this fact if the object of these experiences is illusory and unsubstantial. Nevertheless, for the reasons given, it can only be question of a presumption and not of an apodictic proof.

The Positive Sciences

All *rational proofs of the scientific type* must also be rejected as they suffer from a latent defect in method. By definition, the positive sciences confine their attention to *phenomenal* explanation: they describe and classify phenomena and look for laws of a phenomenal order; they build hypothetical theories, but always on the plane of phenomenal explanation. Consequently, when the

scientist tries to discover the antecedents of any phenomenon or group of phenomena, what he is looking for
is something *in the same order* and the Creator cannot
be found within this order. Hence, whatever reasons may
be advanced in physics, biology, astronomy, geology or
any other positive science, to arouse wonder or the
sense of mystery, they can never be more than *first steps*
in the proof of the existence of God, approaches towards
a reflection of a different order from that of science.

The late P. Auguste Grégoire brought out the impossibility of a "scientific" proof for the existence of God very
well ([1]). When he has shown that God can be neither a
scientific *fact*, nor a scientific *law*, he continues: "But
perhaps science will be forced to bring God in as a
hypothesis? In any case, it would be a very bad hypothesis.
For what is a hypothesis in science? It should be a
principle from which laws and facts can be analytically
deduced. It must, therefore, of necessity, be of the same
order as these laws and facts" (pp. 151-152). P. Grégoire
shows further on that it is not the business of science as
such to bring in God to explain the "irrationals" that it
comes up against: its role is to try to rationalize them
and it cannot declare *inexplicable* what is for the moment
unexplained. The work of the scientist is never-ending.

This is equivalent to saying that science as such is and
should be *agnostic*. This has to be stressed, for it is a
point on which scientists and philosophers agree and
which could be useful in dispelling many misunderstan-

([1]) A. GRÉGOIRE, *Immanence et transcendance*, Brussels-
Paris, 1939, pp. 138-157: Les preuves scientifiques de l'existence
de Dieu.

dings. But Marxist propaganda tries to exploit the agnostic status of science and is never tired of repeating that science is *atheistic*, that it *excludes* a theistic explanation of the universe, that God is a gratuitous invention of "idealist" (they mean: non-materialist) philosophy and religious belief. It is obvious that these conclusions go beyond the premisses. We shall see in a later chapter that, though science, in pursuit of its object, should disclaim all knowledge of God, its *presuppositions* and *results* raise fundamental problems for the *philosopher* that could ultimately lead to the discovery of God.

The Augustinian Proof

Many *rational proofs of a philosophical nature* are also defective and cannot therefore be retained. Here it is no longer the general method that is defective but its application. We have to confine ourselves to the examination of a few typical examples selected from among the better known ones. Without going into a full scientific discussion (not within the scope of this essay) we shall try to point out clearly the weak points that invalidate these demonstrations.

St. Augustine develops a famous proof for the existence of God in the second book of his dialogue *De libero arbitrio*. It can be reduced to the following syllogism: if there is a being above the human mind, that being is God; but there exists a being above the human mind; therefore God exists. The *major premiss* is proved by a long analysis of the life of the mind, whence it appears that human thought is at the summit of all the realities forming the world of our experience and that, if the existence of a reality transcending human thought is proved, it will be easy to detect in it the attributes of deity. To demonstrate the *minor premiss* St. Augustine brings out the transcendent characters of numbers and of wisdom, that is to say, of the principles governing the life of the intelligence; these truths, whose immutability, necessity and eternity we perceive, have not their *raison d'être* in our thought, but reveal the existence of a subsistent Truth, supreme norm of truth for all minds. This eternal, necessary and immutable reality, superior to the human mind, is God.

What are we to think of this demonstration? It contains without doubt valuable elements that can be incorporated into the genuine proof of God's existence. St. Augustine develops perfectly well the primacy of mind over matter and the eminent place of human thought in the universe; he emphasizes admirably the contrast existing between the mutability of concrete things (including thought) and the immutability of abstract truths. But the dialectic of the proof has many weak points and these prevent our giving complete assent to the demonstration.

In the first place, the *major premiss* implies a nominal definition of God which is markedly vague and, indeed, altogether unsatisfactory: God is something superior to the human mind. Augustine was aware of this himself and his friend Evodius expressed the difficulty clearly in these terms: "Non continuo, si quid melius quam id quod in mea natura optimum est, invenire potuero, Deus esse dixerim. Non enim mihi placet Deum appellare, quo mea

ratio est inferior, *sed quo nullus est superior*" ([2]). Augustine
then tries to amend his notion of God and he propounds
what is, in fact, a new nominal definition. "God is an
eternal and immutable being, superior to the human
mind". But Evodius sticks to his guns and demands a
proof for the existence of a *supreme* being, of a being to
which nothing is superior: *"quo nihil superius esse con-
stiterit"* ([3]). Augustine ends by compromising: alright, he
says to Evodius, for either you will acknowledge the
supreme being in the eternal and immutable being,
superior to reason, whose existence I am going to prove,
or you will be obliged to go higher still and discover the
supreme being above it. In any case, the existence of God
will have been established.

As might be expected, the difficulty reappears when
St. Augustine comes to the end of his proof: he points
out himself very fairly the terms of the compromise
agreed by both and he concludes that either subsisting
Truth is God or there exists a reality superior to Truth
and this higher reality is God. But to resolve this
dilemma he seems to have no other resource than faith.
We know by the teaching of Christ, he says in substance,
that there is something that comes before Truth or
Wisdom: this is the Father from whom it proceeds; but

([2]) "No, if I could discover something better than what
is best in my nature, I would not immediately say it was God.
I do not like saying that God is that being to whom my
reason is inferior but, rather, that being to whom none is
superior". *De libero arbitrio, Liber secundus,* VI, 14; ed.
THONNARD, pp. 238-239.

([3]) *Ibidem,* p. 240.

the Father and Wisdom are equal and possess inseparably the attributes of the deity (⁴). This recourse to the light of faith is an implicit avowal: it is the inevitable consequence of the weakness that we pointed out in St. Augustine's manner of stating the problem of God. He set himself only to go beyond the human mind by proving the existence of an eternal and immutable reality, which is Truth. This conclusion, supposing it were established, does not give us knowledge of God that is sufficiently distinct. Is God Truth or a being higher than Truth? Is the Supreme Being one or many? Is He finite or infinite? Is He creator, or first mover, or principle of emanation, or final cause? In putting the problem of God in the terms he chose, St. Augustine made it very difficult, perhaps even impossible, to give a rigorous answer to these questions on the plane of reason.

In the second place, the demonstration of the *minor premiss* of the argument is not beyond question. To prove that there exists a reality superior to the human mind, Augustine relies on the transcendent features of the principles, in the mathematical order, in the moral order and, generally speaking, in all orders in which the normative activity of thought appears. In this he is indeed under the influence of a Platonist idea of knowledge in which the world of Ideas, i.e. the intelligible world, completely cut off from the sensible world and from every contingent reality, is looked on as a real world, claiming the minds submission and obedience. Under the influence of Platonism, Augustine imagines that he discovers this

(⁴) *Ibidem*, XV, 39, p. 290.

intelligible world, that transcends mind, present in the human mind. It would be necessary to show, more clearly than does St. Augustine, why this intelligible world implies the existence of *the* one only subsisting Truth. But the Platonist idea of knowledge is itself very vulnerable. Is the intelligible world more than the collection of principles of the ideal order? Are these anything more than the product of our abstractive intelligence? Are not the "transcendent" features of concepts and judgments explained sufficiently by the nature of concept and the nature of judgment?

It appears that the Augustinian proof is open to serious objections. To admit its validity, one would have to have accepted, to begin with, the Platonist idea of knowledge and then the reduction of the manifold intelligibles to the unity of the supreme Intelligible or of subsisting Truth (⁵).

The Ontological Argument

If we stick to the literal interpretation of the text, the famous proof of St. Anselm in the *Proslogion*, which Kant called the ontological argument, seems to be fallacious.

(⁵) For fuller developments see *Revue néoscolastique de philosophie*, 1933, pp. 239-248. See also R. GARRIGOU-LAGRANGE, *Dieu. Son existence et sa nature*, 6th ed., Paris, 1933, pp. 296-302. A fervent plea for the Augustinian proof can be found in P. F. CAYRÉ, A.A., *Dieu présent dans la vie de l'esprit*, Paris, 1951.

This is how it runs:

We call "God" a being greater than which cannot be conceived ([6]). This nominal definition is admitted by all, not excluding atheists, so that God exists at least in thought.

But a being that is so great that no greater can be conceived, cannot exist in thought alone, for, if that were the case, a greater could be conceived, namely, the same being existing also in reality.

Therefore God exists in thought and in reality.

Anselm saw in this demonstration a quick and infallible way of confuting the atheist. But it was pointed out to him immediately that the proof suffered from a grave logical fault: the author passes unlawfully from the *idea* of the most perfect possible being to its real *existence*.

What are we to think of this criticism? Not every passage from the logical to the real order is unlawful, though people sometimes seem to think so. In a realist philosophy, it is lawful to infer from ideas, the real conditions they necessarily imply: thus, from any idea present to my mind I can infer the psychological reality of the thinking subject, i.e., the reality of an intelligence capable of conceiving it; in the same way, if it were established that we have a positive idea of the infinite, it would be necessary to admit the existence of the conditions necessary to account for its presence in our minds. But in the case of the Anselmian argument, it is not apparent that the existence of the most perfect possible Being is the necessary

([6]) *"Id quo maius cogitari non potest"*.

condition of the idea — a very vague one — that we have of it. This idea could be a product of the mind and, in that case, it remains simply a thought-content until such time as it has been proved, *independently*, that the most perfect possible being *must exist* and St. Anselm doesn't do this.

Can it be done?

I believe that it can, as the existence of the most perfect possible being *is implied in the existence of anything at all*. In other words: if anything exists, then the most perfect possible being exists. For:

Nothing, beyond what exists and what existing things can produce, is possible.

If what exists is only *one*, *single being*, it is the greatest possible being since, beyond it, nothing can come to be except its own effects and these cannot be greater than their cause.

If what exists is *many*, either all are equal and, in that case, all are the greatest possible; or they are unequal and, in that case, the most perfect is the greatest possible.

Therefore, in any hypothesis, the greatest possible being exists.

Does this reasoning save St. Anselm's proof? Alas! no, for it does not lead to a distinct knowledge of God: when we reach the conclusion, we know "the greatest possible being" no better. Is it one or many, finite or infinite, matter or spirit, transcendent cause or principle immanent in the world, personal or impersonal? All these important questions remain unanswered. The real weakness of St. Anselm's proof is, then, that the nominal definition with which it begins is insufficient, more so even than that from which St. Augustine starts in the *De Libero Arbitrio*.

The Avicennian Proof

At the very beginning of his professional career, in the opusculum *De ente et essentia*, St. Thomas Aquinas formulated a proof for the existence of God inspired directly by Avicenna and previously used by William of Auvergne. It has the appearance of a purely metaphysical proof and it can be stated briefly as follows:

Existence is not an *essential* attribute of finite being since it is not included in the definition of any finite being. I can define man or the phoenix, says St. Thomas, without knowing whether they exist in the real world; existence must then be either a *property* resulting from the essence or a *logical accident* ([7]). Now it cannot be a property resulting from the essence, as, in that hypothesis, the essence would be the cause of its own existence before existing, and this is absurd. Existence is therefore a logical accident, predicable of the finite essence for some reason other than the essence itself (*per aliud*), and received therefore from some outside cause. But whatever is relative (*per aliud*) must be reduced to something absolute (*per se*). Therefore all finite essences, owing their existence to an outside principle, are explained by a cause whose

([7]) By applying the Aristotelian doctrine of the five predicables: a predicate that is not an essential element (*genus, differentia* or *species*), must designate a *property* or an *accident* (logical accident).

essence is to exist or who is defined by existence: this universal cause of existence is God.

There is no gainsaying the interest of this demonstration: it is based directly on the analysis of finite being as such (St. Thomas is speaking of subsisting forms, but the argument evidently holds for every finite reality, for every being not defined by existence); its object is to find in the finite essence a mark of metaphysical contingency and it concludes that there exists a cause whose essence is to exist or who is self-existent. Although St. Thomas doesn't do so, it is easy to deduce that this cause is non-finite or infinite (since it is *Esse subsistens*, having no principle of limitation or finite essence) and, consequently, unique.

However, the way the proof is presented gives rise to serious difficulties. Under the influence of Avicenna, St. Thomas speaks as if finite being were an *essence*, of itself incapable of existing, receiving from outside an *esse* that would become united to it as an extrinsic and accidental principle. Now his reasoning depends on this way of putting it. Set the expression right — as it does not respect sufficiently the distinction between the conceptual and the real order — and the demonstration is no longer rigorous. For, in the ontological order, the *esse* of finite being is not an extrinsic and accidental principle compared to *essentia*, but both *esse* and *essentia* are correlative principles, incapable of existing apart, unthinkable one without the other: how can it be proved that a compound like that must be caused? On the other hand, though it may be possible to think of some finite beings (as man, who is mortal) apart altogether from their actual existence,

I can think of none of them apart from existence simply, or from the fundamental perfection that being is, for a *non-existing* finite being would be *nothing*. The perfection of being, common to every existing thing, is the most essential of all attributes. It is impossible to define man or phoenix without saying that they are *beings* of such and such a species; if they are not found, in fact, in the real world, the only conclusion to be drawn is that the definition was purely nominal, without significance beyond the conceptual order.

St. Thomas's argument doesn't prove therefore that finite being as such is contingent: *some* finite beings as, for instance, man, are evidently contingent since they come to be and cease to be. But why could not higher finite beings exist necessarily of themselves, as Aristotle believed? To prove that *every* finite being is a caused being, even in the case of pure spirits, you have to find one or more indices of the dependence of finite being as such.

St. Thomas himself seems to have seen the weaknesses of this proof, for he dropped it in his later writings when he dealt *ex professo* with the existence of God ([8]).

The "Fourth Way"

In a famous passage of the *Summa theologiae*, St. Thomas propounds five "ways" that lead the human mind to

([8]) A fuller discussion of this proof will be found in F. VAN STEENBERGHEN, *Le problème de l'existence de Dieu dans le "De ente et essentia" de saint Thomas d'Aquin*, which

the affirmation of God's existence. With the exception of the Fourth Way, these proofs can be classed with the "approaches" to the metaphysical proof and will be discussed later on. The *quarta via*, on the contrary, is open to very serious criticism.

Here is how St. Thomas reasons. There are degrees (of perfection) in things: they are more or less good, more or less true, more or less noble, etc. But the more and the less refer to a maximum. There exists therefore a maximum of goodness, of truth, of nobility and, consequently, of being. But the maximum in any given order is cause of all its inferiors. Therefore there exists a supreme Being, cause of being, of goodness and of all perfections in other beings.

It is easy to see that this demonstration will not do, as it brings into play two principles that are not only not evident, but are very debatable under the general form which they assume here.

On the one hand, *the more and the less do not necessarily imply reference to a maximum*, but, in most cases, imply a unit measure: a person is more or less rich according to his sterling or dollar holding; a person is more or less tall in proportion to his inches or centimetres; a body is more or less warm in proportion to its effect on the column of mercury in the thermometer which is used to measure it (and not, as St. Thomas said, under the influence of ancient physics, according as it partakes more or less of maximal or of essential heat); even in the

was published in *Mélanges Joseph de Ghellinck, S.J.*, Gembloux, 1951, vol. II, pp. 837-847.

domain of spiritual values, intelligence, memory, will, a child's docility, are measured, not by reference to maxima, but by using tests which can be reduced to unit measures.

On the other hand, *the maximum in a given order is not necessarily the cause of all its inferiors*. Important distinctions should be introduced at this point and St. Thomas makes no reference to them. The richest man is obviously not the cause of the wealth of others. It will be said (even though this is to go beyond the letter of St. Thomas) that in the case in point it is question of a *relative* maximum, of a wealth greater than that of the others, but not of a wealth that is *absolute*. If we grant this, if we even grant that it can be shown that the absolute maximum is cause of all its inferiors (though St. Thomas doesn't do so), it remains true that the *quarta via* has not proved the existence of this absolute maximum.

Here as elsewhere St. Thomas allowed himself to be influenced by the Platonist dialectic of the degrees of perfection. He accepted it without due criticism and, like most of his contemporaries, he fell victim to the mirage lying behind this seductive dialectic.

The Cartesian Proof

The *Cartesian proof by the idea of the infinite* need not detain us long. It seems to be invalidated by the fact that Descartes considers this idea to be *positive* when in fact, no matter what Descartes may say, it is obtained by the negation of the finite. Consequently, the presence in the mind of this idea whose proper content is essentially negative is by no means sufficient to prove the existence of an infinite Being, and less still that of a Creator of the universe.

Even still there are intelligent people who believe in the positive character of the idea of the infinite. Others believe that the affirmation of infinite Being is immediately implied in that of finite beings, the two notions seem to them correlative to such an extent: limitation of finite beings could not be affirmed unless it is seen beforehand, or simultaneously to say the least, that being is of itself unlimited. Here there seems to be a confusion, unnoticed as well as unacceptable, between the conceptual plane and the real plane. On the *real* plane, which is that of experience, we apprehend objects that have a twofold character: they *are* and they are *such*, they resemble one another (in so far as they *are*) and they are opposed to one another (in so far as they are *such*); they are given as "partaking" the same perfection (being) whilst being entirely distinct from one another by their very being. On the *conceptual* plane, we express this situation by conceiving the *idea of being*, the content of which comprehends no limit, precisely because, in its extreme vagueness, it "abstracts" from all the differences perceived between beings although it contains them all implicitly; *less general ideas*, representing modes of being discerned in reality, are therefore necessarily limitations of the idea of being — an idea, moreover, which they determine from within. We see then how the finite character of particular ideas is correlative to the infinite or unlimited character of the idea of being; but that implies nothing more in reality, immediately at least, than the existence, which we perceive, of objects which resemble one another whilst being opposed, which share a common value (being) whilst each one possesses it in its own way. To affirm without more ado the existence of the infinite Being on the basis of these considerations is to confuse the notionally infinite with the really infinite. Up to the present, "participation in being" predicated of finite beings is no more than the translation, on the *conceptual* plane, of the analogical similarity of finite beings to one another: this similarity is expressed as the result of the "sharing" of the one, unlimited perfection *represented* by the idea of being. As can be seen we are still at the stage of *logical participation* and the whole problem is to prove that this is based on an ontological participation, i.e., on the existence of an infinite Being, cause of finite beings.

The Proof of P. Maréchal

These reflections lead us into the sphere of thought in which the proof for the existence of God, proposed by P. Grégoire in his little book *Immanence et transcendance* ([9]), so valuable from many points of view, is developed. The proof draws its inspiration from the philosophy of P. Maréchal and sets out to renovate completely the philosophical solution to the problem of God's existence. It is natural therefore that we should devote special attention to an examination of this essay. When we have outlined the various steps in the proof, we shall indicate the difficulties that it gives rise to.

([9]) A. GRÉGOIRE, *Immanence et transcendance*, pp. 94-130.

P. Grégoire proves first of all that the *objective capacity of the human intelligence* is absolutely unlimited and he concludes from this that the object that adequately corresponds to this capacity can be none other than *absolutely unlimited Being*: this is how the speculative aspect of our intellectual activity appears. On the practical side, i.e., on that of voluntary activity, there is an analogous situation: beyond representation or knowledge, voluntary activity tends towards a *last and absolute end* which can only be *unlimited Being*. It is conceivable, at least provisionally, that the adequate object of the intellectual tendency does not exist outside the intelligence and that this faculty is therefore the victim of the transcendental illusion exposed by Kant; in the order of action, on the contrary, the distinction between "phenomenon" and "ontological reality" has no sense; action is set in the real order straightaway and, consequently, voluntary action implies the *practical necessity of affirming*, not only the reality of those ends immediately pursued, but also *the reality of the final end or of infinite Being*. — Can we get from this *practical* necessity to *theoretical* necessity? In other words, can it be shown that it is *contradictory* to deny the real existence of unlimited Being, the adequate object of the intellectual tendency? P. Grégoire thinks that this can be done if we try to discover the conditions of objective knowledge. He goes on to a transcendental analysis of affirmation and tries to prove that judgment is an act that is "constitutive of the object as such", that judgment "sets up a relation between the given and the absolute unity of thought", that this relation is one of participation in unlimited Being, and finally that the affirmation of unlimited Being is logically necessary under pain of contradiction: the existence of God is therefore implied in every act of affirmation.

This arduous demonstration gives rise, at each one of its three stages, to very serious, perhaps even insurmountable, difficulties.

The *objective capacity of the intelligence* is absolutely unlimited: this we may grant without difficulty, but not exactly in the sense in which it is understood by the author. We are conscious of a capacity of knowing, the formal object of which is the *being* of things, whatever they are: we have in us a desire or tendency which aims at knowing *all that exists*, without any exception, for everything that exists is knowable as being; in fine, we have a *transcendental* (in the Thomist sense of the word) or *unlimited* capacity of knowing, and since we know that there are finite beings, i.e., beings opposed one to another, that limit one another (at the very least the self and the not-self), we realize that the capacity of our intelligence is measured by none of them. — Does anything else exist? Is the *unity* of reality, and consequently that of knowledge, anything more than a *unity of order*, the order of finite beings? Is a non-finite or infinite being possible? Is it not the case that one condition of existence is to be determined by a finite essence? The mere examination of my transcendental capacity is unable to provide an answer to these questions. It would be necessary to repeat here what has been already said concerning confounding the conceptual plane with the real, which can easily enter into our affirmation of the infinite: let us repeat once more that, to speak of finite beings, all that is necessary is to have experience of two beings opposed one to the other, alien

to each other ([10]); to determine the notion of being by
the notion of finite, there is no need to know whether
being is, of itself, infinite, nor even whether it *can be*
unlimited, whether infinite being is not contradictory; it
is sufficient to know that being is a value common to all
finite beings and limited in each of them by what makes
it what it is and sets it in opposition to the others. It is
not immediately evident that this *analogy* of finite beings
and this *logical participation* in the one perfection represented by the idea of being, implies *ontological participation* in one only cause, infinite Being or Fullness of being.
To hold the contrary would be equivalent to returning,
willy nilly, to the ontologist position that the transcendental idea of being comprises some sort of intuition of infinite
Being. The proposition "There exist only finite beings"
is not therefore, as far as we are concerned, *quoad nos*,
immediately contradictory; the contradiction becomes
apparent only when the fundamental relativity of the
entire order of finite beings has been demonstrated.

The second stage of the proof is open to objections
that are exactly parallel. The *object of the will*, the intellectual appetite, is co-extensive to that of intelligence: as
intelligence tends to know all that is, will aspires, beyond
all partial enjoyment, after *enjoyment of the universal order*
possessed by the intelligence. It is obvious that this final
objective cannot be attained, especially in any stable and

([10]) This means that we cannot admit what P. Grégoire
writes on p. 108:"There is therefore only one way to explain
our awareness of the limitation of objects and that is to
admit, in the intelligence, a *tendency* which, of itself, goes
beyond all finite objects".

definite manner, in our present condition and that is quite
sufficient to explain the profound *restlessness* of our will,
always borne towards something beyond what it actually
embraces. As for discovering in this restlessness a positive
tendency towards unlimited Being, final and absolute end
of the knowing subject, the attempt would seem doomed
to failure.

Much could be written about the theory of judgment
which forms the third stage of the demonstration given
above in abridged form, but we cannot here introduce a
detailed critique of this conception, directly inspired by
Kant. We shall confine ourselves to the central point
which is of special interest to the proof of God's existence.
According to P. Grégoire every judgment sets up a relation of the given to the absolute unity of Thought (p. 117)
and "in every judgment, the reality of absolutely unlimited
Being is implicitly affirmed" (p. 122). Let us take as an
example the judgment proposed by the author himself:
when we say, about anything at all, "that is", we acknowledge and we express that the subject "that" has the
fundamental value of "being" and occupies, by that fact,
a place in the order of beings that it can never be deprived
of: nothing could prevent "that" from existing when
"that" exists, prevent "that" from having existed when
it had existed, were it only for one fleeting moment. There
is therefore something *absolute* in every affirmation of
existence and, generally speaking, in every *true* affirmation: it forces itself on every intelligence, for every intelligence must, under pain of self-negation, affirm *what is*.
This absolute character of affirmation derives therefore
from the given and not from the subject, and it immediately

implies no reference to anything beyond the given which possesses *in itself* the value of being on which the affirmation rests. However, the given in question is not alone: it is part of a world of finite realities all of which, as we have seen, have the value of being, the formal object of the intelligence: consequently, when we affirm "that is" we unite the "that" to the *real unity* that is formed by the order of finite beings and, at the same time, to the *unifying principle of my thought*, i.e., to the transcendental idea of being (¹¹). Must this unity be carried further still? The answer is not immediately evident. To find it, it is necessary to ask whether finite beings, possessing *in* themselves the value of being, can possess it *from* themselves, so that the order of finite beings can coincide with the Absolute and be the ultimate reason for all things. This problem is precisely the problem of God. It must *be solved* before we can know that the unity of thought is ultimately explained by the unity of infinite Being and that every judgment, by attributing being to anything whatever, implicitly affirms the existence of infinite Being, the ultimate explanation of all reality.

As can be seen, the method advocated by P. Maréchal

(¹¹) P. Grégoire tries to show that the unity to which every judgment contains a reference is not the "sum or product of finite objects" because "it is not the addition or juxtaposition of contents of consciousness that defines its objective form" (pp. 118-119).—The ontological *order* of finite beings is something entirely different from the sum, the juxtaposition or addition of parts and it is not immediately evident that unity of order cannot be the keystone of reality and the foundation of the unity realized in thought through the transcendental idea of being.

in the search of God seems unable to meet the demands that the mind can rightfully make. When you read the long exposition of it given by P. Grégoire, the first impression is that the new itinerary is strangely complicated and that it makes access to God more difficult than ever. After a while the uneasiness becomes more defined, objections take shape, and in the end you ask yourself if the author, after having subscribed to the hypercritical ideas of J. Laminne in the discussion of the principle of causality, is exacting enough when it comes to discovering infinite Being at the term of the dynamism of the intelligence. The subtle and penetrating explanations with which he surrounds his deduction do nothing to correct this impression ([12]).

P. Isaye defended P. Maréchal's theses in a study that can be heartily recommended to keen students of philosophy ([13]). We must confess, however, that our principal difficulty remains: suppose that only finite being existed,

([12]) P. Maréchal's proof has been given by P.J. DEFEVER, S.J. in *La preuve réelle de Dieu*, Brussels, 1953, under a slightly different form. This little volume is full of penetrating insights and valuable suggestions, but the proof propounded gives rise to difficulties analogous to those we encountered when discussing the work of P. Grégoire. — An interesting discussion of P. Defever's work can be read in F. GRÉGOIRE, *La preuve réelle de Dieu. Étude critique*, in *Revue philosophique de Louvain*, February 1956, pp. 112-129. P. Defever replied in a long article: *Idée de Dieu et existence de Dieu. Réponse à une question*, in *Revue philosophique de Louvain*, February 1957, pp. 5-57.

([13]) G. ISAYE, S.J., *La finalité de l'intelligence et l'objection kantienne*, in *Revue philosophique de Louvain*, February 1953, pp. 42-100.

i.e. beings opposed one to the other, the *total order* of finite beings would have to be called *infinite* or *unlimited*, since it would be opposed to nothing; consequently, even in this hypothesis the formal object of the intelligence is *being as being, excluding all limit.* It remains, therefore, to show in some other way that the order of finite beings cannot be absolute or uncaused ([14]).

Conclusion

At the end of this discussion, that covered some of the best known attempts at proving God's existence, I feel it necessary to apologize for what may appear to have been a too summary treatment. As we pointed out in the foreword, this work is just a sketch, a bird's eye view. It is understood of course that views stated, where not supported by thorough discussion, are the sincere personal opinions of the author. It is up to the reader to examine at his leisure the validity of the criticisms made. We are well aware that experienced philosophers and even in some cases eminent thinkers still look on the Augustinian or Anselmian proofs, the *quarta via* of St. Thomas or the proof of P. Maréchal, as valid. It will be remarked that in many of these instances the point at issue is the Platonic dialectic of ascent to the Infinite; there are some minds who remain — and no doubt always will remain —

([14]) See F. Van Steenberghen, *A travers la littérature thomiste récente*, in *Revue philosophique de Louvain*, February 1954, pp. 142-144.

attracted by this form of thought. While respecting this attraction and the option it entails, I feel that intellectual honesty compels me to pronounce it illusory.

Philosophers therefore disagree — even theistic philosophers — on a problem as fundamental as that of the existence of God. This will perhaps tempt some to draw a *sceptical* conclusion; young people, especially today, are easily shocked by what has sometimes been called the scandal of the history of philosophy, i.e. the disappointing spectacle of innumerable differences of opinion dividing philosophers on vital problems as well as on less important ones.

But this impression is superficial; if you probe deeper you are struck rather by the strange convergence of ideas to be found in the case of most of the great thinkers, in spite of differences of temperament, of environment, of formation, of interests, of language, of technical vocabulary, which make communication between mind and mind often so difficult. This substantial convergence it is that, in the sphere of knowledge of God, enables us to speak of *a morally universal consent of great philosophers* in affirming the existence of a supreme Being.

This is the reason for insisting on the *considerable amount of truth* contained in each of the proofs we have criticized. Thus, the *quarta via* is made up of propositions each of which is *true* provided it is properly understood. But they are not evident *quoad nos*; and it seems to me that, in the proof we are dealing with, they have not been satisfactorily proved in fact, and that they cannot be so before the existence of an infinite Being has been demonstrated. Similar remarks could be made about the other proofs criticized; all contain valuable points and useful suggestions.

But when all is said and done the methods, formulae, principles, employed in the course of history in the proof of the existence of God are manifold and not universally approved. This is an inevitable consequence of the plurality of metaphysical systems. Can one look forward hopefully to the day when the progress of metaphysical speculation will have reduced this plurality and brought about a greater degree of agreement in this domain? We shall return to this point in the conclusions of Chapter IX, devoted to the metaphysical proof of God's existence.

Chapter VI

THE ROLE OF THE POSITIVE SCIENCES

We have come accross the positive sciences many times already on the road that should lead us to the discovery of God.

They appeared at first as formidable *allies of agnosticism*: science will soon have explained all the riddles of the universe and any appeal to a transcendent principle will be obviously superfluous (¹).

On the other hand, when we were making an inventory of the *methods* used in elaborating proofs for God's existence, we noticed that many attempts were made to prove it by the help of the positive sciences (²).

When dealing with *psychological preparations* that advance the search for God, we observed that the natural sciences can stimulate the human spirit very effectively by revealing either the imperfection of corporeal things or the wonderful order of the cosmos. In both cases, the positive sciences direct the mind towards the discovery of a higher Reality that explains both the existence of

(¹) Cf. *supra*, p. 18.
(²) Cf. *supra*, p. 42.

creatures in spite of their precariousness and the marvelous finality traces of which can be found in the organization and evolution of the universe (³).

Finally, when considering some of the *unsuccessful attempts* that have made their appearance in the course of history, we dismissed all rational proofs of a scientific kind, and we did so in the name of the method of the positive sciences themselves (⁴).

At the present day this last point is admitted by everybody: nobody believes that it appertains to science as such to prove the existence of God. God is not a "fact" of the scientific kind, nor a "law", nor a "hypothesis", nor the object of a scientific "theory". By definition the "provident Creator of the universe" cannot belong to the phenomenal order, which is that of the positive sciences. There is no need to dwell at greater length on this negative aspect of the reply to make to the question: what role can the positive sciences play in solving the problem of the existence of God?

On the other hand, this is the place to resume, *ex professo*, the study of the positive aspect of this reply, for a few ambiguities have to be cleared up and questions restated if we are to avoid taking a wrong turn and finally going astray despite the best intentions.

To keep the discussion topical and interesting, it will centre on two documents of uncontestable value, considering who the authors are: the little book of Sir Edmund Whittaker, *Space and Spirit*, and the memorable discourse of Pope Pius XII to the meeting of the Pontifical Academy

(³) Cf. *supra*, p. 54.
(⁴) Cf. *supra*, p. 57.

of Sciences on November 22nd, 1951. Afterwards we shall see what conclusions have to be drawn.

The Opinions of Edmund Whittaker († 1956)

E. Whittaker was a well known Scottish mathematician. He was received into the Catholic Church in 1930 and was one of the most respected members of the Pontifical Academy of Sciences. In 1946 he published a small volume with the puzzling title *Space and Spirit*. Its sub-title clearly revealed its object: *Theories of the Universe and the Arguments for the Existence of God* (⁵). A brief analysis of the work, followed by a few critical remarks, will not be without interest, since the position taken up by the author is fairly typical and discussion of his opinions will help to emphasize some aspects of the problem of the existence of God.

The conferences of E. Whittaker (they were lectures delivered in Trinity College, Dublin) were the result of a dialogue between a clergyman and a young agnostic who came to him to receive religious instruction. The clergyman explained to him the *quinque viae* of St. Thomas, but remarked that they made little or no impression on the young man, a graduate in physics, whose mind was closed against the assumptions from which St. Thomas's proofs started. E. Whittaker was impressed by this incident and decided to point the lesson it contained: St. Thomas

(⁵) Sir Edmund WHITTAKER, *Space and Spirit*. London, Nelson, 1946. French translation: *L'Espace et l'Esprit*. Paris, Mame, 1952. Our quotations are from the original.

started from the conception of the universe that prevailed in his day; but the science of nature has profoundly changed since. If he were alive now, there is no doubt that he would adapt his premisses to the present state of physics; what consequences would this entail for the problem of God's existence?

To answer this question, E. Whittaker gives a historical sketch of the evolution of physical theories and, in parallel manner, of the evolution of the cosmological proofs for the existence of God from antiquity to the present time.

The idea of seeking God as the author of nature or of the order in the cosmos can be found in Greek and Jewish literature before the time of Christ. It occupied a prominent place in that of the Stoics. Unfortunately Neoplatonism triumphed from the second century onwards; its contempt for matter, its disdain for experience, resulted in making arguments of the cosmological kind unfashionable and we find men like St. Anselm trying to prove God's existence by pure reason. From the twelfth century, thanks to the translations of Greek and Arabic scientific works, there was a renaissance of experimental science and especially of the physics of Aristotle [6]. St. Thomas adopted Aristotle's principles; hence he brought about a radical change of orientation in natural

[6] The author gives a very misleading account of the Aristotelian theory of hylomorphic composition: matter and form would seem to be mere concepts, mere abstractions (p. 18). For Aristotle and the scholastics they were real concrete constituents of material substance.

theology and the *Five Ways* start from the observation of the material universe (⁷).

What are we to think of the *Five Ways*? Science is familiar with different kinds of proof, such as mathematical demonstration, induction in physics, criticism of testimony in history. The *Five Ways* belong to none of these types; they rely on the existence of the cosmos and bring into play the principles of causality and analogy to carry us beyond experience, into the domain of metaphysical entities. This explains why the proofs have no coercive character. Moreover, they are no longer suited to our culture and objections have been brought against them at various times. From the fourteenth century the principle *omne quod movetur ab alio movetur* (⁸) was attacked in the name of dynamical science (*prima via*). Later on the idea of cause and the principle of causality were called in question (*secunda via*), the ideas of contingency and necessity (*tertia via*), the principles invoked in the *quarta* and *quinta via*. To sum up, the *Five Ways* bring into play Aristotelian doctrines and we are entitled to ask how these have been affected by later developments of natural philosophy.

Side by side with Thomism, there flourished in the thirteenth century a different type of philosophy in which

---

(⁷) The author says, without explanation, that the *tertia via* is inspired by Plato (p. 30). The Fourth Way reminds him of Chrysippus (p. 31). The Fifth Way, ascribed by St. Thomas to St. John Damascene, can be traced back to Jews and Stoics, to Plato in the *Timaeus* and even to the pre-Socratics (pp. 31-32).

(⁸) Whatever changes is moved by a cause.

we can see a direct ancestral form of modern science: this is the Franciscan school founded by Robert Grosseteste and rendered illustrious by Roger Bacon ([9]). They avoided, in a greater or less degree, the erroneous Aristotelian physics and advocated the use of experimental methods in physics. Ockham and his followers gave added impetus to this twofold movement and very soon, with the Renaissance, Aristotelian physics fell into decay. The Renaissance sees a return to Platonism. But, unlike the old, mystical, Platonism, that of the Renaissance was turned towards nature and contributed powerfully to the flowering of experimental science and of the fine arts. The Aristotelians were the innovators in the thirteenth century; in the sixteenth the Platonists were the party of progress. The revival of Platonism was accompanied by a return to mathematics and to the use of mathematics in physics. Soon, the great modern physicists, Copernicus, Tycho, Kepler, Galileo, dealt the death blow to scholastic physics.

To safeguard their philosophical theses, the Aristotelians tended to dissociate metaphysics from the observational sciences and to make of it a purely notional science (p. 67). They claimed that the ruin of Aristotle's physics by no means entailed that of metaphysics, which is independent of the development of experimental science. What is more, since metaphysics is the supreme science, a physical theory that contradicts the laws of metaphysics should be rejected. The *quinque viae* have a pure metaphysi-

---

([9]) As we can see, the author is speaking exclusively of the Oxford Franciscan school.

cal character and consequently are beyond the reach of the discoveries of experimental science. E. Whittaker comments that this robs St. Thomas of one of his chief titles to honour, i.e., his service to apologetics in providing it with proofs that started from concrete facts duly observed in the external world. A purely metaphysical proof is of little value in apologetics since "most men will always be more ready to believe in God than to believe in any system of metaphysics" (p. 68). Moreover, the claim that metaphysics need not be based on observational science cannot be admitted. A science of all being cannot afford to ignore any region of being regarding which knowledge is available — regions which go far beyond the immediate sensorial data. The impossibility of making a complete separation between Aristotelian metaphysics and experimental physics is shown by the fact that their explanations of the same facts are sometimes contradictory (and therefore incompatible). According to Aristotelian metaphysics the action of a material agent consists in bringing to 'act' a determination that the 'patient' already had in potency; the movement does not pass from the billiard cue into the ball but the cue actuates the movement *already existing in the ball* in potency *(sic,* p. 70*)*. It is obviously impossible to reconcile such doctrines with modern physics ([10]).

([10]) The author did not understand correctly the teaching of the medieval Aristotelians on this point. According to them the billiard cue is an *instrumental cause* and the player the principal cause. The cue exerts a *transitive action* on the ball and this presupposes *contact* between the two bodies, the *agent* and the *patient*. Its result is to communicate to the

Fresh progress in our knowledge of the physical world resulted from the "cartesian revolution" with its mechanical conception of matter and from the theory of space developed by Gassendi and Newton. The Newtonian conception of infinite space dominated physics for three centuries, from the rejection of the finite space of Aristotle to the introduction of the finite non-Euclidean space of Eddington.

The discovery of the law of gravitation by Newton called for certain changes in the presentation of the *quinta via*. St. Thomas accepted the Aristotelian cosmos governed by the heavenly intelligences. But the argument was strengthened rather than weakened, for the *laws* of nature, the law of universal gravitation, for example, provided far clearer evidence of mind than the hypothetical system of Aristotle. According to Newton, the new physics implied the existence of a Voluntary Agent as ultimate explanation of movement, but it seems that his inter-

patient a *new determination* (*actio est in passo*), in this instance, to bring it from the state of *rest* to the state of *movement* (local). When it is said that the cue "brings the ball from potency to act" (speaking of local motion), or that the motion "existed in potency" in the ball, this does not mean that the ball "at rest" already possessed motion in itself under some diminutive or imperfect form. It simply means that the ball at rest is a reality "capable of being set in motion". Remark finally that transitive action enables us to explain the *communication of movement* without the need to introduce an accident passing from one subject to another. The scholastics were right in considering this hypothesis absurd having regard to the metaphysical doctrine of substance and accident.

vention was necessary only to set things going at the beginning and this led to the idea of an absentee God.

At the same time, as the laws become more general and more perfect, they tend to reveal a natural and ontological order (p. 96), transcending the range of experimental facts. Thus it becomes possible to assert from pure theory the existence of effects previously unknown — a typical example is Hamilton's discovery of conical refraction. To sum up, *physics, at first purely descriptive, eventually becomes asymptotic to a metaphysics* (p. 100).

At the beginning of the twentieth century, classical physics gave way to the relativity theory and to the quantum theory. This called for a new metaphysics, for *metaphysics must originate with reference to physics*, since it is the conceptual framework into which our experience of Nature is to be fitted. Indeterminism in atomic physics has proved that the principle of causality interpreted in the light of Newtonian physics is worthless (pp. 106-107).

Finally contemporary astronomy enables us to estimate approximately the age of the material universe. The universe as we know it did not always exist and we can calculate when it began. That brings us to the idea of "creation" of the material world (p. 118). From the point of view of natural theology, the introduction of the idea of "creation" into the scientific image of the cosmos is of immense significance. St. Thomas believed in the creation of the world [11] solely on the ground of revelation. Now creation is scientifically established and we

[11] E. Whittaker means to say: believed in a *beginning* of the world.

can return to the *Five Ways*, and in particular to the second one, the proof from causality. But we must get rid of its essential dependence (p. 124, note 3) on discredited Aristotelian physics and restate it in the light of contemporary physics (pp. 121-126). The *Fifth Way* can also be modernized by substituting the idea of law, especially the idea of mathematical law, for that of finality. A world governed by scientific laws is obviously the work of an intelligence (pp. 127-132).

The general attitude of physicists during the last two hundred years has been to ignore metaphysics and to look on their study as independent of all metaphysics. This "isolationist" outlook can be justified in a certain sense, but it condemned science to cut itself off from life and thought, exercising only an indirect influence through its applications. In recent years, scientists have become more broad-minded and some have tried to systematize the metaphysical presuppositions of modern scientific theories. The metaphysics which appeals to them is neither materialism nor idealism, but rather the realism of traditional philosophy.

To sum up, E. Whittaker recalls that the aim of his work was to indicate to *theologians* what the obstacles are to natural theology on the side of science, and to *scientists* that these obstacles are less formidable than has sometimes been supposed; moreover, the deeper understanding of the nature of the material universe has opened up new prospects and possibilities in favour of belief in God.

In a brief appendix the author discusses the scholastic maxim *quidquid movetur ab alio movetur*. Side by side

with perfectly apposite criticisms of the unfortunate applications of this maxim and of others like it (e.g., *nemo
dat quod non habet*) by Aristotelians, a few of his remarks
reveal a pretty radical empiricism: a metaphysical law has
no value *a priori* and can be justified only by an induction
based on observation of the real world (p. 140). The
principle that asserts that nothing is at the same time and
in the same respect both in potency and in act can be
rejected without fear of contradiction for it regards the
conditions of the existence of things, their constitution,
but the principle of contradiction relates only to *propositions* (p. 141) ([12]).

E. Whittaker's interesting statement excites in the
reader's mind various reflections and questions. We
cannot enter into a discussion of all of them, but there
are a few observations that ought to be made with a view
to defining, at least in its main outlines, the position that

([12]) The distinction the author introduces at this point is
entirely illusory and inoperative. It is true that the principle
of contradiction, at least as it is usually understood, refers
formally to propositions and, through propositions, to
judgments: "one cannot contradict oneself", "the same
predicate cannot both be affirmed and denied of the same
subject at the same time". But it is obvious that a reality
that would be determined in itself as in E. Whittaker's supposition, i.e. a reality that, in its inner constitution, is both
act and potency at the same time and in the same respect,
would of necessity give rise to two contradictory judgments.
The hypothesis in question is therefore meaningless.

one has to adopt in face of the fundamental problem raised by the author. The reader will easily see where the two attitudes converge or diverge.

To do this there is no need to go into the historical sketch given by E. Whittaker. It contains lacunae, over-simplifications and inaccuracies, at least where it covers ancient and medieval philosophy. But it is only a sketch, a mere outline; though concise, it is, on the whole, satis-factory and certainly very suggestive. On one point, however, the gravest reservations have to be made, namely, when the author states that the *quinque viae* of St. Thomas are *essentially* dependent on Aristotle's physics. Aristotle's "physics" are a hybrid mixture of science and philosophy. Now it is obvious that the progress made by St. Thomas was in the sense of an emancipation of the metaphysical principles mixed up with the worthless theories of peripatetic science. Thus, the proof for the existence of God from motion is expound-ed in the *Summa contra Gentiles* with all the wealth of the physical and astronomical theories of Aristotle, whereas, in the *Summa theologiae*, it is developed alto-gether on the metaphysical plane. It seems undeniable that, in the *Summa theologiae*, the connexions between the *quinque viae* and the outmoded theories of Aristotelian science are purely accidental: act and potency, becoming or motion considered as the actuation of a potency, the principle of causality, cause and effect, contingency and necessity, degrees of perfection, participation, finality, order and intelligence — all these notions are completely independent of Aristotelian science, both as regards meaning and as regards validity. But here we come up against the problem of the relations between science and philosophy and this is a matter that we shall return to later on.

In regard to E. Whittaker's theories, they are undoubtedly highly interesting and we can to a large extent make them our own.

In the first place, this eminent scientist sees no opposition between science and belief in God. Far from believing that metaphysical explanation will be eliminated by the progress of science, he is perfectly well aware that science itself raises fundamental problems that it is unable to solve by sticking to its own methods.

In the second place and consequently, he admits that positive science cannot, with its own methods only, solve the problem of the existence of God.

It might appear at first glance as if he is prepared to admit *scientific* proofs of God's existence and so doing would contradict the view that these proofs are radically impossible ([13]). However, the disagreement on this point is more apparent than real, for he would agree that physics, in the strict sense, whether experimental or theoretical physics, cannot arrive at affirming the existence of God. Physics discovers and defines the laws governing the cosmos; it tries to explain them, at the phenomenal level, by reducing them to ever more general and ever simpler laws from which the facts can be deduced; in the end, it aims at embodying all these laws in a general theory of the universe. That is all. The methods

([13]) Cf. *supra*, p. 57.

of the physical sciences will not allow us to go further and ask, for example, what *non-phenomenal* antecedents are necessary to explain these facts.

More concretely, as regards the historical origin of the material universe, contemporary astronomy is inclined to show that the actual state of the universe is the result of a determined evolutionary process the starting point of which can be dated with some degree of accuracy. That is all it can say.

In the third place, E. Whittaker believes that scientific conclusions can serve as starting points for reflection of another type and this can reach fresh conclusions of great metaphysical and religious significance. Here once again we can follow him.

For the physicist is a man and every man is a meta-physician at times. Who would dream of telling the physicist not to speculate about "transphysical" problems suggested either by the presuppositions or by the conclusions of physics? On the contrary, E. Whittaker has every right to want physicists to lay aside the isola-tionism of the past few centuries and to become more "human" in their intellectual restlessness. Once he has reached the end of his astronomical calculations on the approximate age of the universe and on the starting point of its evolution, he brings in the idea of "creation": it is clear that he is no longer speaking as a physicist.

It is wrong therefore to say (p. 100) that *physics tends to become metaphysics*: by virtue of its formal object and method, physics always remains on the plane of phenome-na or of laws and theories from which phenomena can be analytically deduced; that means that the laws and theories must belong to the same order as the phenomena. There comes a time then when the physicist has to *leave the field of science* to explore other regions of human knowledge. The whole difficulty is how to set about the task of getting beyond the strictly physical. What means have we at our disposal to cross the frontiers of empirical knowledge? To what methods should we have recourse in order to solve the "metempirical" problems that the starting points and conclusions of science pose to the human spirit? It makes little difference whether you talk about the "philosophy of nature", or about" metaphysics of the material world", or even about "metaphysics" without addition; how is this knowledge, of a different order, to be gained? On the basis of physics and in dependence on it? In what sense? Why? and to what extent? These questions lead us to the consideration of a different aspect of E. Whittaker's thought.

In the fourth place, a valid metaphysics can be raised only *on the foundation* of the conclusions of positive science, especially of physics, and the chief merit of St. Thomas was that he rejected the aprioristic theories of Neoplatonism in favour of Aristotelian empiricism.

This time we cannot follow E. Whittaker. Let us try to determine the precise area of disagreement.

It is true that the presuppositions and conclusions of science at a particular epoch can be the object of philosophical reflection and can give rise to one kind of "philosophy of nature", or of "cosmology". What is the object of this philosophical discipline? How far is it possible? How is it built up? What are its relations to the physical sciences on the one hand and to ontology or general metaphysics on the other? This complex problem has no direct bearing on the question of God's existence. Let us confine ourselves to observing that a cosmology so conceived is inevitably bound up with the state of scientific opinion at a given moment and is therefore essentially provisional in character.

The same is not true of ontology and here we must take a firm stand against E. Whittaker's views by defending the rigorous autonomy of ontology vis-à-vis the positive sciences and, as a consequence, the complete independence in regard to physics of the proof for God's existence.

E. Whittaker rightly condemns the abuses of idealism and rationalism at all periods of history. It would be an easy matter to complete the picture by showing in detail the mistakes of Platonic idealism, the shortcomings of the extreme intellectualism of the neo-Platonists and indeed of St. Augustine, the abuse of logic and aprioristic reasoning in the Middle Ages, especially after the thirteenth century, the tendency of the scholastics to solve by dint of syllogizing, problems demanding observation and experimental treatment, and finally the deviations of modern rationalism since Descartes's time.

But between the aberrations of rationalism and empiricism there is a happy medium. Ontology is not the science of the *idea* of being and it is not an unrolling of concepts. It is the science of the *real*, of what *exists*. It is indeed the only science that studies things precisely as *existents*. That is its formal object; it begins in an *experience*, with a *given*. But its preoccupation with the most general laws of the real, the existential conditions common to all beings, does not entail that it has to take account of the complex data provided by physics or any other positive science.

When E. Whittaker infers from the universality of its object that metaphysics has to keep up with the discoveries of physics, he is confusing its material and formal objects. The object of physics is an integral part of the *material* object of ontology, but the *formal* objects of ontology and of physics or of any other positive science are completely different. It would be a good thing for the metaphysician to be aware of scientific methods and advances; it would give him a broader outlook and keep him from being too narrow-minded. But science itself has nothing to offer metaphysics. The starting points of metaphysics are very simple data and, for that reason, beyond question: something exists — something that is diverse and, in a certain sense, many; I am opposed to the surrounding world (the not-self); the existent is an object of knowledge and of desire or tendency; reality evolves; I myself am active. These data are sufficient; considered under the light of the intellect they reveal the general structure of the universe and the general laws governing the whole order of finite beings, of every kind. Straightaway the road that leads directly to the discovery of God, is indicated and, subsequently, to the deduction of his essential attributes.

The autonomy of metaphysics cannot be rated too highly: if this study, so important in the life of the spirit, depended on the ever provisional results of science, we would have to give up forever the task of setting on a secure basis those truths that command our conception of human life and destiny. That is why St. Thomas deserves to be praised no less for having set his meta-physics (and, at least to a large extent, his *Five Ways*) free from every essential link with the physical theories of Aristotle than for having refused to compromise with Platonist or even Augustinian idealism. If his metaphysics were bound up with these theories, it would no longer have any value.

This achievement of St. Thomas is all the more re-markable and meritorious when we recall that in the thirt-eenth century ideas concerning the distinction between philosophy and science were still very rudimentary, not to say non-existent. Besides, his views on the nature and genesis of human knowledge led him to believe that "physics", or the science of changeable being (*ens mobile*, sensible or corporeal being) was just one stage in know-ledge preceding metaphysics or the science of being as such. To his eyes, in any rational scheme of education, philosophy of nature, hardly distinguishable from the natural sciences, must come before metaphysics. It pro-vides it with some basic notions (such as potency and act, movement, matter and form, causality), it provides some conclusions (the existence of the Prime Mover). These will be incorporated into a new synthesis by the metaphysi-cian. In spite of all this St. Thomas succeeded in sepa-rating, in Aristotelian "physics", its pseudo-scientific theories that have lost all value (the four elements, incorruptible heavenly bodies, the theory of light etc.) from its metaphysical principles that have retained their full value.

It is true that the great scholastics of the sixteenth century, who were witnesses of the irremediable ruin of ancient physics, were forced to stress the autonomy of metaphysics so as to save it from the lot of physics. In the nineteenth century, on the contrary, there is a return to empiricism. The encyclical letter *Aeterni Patris* advised Thomists not to remain aloof from the contemporary scientific movement, but to rebuild Thomism, taking into account all that scientists as well as philosophers had achieved since the end of the Middle Ages. Thus Mgr Mercier, attentive to the counsel of Pope Leo XIII, and also under the influence of the Scientist and Positivist climate of the time, gave to his philosophy an unmistakable empiricist bias. Ontology, in his scheme, comes as the final crown of the edifice of philosophical sciences, raised on the foundation of the positive sciences.

At the present time Thomists have almost without exception left these conceptions behind. There has been a strong reaction, for a considerable time now, against any concession to empiricism. Thomist ontology, now no longer tied to positive science, has attracted the attention of contemporary thinkers more and more. Of course, in neo-Positivist circles (E. Whittaker knew them well since they are very influential in British universities), metaphysics is still treated as a science without meaning or object. This frame of mind necessarily entails radical agnosticism as regards religion. The method recommended by E. Whittaker is no less unsuccessful against this negative, narrow and obstinate stand than that of an autonomous metaphysics.

To say that Thomism as a metaphysical synthesis is independent of the positive sciences is not to say that there is any *incompatibility*. No antagonism is possible as long as each remains true to its own methods and objectives. On the contrary, ontology can and should provide the principles of a philosophy of nature having for object to deal with the *philosophical* problems raised by the presuppositions and conclusions of the sciences.

Let us now return to the proof for the existence of God traced in *Space and Spirit* and based on contemporary astronomy. While admitting the autonomy of metaphysics and the possibility of a strictly metaphysical proof for the existence of God, could we not also admit a proof directly inspired by the results of scientific investigation? Despite its connexion with the present state of science, such a proof has an appeal for those formed to positive methods who might very easily be put off by purely metaphysical speculations.

It is necessary to make an important distinction at this point. Consideration of the results of science can form a really valuable *introduction* or *psychological preparation*. It can bring home to those who are hypnotized by positive methods that science, far from solving all problems, issues in mystery. This leads these positive spirits to try a reflection of a different kind. The results of science can also serve as illustrations to bring out better the empirical starting points of the metaphysical proof for God's existence (later on we shall see some examples of this). However, it is important to see clearly that in its essential features this metaphysical proof is entirely independent of the results of any positive science whatever. To introduce these results into the proof at any cost is a needless complication and risks stating the problem in terms that are too narrow.

We shall try to show that this is indeed the case by considering the results of E. Whittaker's effort to give new life to the *Second* and *Fifth Ways* with the help of modern physics.

In the case of the *Second Way*, he shows that the "chains of causality" connecting events in the material world cannot be *closed*, for the relation of cause to effect is *strictly monotonic* or irreversible. Besides we know at present that the duration of cosmic evolution is finite and when it started can be approximately fixed, whereas St. Thomas had to prove that the chain had a terminus. We are forced therefore to admit the existence of the First Cause.

But E. Whittaker seems to move too quickly in the final and most important stage of his argument. We are not really forced to admit the existence of a First Cause but to ask what exactly took place at the commencement of our present evolving universe and what were its antecedents. To this query physics can give no answer. As regards metaphysics, all it can do is point to the signs of dependence displayed by the material universe in all its elements because of its finitude. We are thus brought back to the main metaphysical proof of God's existence. We shall see soon that this is identically the critique of finite being as such and consists in showing that all finite beings, no matter what they are, are 'caused causes', i.e., effects of one infinite Cause.

As for the *Fifth Way*, E. Whittaker is right in saying that present day as well as ancient astronomy presents the world as a cosmos and not a chaos. Mathematics, which is a system of abstract thought, has the power of solving the problems raised by physics regarding the concrete material world. This world has a character of rationality. Hence, from the existence of mathematical law, it is not unreasonable to infer that there is a Mind, analogous to our minds, in or behind material Nature, just as we infer that other human beings are intelligent from observing how they behave. The unity and coherence of the cosmos, the adaptation and co-ordination of its parts reveal an intelligible finality and exclude polytheism. Lastly, the contingency of the material world — this is an immediate corollary of the fact that it had a beginning — shows that the Designer to whom it owes its harmony is not immanent (that would entail that He too is contingent), but transcendent.

This exposé contains some valuable insights. But its inadequacy appears immediately a few questions are asked. For example, are the laws governing the evolution of the cosmos not satisfactorily explained by the nature of its constituents? It is *not unreasonable*, says E. Whittaker, to infer that there is a mind or intelligence behind nature. But is that the *only* explanation? It may well be the case but it has to be proved. Is not the present cosmic order, which had a beginning, the result of a previous order about which we know nothing at all? ([14]). Even granting that cosmic order implies a transcendent Intelligence, is it a creative Intelligence or does it do no more than

[14] We shall see later how protagonists of atheistic material- ism reject the argument from the age of an expanding universe.

organize? Are other worlds, results of a different First Cause, possible? What relation is there between the world of spirits (human or others, if others exist) and the Intelligence that explains the cosmos?

By proving the radical relativity of *every* finite being, both in its being and in its action, the metaphysical proof sets itself immediately at the core of these problems and solves them simply and easily: there exists an infinite Being, creative thought and love, sole source of the whole order of finite beings. All else is needless complication or useless digression. The results of the positive sciences can *direct the mind* towards the search for God, by raising problems, by awakening wonder and even by suggesting solutions. To that extent science has a valuable contribution to make in the domain of psychological preparations for the proof of God's existence. But the proof itself is set beyond the domain of science, on the plane of metaphysical reflection.

E. Whittaker is afraid that a purely metaphysical proof would lack the coercive character of scientific demonstrations to which scientists readily and unanimously assent. He is even afraid that people accept more readily God's existence than the metaphysics which sets out to prove his existence rationally.

The remarks, to the extent that they refer to the present-day, are pertinent. But they transport us to a different sphere, to that of psychology, and they raise other problems that have to do with, e.g., the subjective conditions of certainty, how to make metaphysics popular — if that is possible and advisable, the historical and psychological explanation of the present distrust of metaphysics, ways of leading people towards the problem of God and towards a rigorous solution to this problem, what contribution experimental methods may eventually make to the quest for God (experience of mystics, sanctity, miracles etc.). No matter what the solution to these problems may be, it has nothing to contribute to the solution of the more theoretical problems discussed previously: the relations between physics and metaphysics and their relative competence in the problem of God's existence.

If a proof of the existence of God, directly stemming from the results of science and easily capable of rallying the assent of all, were possible, we would have no hesitation in admitting it. But the process of reasoning by which we raise ourselves up to the Creator is of its very nature of a higher order and it can easily be understood how, in spite of the rigour of the proof, the mind feels itself ill at ease. In the case of metaphysical and especially of religious knowledge, more than in that of scientific knowledge, psychological and even moral dispositions are demanded. These are very often lacking. In consequence, unanimity of minds in these matters is a utopia.

The teaching of Pius XII

The address of Pope Pius XII to the Pontifical Academy of Sciences on 22nd November, 1951, had for its object "the proofs of the existence of God in the light of modern science". The main outlines of the argument are as follows ([15]). It has often been claimed that science estranges

([15]) The Italian text appeared in the *Osservatore Romano*,

man from God. But, in reality, "the more it progresses, the more it discovers God as though God were waiting behind every door opened by science". The scientist is first to profit by this progressive discovery of God "when he thinks as a philosopher". Philosophers, too, profit from these discoveries, for "by taking these scientific conquests as the basis of their rational speculation, they draw from them a greater assurance in their conclusions, clearer lights to dissipate eventual shadows, more convincing assistance to give an ever more satisfying answer to difficulties and objections. Thus stimulated and guided, the human intellect tackles the demonstration of the existence of God".

That is the essential thesis of the address.

To prove it the Pope recalls that tradition presents us with various philosophical arguments in favour of the existence of God and that they have taken shape in the Five Ways propounded by St. Thomas. These *philosophical* proofs are not, for all that, aprioristic, since they "are based on concrete realities and guaranteed by the senses as well as by science, even though they derive their demonstrative force from the power of natural reason". The progress of science throws more light on the facts which the traditional proofs take as their starting point. It is therefore useful to inquire "in what degree a more profound knowledge of the macrocosm and of the microcosm helps to reinforce the philosophical argu-

November 23rd, 1951, pp. 1-2; English translation in *The Irish Ecclesiastical Record*, January, 1952, pp. 60-71. [I have modified this translation where I thought necessary. Translator].

ments"; or, on the contrary, "to what extent they have been weakened, as is sometimes said, by the fact that modern physics has formulated new basic principles, abolished or modified some ancient ideas". Consequently, "the question is not one of revising the philosophical proofs, but rather of examining the physical bases from which these arguments derive".

Having pointed out the advantages to be gained from an examination of the empirical starting points of the proofs from *motion* (First Way) and from *order* (Fifth Way), Pius XII confines himself to the first, that from motion.

The progress of science has revealed to man "the fact of *mutability* in the deepest recesses of nature, where previously no human mind could even suspect its existence and extent". And when we think of the actual results of physics on the *direction* of the changes affecting the material world, there seems to be more than a mere confirmation of the traditional proof: these results seem "to reach almost the structure and rank of a physical proof, in great part new and, for many minds, more acceptable, more convincing and more satisfactory".

The Pope next goes on to give a remarkable summary of the scientific discoveries concerning the essential *mutability* of the corporeal world. The famous dictum attributed to Heraclitus: "Everything flows" receives fresh confirmation daily: physico-chemical transformations affecting, contrary to the belief of the ancients according to whom the heavens were incorruptible, the celestial as well as the terrestrial world, transformations inside the atom and even in the nucleus of the atom, possibility of splitting the atomic nucleus. Matter is therefore marked in its innermost structure with the seal of mutability and "consequently, its existence and subsistence demand a reality entirely different and by nature immutable"; so that "the image of eternally immutable Being emerges, clear and resplendent, from the torrent which bears away with it all material things".

But modern science "also provides us with valuable indications on the *direction* followed by the processes of nature". A hundred years ago "a continually recurring renovation and rejuvenation of the cosmos was regarded as possible". But the discovery of the law of entropy showed that the corporeal world is irremediably being consumed and is slowly moving towards its death. "This fatal destiny, from which only gratuitous hypotheses endeavour to save the universe, eloquently postulates the existence of a necessary Being". A law analogous to the law of entropy obtains in the microcosm. There is a constant diminution of the utilizable energy and "up to the present we know of no process to compensate or annul this loss through the spontaneous formation of nuclei having high energy value".

The logical implications of these facts are of capital importance both for the past and for the future of the universe. The world is growing old, "matter is approaching the state of an extinct volcano". On the other hand, "everything seems to indicate that the material universe possessed, in finite times, a powerful initial élan, charged as it was with an incredible superabundance of reserves of energy, in virtue of which, at first rapidly, then with increasing slowness, it evolved into its present state". By various means "more or less independent of each other, though all convergent", science can give an order of magnitude for the age of the world: between 5 and 10 milliard years. These conclusions agree with the opening words of *Genesis*: "In the beginning God created heaven and earth" and the figures cited "give to these words a concrete, and almost mathematical, expression". With regard to the "state and quality of primitive matter", the question is an arduous one to which natural sciences can give no answer. Philosophical reflection "penetrates more deeply into the problem". What solution does it find? "It is undeniable that a mind enlightened and enriched with modern scientific knowledge... is led to break the circle of completely independent matter... and to ascend to a creating Spirit", whose "*fiat*", pronounced milliards of years ago, called into existence matter bursting with energy, "It seems in fact that present-day science, stepping back across millions of centuries, has succeeded in being witness of the initial "*fiat lux*", of that moment when, together with matter, there arose out of nothing a sea of light and radiation, while the particles of the chemical elements split and formed into millions of galaxies".

Having reached the summit of his discourse, Pius XII corrects himself and puts a damper on what he has just said: "It is quite true that the facts established up to the present time do not constitute an absolute proof in favour of creation in time". These facts "await still further research and confirmation, and the theories based on them are in need of further development and proof before they can provide a sure foundation for a process of reasoning which is, as such, outside the proper sphere of the natural sciences. Nevertheless, it is remarkable that modern scholars, versed in these sciences, regard the idea of the creation of the universe as perfectly compatible with their scientific conceptions and that they are rather led spontaneously to this conclusion by their research. Yet a few decades ago any such 'hypothesis' was rejected as irreconcilable with the present state of science". And the Pope opposes to the peremptory statements of Arrhenius (1911) and of Plate (1907), the suggestions of Sir Edmund Whittaker in *Space and Spirit* (1946).

In conclusion, Pius XII observes that modern science "has broadened and deepened considerably the empirical bases on which the argument for the existence of an *Ens a se*, immutable by nature, rests. Besides, it has followed the course and the direction of cosmic developments and, just as it glimpsed their inevitable end, so too has it indicated their beginning in time some five milliard years ago. Thus, with that concreteness which is peculiar to physical proofs, it confirmed the contingency of the universe and the well-grounded deduction that, towards that epoch, the cosmos came forth from the hands of the Creator".

The address ends with considerations on the fruits of the knowledge of God obtained by reason and revelation.

*
* *

Pius XII was vividly struck and obviously carried away by the recent discoveries in physics and the new direction they gave to the cosmogonic theories of scholars.

Physics, far from contradicting the theses of traditional philosophy or the data of Christian revelation, brought to light *facts* which reinforced the empirical starting points of the philosophical proofs for the existence of God. Physics, too, reaches scientific *conclusions* that "almost" meet the assertions of philosophy and of faith touching the creation of the world. On this last point science does more than confirm the data relied on for a long time by philosophers: it presents us with new facts (the age of the world) from which it "almost" constructs a "physical proof for a great part new".

However, the reader will have noticed, each time his admiration for the discoveries of science risks leading him to make imprudent statements, he stops in time and adds the necessary reservations and nuances. Taken alone, he says, science cannot prove the existence of God. The scientist, to reach this point, must think as a philosopher. The data of science are bases for philosophical speculation but, ordinarily, do no more than confirm starting points long admitted by the scholastics. As regards the enigma of primitive matter, it can be solved only by philosophical reflection.

The Pope is extremely discreet when he speaks about the philosopher's task: it was not the object of his address and there is no reason to be surprised at the omission. His silence leaves the field free for the inquiries of philosophers, who have to determine the nature and value of the so-called cosmological proofs, erected on the basis of the scientific facts and conclusions high-lighted by Pius XII. Why does the radical mutability of matter entail the existence of an immutable Being? Why one immutable Being and not several? Is he "creator" or merely "mover", first cause of movement? What is the value of the principle "*Quidquid movetur ab alio movetur*" (Everything that changes is moved by a cause), which is the key to the First Way, but which E. Whittaker thought outmoded ([16])? Where does primitive matter, the starting point of the evolution of our universe, come from? Why can it not be considered absolute or uncaused? Does science prove that the primitive atom *began to exist* or simply that it *burst* at that moment? Finally, it will have to be explained why Bertrand Russell is wrong when he writes: "I think we ought provisionally to accept the hypothesis that the world had a beginning at some definite, though unknown, date. Are we to infer from this that the world was made by a Creator? Certainly not, if we are to adhere to the canons of valid scientific inference" ([17]).

It is clear then that, at the end of this brilliant exposition of Pius XII, the proof for the existence of God is scarcely under way. Does that mean to say that the address was a waste of time? By no means. But, once again, it proves that the role of science in this field is one of introduction, of preparation and of suggestion. Once this task has been done, the essential yet remains to be done.

The address of Pius XII did not escape the attention of communists engaged in the anti-religious struggle. They

([16]) Cf. *Space and Spirit*, Appendix, pp. 139-143.

([17]) B. RUSSELL, *The Scientific Outlook*, London, 1931, p. 122.

realized its significance and did their best to neutralize its effects by refuting the Pope's arguments ([18]).

The defenders of dialectical materialism say that the theory of the universe expanding as the result of the explosion of the primitive atom is naive and anti-scientific. It reminds one of "little Fritz": he saw an aeroplane flying and, because he had never seen a landing or a take-off, he imagined that it was in perpetual flight. The distance of the spiral nebulae is a phenomenon affecting a limited part of the universe, that accessible to our instruments, and this fact does not authorize us to judge the whole universe, which is spatially unlimited. It is possible that in other parts the universe is going through a process of contraction and also that, after millions or milliards of years, the movement of expansion of the universe which we observe will give way to the inverse movement. The facts do not justify the conclusion that the universe had an absolute beginning.

As far as the law of entropy, as understood by the Pope, is concerned, it might be asked in the first place what its meaning could be in the finalist conception favoured by Pius XII: God would have created an order that tended necessarily towards its own destruction. In fact, the law of entropy holds good only in a finite and closed system. If the world is spatially infinite, the process of the diminution of utilizable energy will carry on indefinitely and, since the reserve of energy is infinite,

([18]) Cf. O. KLOHR, *Naturwissenschaft, Religion und Kirche*, pp. 53-61; H. PFAFFE, K.-H. NEUMANN, *Kein Platz für Gott im Weltall*, pp. 42-48; R. ROCHHAUSEN, *Der Sputnik und der liebe Gott*, pp. 19-20.

will never reach extinction. Secondly the law of entropy is not universally applicable. Finally, it may be supposed, if we are to rely on the latest findings of astrophysics, that there exist some unknown processses by which energy is reconstituted.

To sum up, Pius XII made use of uncertain scientific conceptions and hypotheses as bases for the dogma of the creation and of the beginning of the world.

This, substantially, was the reaction of Marxist propaganda to the discourse of Pius XII. It calls for a few comments.

The orientation of astrophysics in the free world, under the influence of a number of first-rate scientists, embarrasses Marxist philosophers and forces them on the defensive. They are compelled to appeal to the more than gratuitous hypothesis of a universe that is spatially infinite, to the unwarranted hypothesis of an alternative movement of expansion and contraction and, lastly, to the still more gratuitous hypothesis of the reconstitution of energy. This adds up to a great many hypotheses for people who pride themselves on admitting only duly established scientific facts.

On the other hand, the disadvantages of a proof for the existence of God that depends on the uncertain conclusions of science is obvious. As long as we are not dealing with definitive and universally admitted truths, the use of these conclusions involves risk and the theistic thesis remains vulnerable. This goes to show how opportune were the reservations voiced by Pius XII himself.

Conclusions

It now remains to draw the conclusions of this chapter. They may be set out as follows.

1. Science raises *no obstacle* to the philosophical demonstration of the existence of the Creator, and *no objection* to the teachings of Christian revelation regarding the existence and attributes of God. On this point, the claims of some scientists must be rejected out of hand. Science studies the phenomenal order and is not competent to decide other questions.

2. Science, far from providing an adequate explanation of the real in such a way as to eliminate God as a useless and therefore superfluous hypothesis, *raises more problems than it can solve*. Progress has been made in science in the course of history, and will continue to be made, at the expense of myths, superstitions and philosophical pseudo-explanations of phenomena. This boils down to saying that science patiently takes possession of its own domain, unlawfully occupied by usurpers. But progress in science does not get rid of the problems raised by its presuppositions and its conclusions. These problems are of a different order. Science can tell us nothing either about the ontological nature of matter and its properties, or about the origin of matter, or about the eventual finality of the cosmos. Scholars and especially amateur scientists are often uncritical in their naive admiration for the conquests of science and seem to forget the essential limits of positive knowledge [19].

[19] The pages devoted to the relation between science and

3. If positive science lacks competence and jurisdiction beyond the phenomenal order, then *there can be no scientific proofs* for the existence of God. All such proofs suffer from a hidden defect in method. Scientific explanation is always on the phenomenal plane and the Creator is not on that level. Consequently, all considerations that may be urged in physics, biology, astronomy, geology or any other positive science with a view to arousing wonder or a sense of mystery are no more than *first steps* towards the proof of God's existence, approaches towards a kind of reflection that is not on the same plane as that of science. The results of science concerning the radical mutability of matter, the law of entropy, the diminution of utilizable energy, the probable age of our universe, the irreversible chains of physical causality, the unity, order, finality of the cosmos, provide philosophers with interesting *themes for reflection* that can serve as *a starting point* in the quest for God. It is up to the philosopher to trace the subsequent itinerary of this quest [20].

4. On the other hand, once the existence of a personal and provident Creator has been proved, the scientific study of the inexhaustible wonders of the created world will *help us to glimpse and admire the power, wisdom and generosity of the divine Artist* who conceived the universe and brought it into being.

the philosophy of nature by F. RENOIRTE (*Cosmology*, New York, 1950, pp. 175-181) can be read with profit.

[20] "Science is the formulation of the order of the world. And this order is one of the signs of the infinite Intelligence of God". (J. VIEUJEAN, *L'acte de foi et son mystère*, Collection *Appels*, 2e série, 5, Liège, 1955, p. 7).

5. Not only has science never proved nor been able to prove anything that precludes creation and creation in time, but also recent discoveries in physics on the probable age of the universe raise problems that *immediately suggest the hypothesis of a temporal creation*. To say the least, this would be the simplest and easiest explanation of the facts uncovered by science. In any case, there appears to be, at the present time, a fresh *harmony* between the conclusions of physics on the one hand and the theses of traditional philosophy and the teachings of Christian revelation on the other. In the eyes of well-informed people science no longer appears as the ally of atheism; this idea should be relegated to the arsenal of Marxist postulates and dogmas of the religion of communism.

The following lines of Michel Carrouges sum up these conclusions very well.

"It is not true to say that matter is mute and the heavens silent. No mystical ecstasy is necessary to hear the canticles of the worlds... Matter is the cosmic book that man is learning to open and read. This is what Science, willy nilly, is never tired of telling us."

"Brute matter exists only in the naive sensation of the solid and of the inert, in the retrogressive thinking of materialism which stops at this primitive intuition. Matter may be hard and real, but it is not an impenetrable wall, the inert bed-rock of reality. To mind, it is completely porous. Everywhere mathematical physics is uncovering the secrets of the atoms as well as those of the stars,

discovering their numbers page after page like Champoll-
ion learning to decipher Egyptian hieroglyphics''.

But, of itself, positive science cannot draw the conclusion:

"When Einstein asserts: 'What is most incomprehensible
is that nature is comprehensible', he speaks as a physicist
who affirms the intelligibility of nature, but who stops on
the threshold of metaphysics'' [21]. Metaphysics alone is
competent to interpret the conclusions of science.

[21] Texts of Michel CARROUGES in *L'Age nouveau*, January,
1955, reprinted in the collection *Appels*, 3e série, 8, Liège, 1955,
p. 3 of cover.

INCOMPLETE SOLUTIONS

Our quest is becoming more definite and the contours of the territory we are exploring are becoming sharper. We have found numerous tracks leading to the main highway — "psychological preparations" for the proof proper. We found other tracks that turned out to be blind alleys, leading nowhere — the fruitless attempts. The paths traced by the positive sciences must also be numbered among the psychological preparations; the best they can do is give access to materials that can be used in building the main highway.

At this point in our inquiry, we reach the start of the highway, i.e. the philosophical demonstration of the existence of the Creator of the universe. Fresh partial disappointments await us here: the first sections of the road have the appearance of being unfinished and, strictly speaking, seem to be nothing more than "approximations" to the proof of God's existence. We refer to considerations and reasonings that can be considered as elements of the real proof. If they are numbered among the unsatisfactory answers to the problem of God's existence, it is either because they are to some extent incomplete or because they are imperfectly and inaccu-

rately presented. We shall confine our attention to those
that are known best: the "Ways" St. Thomas outlines
in the *Summa theologiae*. But we shall not again discuss
the Fourth Way, which we included among the ineffectual
attempts.

The Proof from Movement

St. Thomas took up the Aristotelian proof of the
existence of a First Mover for the first time in *Summa
contra Gentiles* ([1]). He here expounds Aristotle's argument
at great length in the framework of the Philosopher's
cosmology. In the *Summa theologiae* this proof becomes
the *prima via*, *ex parte motus* ([2]). But here it is no longer
associated with Aristotle's physics and has become a
purely metaphysical proof. Movement is considered in its
ontological nature and in an absolutely general sense.
This is how the proof runs. There is movement, i.e.
change, in the world. Now everything that changes is
subject to the influence of a cause that moves it and there
cannot be an infinite series of "moved movers", for, if
there were, movement would remain without explanation. We must therefore reach an unmoved mover, i.e.
a First Mover.

The dialectic of the *First Way* is faultless and, on
condition that the terms used by St. Thomas are properly
understood, it is easy enough to answer the objections

[1] *Summa contra Gentiles*, I, c. 13.
[2] The *First Way*, based on movement.

raised, e.g. by E. Le Roy, or those that could be raised by a physicist in the name of the principle of inertia. I repeat once again: we are discussing the *ontological reality* of change, the indubitable fact that there are things that cease to be what they are or become what they were not. It is impossible for a thing, without outside help, to acquire what it did not possess.

But what exactly does the *First Way* prove? It proves that we must look beyond our world of becoming for an absolute, immutable reality. Is this reality one or many? Is it finite or infinite? Is it a creative Cause? Personal or impersonal? The *First Way* answers none of these very important questions and when St. Thomas concludes: "*et hoc omnes intelligunt Deum*" (and everyone knows that this First Mover is God), he is well aware that his statement is elliptical and needs to be explained.

From the fact that every changing being is dependent, it follows that there exists *at least one* unchangeable Being, source of all changes that take place in the universe. But how are we to prove that there exists *only one*? Aristotle proved that there is only one first source of all movement by means of considerations taken from astronomy regarding the unity of the cosmos and the unicity of the "primum mobile" or "first heaven". He was followed in this by St. Thomas at the start of the *Contra Gentiles*. But, fortunately, in the *Summa theologiae* he leaves out these considerations taken from Aristotelian astronomy. With them however goes the proof for the unicity of the Prime Mover [3]. As for proving that the Prime Mover

[3] The impossibility of proving the unicity of the First

is also a personal Creator, it is obvious that there is no question of it in the *First Way*.

If the *First Way* is to prove the existence of God, it must be completed and is, in fact, completed by St. Thomas in the third and subsequent questions of the *Summa*, where he develops the deduction of the divine attributes. The deduction is not at all easy if one starts from the conclusion of the *First Way*, for the difficulty is to get from the first principle or principles of becoming to the unique creative Cause. This can be done validly only by proving that *every* finite being is subject to change, at least in its activity, and that therefore the unchangeable Principle of change is necessarily the *infinite* and unique Being, creative cause of all finite beings. In short, the *First Way* is rather an approach to the genuine proof, which begins where it leaves off.

Proof from the Hierarchy of Causes

Like the *First Way*, the *Second* draws its inspiration from Aristotle. It can be summarized as follows. There is in the universe a hierarchy of causes and effects. This hierarchy cannot be reduced to a series of caused causes, i.e. of cause-effects, even if the series were infinite, for, without an initial uncaused cause, the whole series is incoherent and impossible. We must therefore have

Cause by means of the First Way had already struck Siger of Brabant, the contemporary of St. Thomas. Cf. C.A. GRAIFF, *Siger de Brabant. Questions sur la Métaphysique*, Louvain, 1948, p. 95.

recourse to a first uncaused cause and this is God. The reasoning gives rise to no difficulty once it is shown to begin with that a hierarchy of causes does in fact exist. It is obvious that the Aristotelian system of causes is completely out of date — immaterial movers, celestial spheres, sublunary bodies etc. But we have heard a scientist as alert as Sir E. Whittaker declare that this archaic system could be replaced by up to date scientific data about "chains of causes" in the material world (4). In any case, the essential fact on which the *Second Way* rests is beyond all question: "caused causes", i.e. realities that exist and develop due to the action of other realities, do exist in the world. Not all the subtleties of phenomenalism, idealism or neo-positivism can prevent any man of common sense from believing that every living being is "produced" by other living beings, that a falling stone "caused" the death of such and such a person, that fire "destroyed" such and such a building, that some microbe "caused" a particular disease etc. If caused causes exist, beings that "receive" before "giving", it is impossible to avoid the affirmation of the uncaused, unconditioned, absolute. Even if an *infinite* series of subordinate causes was not absurd, multiplying to infinity the inadequacy of every "caused cause" explains nothing: the difficulty is merely multiplied to infinity. The same holds true if you imagine that the causal chains existing at present in the universe constitute a closed circuit and that all that happens is nothing but an exchange within the circuit (the hypothesis is in conflict with the findings of present day science);

(4) See *supra*, p. 102.

you will still have to go back to a first cause, to a being that "gives" without having "received". It would then remain to show that such a cause is not involved in the circuit of caused causes, but transcends it.

The reasoning in the *Second Way* is therefore incontestable. But what exactly does it prove? It proves that you must seek the absolute beyond dependent or caused causes and that there exists therefore *at least one* first cause. But is the first Cause one or many? Is it finite or infinite? Creative or merely transforming? Corporeal or incorporeal? Personal or impersonal? The text of the *secunda via* provides no answer to these questions, though they are very important to the theistic theory. Here, too, we find ourselves in presence of a demonstration that is incomplete and that calls for indispensable developments. St. Thomas is fully aware of this since, in the deduction of the divine attributes, he goes to the trouble of proving that *every finite being* is caused and that, consequently, there exists an *infinite* Being, sole cause of the order of finite beings. We shall return to this point.

Proof from Contingency

It has been shown recently that the real source of the *Third Way* was not Moyses Maimonides, as had been believed up to the present, but, just as was the case in the *First* and *Second Ways*, Aristotle ([5]). Here is how the

---

([5]) Cf. H. HOLSTEIN, *L'origine aristotélicienne de la «tertia via» de saint Thomas*, in *Revue philosophique de Louvain*, August 1950, pp. 354-370.

argument is given in the *Summa theologiae*. There are in the world contingent beings, i.e. beings that do not exist necessarily since they come to be and pass away. But it is impossible that all beings should be contingent: for the duration of that which is able not to exist is limited. If, then, all things were contingent, the whole world would have a limited duration and, retracing the course of time, a point would be reached when nothing existed. But if ever nothing existed, nothing would exist now: what does not exist can come into existence only under the causal influx of an existing being. Therefore all things cannot be contingent and something is necessary. On the other hand, the necessary is so either of itself or in virtue of a cause. But the series of beings whose necessity is caused cannot be indefinitely prolonged in the past. There exists, therefore, a Being who is self-necessary and this is God.

The starting point of the demonstration gives rise to no difficulty: it is evident that contingent beings, in the sense of the word here used by St. Thomas, exist, i.e. beings that begin and cease to be and, therefore, do not necessarily exist. To avoid all ambiguity it should be carefully noted that St. Thomas is making use of typically Aristotelian notions that connote that whatever is *necessary* is *eternal* and whatever is *contingent* is *temporal*. This it is that enables him to continue the argument by declaring that "whatever is able not to be, has limited duration" [6].

[6] *Quod possibile est non esse, quandoque non est.* The *Third Way* starts therefore from *physical* contingency, which is a fact: we see that some being has a temporal, limited existence and we conclude rightly that this being does not exist of

But what is the value of the following principle: "if all things were contingent (in the sense indicated), the whole would have limited duration" ([7])? Anyone that believes that an *infinite* series of successive contingent beings is impossible will find the principle obvious. But when St. Thomas comes to discuss the question of the eternity of the world in the past, he denies that any valid rational argument can be advanced to disprove it. Faith alone tells us that the world had a beginning ([8]). Once you hold this, you can no longer say that it is impossible to conceive an infinite and eternal series of successive contingent beings and, in consequence, you cannot argue that at a certain point in past time nothing existed. By that very fact the whole argument of the *Third Way* loses its value.

Fortunately, the consequences of this are not serious as it is easy to put things right. All that needs to be done is to go back to the version of the *Third Way* given in the *Summa contra Gentiles*. Here the first part of the proof takes the following form: Contingent beings exist; but

necessity, since it does not always exist. If it existed necessarily, it would always exist.

Metaphysical contingency, the mark of a being whose existence is truly optional, presupposes that this being is produced by a free cause, and is not in question here. In an emanationistic metaphysics, such as that of Avicenna, for example, beings that are contingent in the physical sense are necessary in the metaphysical sense, since they make their appearance at a certain point of cosmic evolution *necessarily*.

([7]) *Si igitur omnia possibilia sunt non esse, aliquando nihil fuit in rebus.*

([8]) Cf. *Summa theologiae*, I[a], qu. 46, art. 2.

every contingent being is caused; an infinite regress in the series of caused causes is impossible; therefore, we have to come to a non-contingent, i.e. a necessary, being (⁹). In this case the demonstration is satisfactory as the minor premiss can easily be proved. St. Thomas proves it by observing that the contingent is indifferent towards being and not-being. It cannot overcome this indifference without the intervention of a cause. Let us say simply that an uncaused, absolute, self-existing being cannot be contingent. The self-existent is obviously necessary and every contingent being is, therefore, caused.

When set right with the help of the *Summa contra Gentiles*, the *Third Way* doubtless gives us a satisfactory proof. But a proof of what? A proof that there exist one or many absolute beings (i.e. self-existent and, therefore, necessary beings) and that the absolute is not to be sought among the contingent realities (in the physical sense) of the corporeal world, but beyond them. It is not a proof that the absolute is unique, that it is creative cause, that it is immaterial, that it is personal. In fine, it is not a proof of the existence of the true God, provi-

(⁹) The argument we develop here is given in the *Contra Gentiles* (I, c. 15: *Quod Deus sit aeternus*) as a proof of the eternity of God. But to turn it into a proof for the existence of God all that is necessary is to suppress the final phrase, as in the *Summa theologiae*.

Why St. Thomas ever abandoned the simpler and more satisfactory formulation of the proof given in the *Contra Gentiles* (begun in 1258) to become involved in the curious and complicated considerations of the *Third Way* (written towards 1266) is a historical enigma to which we shall return.

dent Creator of the universe. It is just one more incomplete proof that requires further development.

The Proof from Finality

The *Fifth Way* provides us with one last example of an incomplete proof. It is the well-known proof from the finality exhibited in the universe. Let us call to mind its main lines. Some beings without knowledge tend towards the realization of an end. This implies direction by an intelligent cause just as the flight of the arrow reveals the archer's hand. There exists, therefore, an intelligence or a providence that guides every being in nature towards its end.

Observe, in the first place, that the analogy of the arrow is misleading: of itself the arrow has no motion and, a fortiori, it has no fixed motion, except perhaps the downward motion due to the forces of gravity. If it goes in one particular direction, this can only be due to some outside agent and if the direction betrays purpose, the agent must be intelligent. But "natural" beings have a fixed *nature* and can act therefore only in accordance with their nature. It is not surprising that the rose bush should produce roses; it would be a surprise if it did not. In this instance the nature provides a satisfactory explanation (proximate, at least) of the activity in question. Of course, St. Thomas is not unaware of the difference between the two cases ([10]). But it would perhaps have been as well if

([10]) He even states it clearly and explicitly: cf. *Summa theologiae*, I^a, qu. 103, art. 1, ad 3^m.

he had mentioned it here and so forestalled the objection that springs immediately to mind.

Be that as it may, the analogy lies in the fact that, like the arrow, natural beings are without intelligence and St. Thomas concludes that the finality manifested in both cases is evidence of the action of an intelligent cause.

The views soberly expressed by St. Thomas in the text of the *Fifth Way* are right and profound. Parallel texts, where he develops his ideas more fully, can help to clarify and interpret them. The fact will then appear that, for the Angelic Doctor, the Intelligence that guides all natural beings to their end is the creative Intelligence that conceived these natures or principles of fixed activities and realized them *with a view to* obtaining the harmonious results with which we are familiar.

A fuller discussion of the principles brought into play in the *Fifth Way* is, nevertheless, indispensable if we wish to convince a modern reader and dispel his latent prejudices.

The proof sets off from a fact, a datum of experience: natural bodies act for an end [11]. This fact is itself the fruit of a twofold observation: these bodies always, or at least very frequently, act in the same way and by their action they obtain the optimum result [12].

These two things are indisputable and can easily be illustrated by examples from the most up-to-date scientific

[11] *Videmus enim quod... corpora naturalia operantur propter finem.*

[12] *Quod apparet ex hoc quod semper aut frequentius eodem modo operantur, et consequuntur id quod est optimum.*

discoveries. The first has for object *determinism*, the stability of the laws of nature, which is the indispensable foundation of science in all its forms. The second has to do with the *success* of nature as a whole, the marvellous evolution of the cosmos. Two principal aspects especially of the finality in the corporeal universe should not be overlooked:

1. In the *world of animate beings* (where alone we can discern "individuals" with certainty, i.e. beings that possess real unity and a certain autonomy), finality appears in the *internal harmony* of the organism, in the equilibrium of functions and in the way that all the biological activities wondrously concur for the good of the individual and of the species ([13]).

2. In the *corporeal world as a whole*, finality appears in the *pre-established harmony* of the natures that go to make it up, in the *affinities* of all kinds manifest between bodies on whatever scale you care to observe them ([14]): exchanges on the physico-chemical and biological levels, mutual adaptation of animate beings, adaptation between animate beings and inanimate matter, evolution of the world of stars ([15]).

St. Thomas sums up all these considerations in one

([13]) It is this first aspect of finality that seems to have been in St. Thomas's mind in the text of the *Summa theologiae* (*Fifth Way*).

([14]) This second aspect of finality, the order of the inter-relations of natures, is referred to in the *Summa contra Gentiles*, I, c. 13, final paragraph.

([15]) It will be recalled that Sir E. Whittaker prefers this last category of facts whence it appears that intelligibility permeates matter. Cf. *supra*, pp. 89-91.

short sentence: "natural bodies act for an end". He seems to think it evident that the tree is organized *so as to* bear fruit, that the roots are made *to* feed the plant, the leaves *to* allow it to breathe, the stem *to* support the rest and *to* ensure the circulation of the sap. All that, in his eyes, immediately betrays the presence of an intelligence. And since natural bodies are not themselves endowed with intelligence, the immanent finality they manifest reveals the existence of a transcendent intelligence.

What is the value of this demonstration?

Remark, in the first place, that the stability of the laws of nature or determinism implies, immediately, nothing more than the existence of *fixed efficient causes* or *natures*. *Agere sequitur formam*, said the scholastics: a being's activity is specified by its form, i.e. by its nature. If the world is made up of a multiplicity of fixed natures, these will of necessity produce fixed activities. These activities will realize the agent's perfection or ontological plenitude since activity is the development of the agent, the unfolding of its virtualities, its full realization.

In short, the *immediate* explanation of all that happens in the universe is to be found in the fixed "natures" or efficient causes that make it up. These, principles of a fixed activity, bring about the order we observe and could bring about nothing else. This is what the sciences set out to show with a success that increases from one day to the next.

It seems to me that it is important to stress this fact as it enables us to dissipate serious misunderstandings and to find some common ground with those who believe that they have to defend the prerogatives of science against the encroachment of philosophers or theologians. It is taken for granted therefore that final causes cannot enter into scientific explanation properly so called.

Must we stop here and give up the quest for final causes on the plea that present-day science knows nothing about finality or that, in the eyes of many scientists, any appeal to final causes is an obstacle to scientific progress?

This would be equivalent to making the naive assumption that positive science exhausts all that can be known about reality. Science, by virtue of its methods, aims at understanding and explaining the "how" of phenomena: how physico-chemical reactions take place in some living organism, how organisms grow and reproduce themselves and, eventually, how biological evolution took place in the course of past millenniums. Hasty appeals to finality and to divine providence would entail the risk of these problems, that demand to be answered on the level of secondary causes, being overlooked, i.e. (for anyone admitting the existence of the Creator) the explanation of the marvellous devices conceived and created by Providence for the execution of its designs.

The fact that science leaves the problem of finality out of account does not mean at all that the problem does not exist. The many splendid triumphs of nature in every field and the magnificent design of beings in view of realizing what is best for them — these are the things that reveal finality and prompt us to look for its source.

As a matter of fact only *purely materialistic pantheism* in all its forms (Marxism is one) claims to be able to explain the universe without having recourse to intelligence. What, briefly, is the philosophical stand taken by materialists? They say that the idea of an *Absolute Nature*, impersonal and unconscious, unfolding its potentialities in the course of cosmic duration, is no more mysterious and no less acceptable than the idea of a transcendent personal and provident Creator. They even say that it is a better explanation of the facts observed; the harmony (relative in any case) of beings is explained since they are simply partial and complementary constituents of one reality, namely, Nature, and, on the other hand, the disorder, the waste of energy, the numerous deviations that we observe are due to the fact that Nature, unconscious and blind, merely gropes forward and advances only by multiple trials and errors.

The position will not stand up to criticism. This can take two lines that ultimately meet.

In the first place, it can attack the idea of *Absolute*, or uncaused, *Nature*. "Nature" is an abstraction. In the concrete, innumerable beings exist, finite, active, individual things, opposed one to another and nevertheless acting and reacting one on another. Ontology proves that natures like these cannot be absolute or uncaused, but are basically dependent on a non-finite or infinite Being. It can then be proved that this Being is intelligent and provident [16].

Criticism of the materialist position can also be pursued along the lines of the Fifth Way. It is impossible to deny the immanent *finality* that the universe displays,

[16] Cf. Chapter IX. — The finality that appears in the activity of natural beings is one of the marks of dependence that serves to prove the relativity of these beings.

i.e. the *relation of means to end* that appears with dazzling brightness in every sector of the cosmos. This immanent finality remains without any explanation in Materialism and is attributed to chance. Ultimately, materialists say, it is the chance encounter of atoms or fortuitous combination of molecules that gave rise to plants with all the marvels of their morphology and physiology, and to animals with the wonderful structure of their tiniest organs and their exquisite adaptation to the functions they perform. This runs counter to common sense. Anyone who observes without prejudice the facts revealed by science is forced to admit that natural beings were *conceived* and *constituted* as they are so as *to* bring about by their activity the cosmic order that we admire. In other words, they are the work of an *Intelligence,* i.e. of a being endowed with knowledge and, consequently, able to put before him an end to be attained, an ideal to be realized, and able to choose the means best adapted to the pursuit of this end.

It would be well to remark that this conclusion is perfectly compatible with the theory of evolution even in its most radical forms. Granted that our actual universe is the result of the *natural* evolution of matter from some primitive atom containing in its stupendous potentialities all cosmic energies and all chemical, vegetable and animal species, this primitive atom would imperiously demand the existence of an intelligent Being able to conceive it and "construct" it with all its unheard of resources and the inner law of its evolution.

This is how Michel Carrouges expresses it:

"There is but one way to understand how nature can

be intelligible and that is to acknowledge that it is the work of a supra-cosmic Intelligence. For nature is no more an intelligence than it is brute matter; it is matter modulated by the creative Word... There is no reason why the human word should be able to interpret nature if a same divine Word did not bring into being both the order of matter and the order of spirit" ([17]).

In sum, whether one criticizes the idea of *Absolute Nature* or deduces what is implied by the *immanent finality* of the cosmos, the conclusion is the same: the existence of natures (or of determined efficient causes), whose activities concur for the good of biological individuals and the evolution of the cosmos as a whole, is not self-explanatory. The order of natures is not self-existent. It needs a cause, and an intelligent cause.

Let us leave aside for the present the first of the two lines that we have discussed: we shall show later that this way, the metaphysical critique of finite natures, can lead us to the existence of the provident Creator of the universe. But let us return to the second line, which is that followed by St. Thomas in the *Fifth Way*: the finality immanent in natural beings betrays an Intelligence.

Does this bring us to the end of our quest? Have we proved the existence of God, i.e. of the provident Creator of the universe? All we have to do is to interrogate the history of philosophy to see that at the end of the *Fifth Way* serious problems still remain to be solved. How

([17]) Text of Michel CARROUGES in *L'Age nouveau*, Jan. 1955, reproduced in the series *Appels*, 3rd series, 8, Liège, 1955, p. 3 of the cover.

should we describe the Intelligence that explains the finality of the cosmos? Is it *one* or *many*? *Immanent* or *transcendent*? Is it like a *Demiurge* that fashions natures from a pre-existing matter or is it a *Creator*? Do not the evil and the disorder we find in the universe suggest the idea of an *Evil Principle* struggling against a *Principle of Good*, i.e. a *dualistic* conception of the universe?

Let us take a closer look at these hypotheses. Firstly, how are we to show that everything depends on *one* intelligent Being alone, on a *single* First Cause? We can admit without difficulty that *our* universe is *one*, forming *one order*, and that it depends, therefore, on one single Principle of order. But do not other universes, with which we have no known relation, exist?

Some pagan philosophers admitted the existence of pure spirits or "intelligences". Are these beings caused or uncaused? Is the intelligent Principle of our cosmos one of them, as Avicenna thought, for example? If they are all uncaused, are there then many independent First Causes?

It will not be out of place to observe here that the Aristotelian system comprises, at the top of the hierarchy of beings, a series of intelligent beings, immaterial substances and movers of the heavenly spheres. The "First Mover" is first only in perfection and rank in a hierarchy of spirits that are limited. All are uncaused, though in some mysterious way they are subordinate one to another as are the celestial spheres they move. Aristotelian cosmology therefore implies some kind of polytheism. It is not unlike materialistic pantheism, as the First Mover is not efficient cause of natural beings and does not know them.

It moves as final cause, as an "object of love", but the natural beings that "tend" towards it are (with the exception of man) unconscious beings. What is there in this system to explain the immanent finality displayed by natures?

Another question: Is the Intelligence that explains the finality of the cosmos immanent in the world or does it transcend it, i.e. is it separated from the world, above it and independent of it? Some are of the opinion that an Intelligence immanent in the universe, a *World Soul*, vivifying and organizing matter, transforming it more and more in its own likeness and realizing itself more and more fully in it, provides the key to the enigma of nature. A theory like this would (unlike materialistic pantheism) explain the finality that evidently governs cosmic evolution; on the other hand, it accounts, better perhaps even than creationism, for the tragic waste and partial failure that is undeniable in the works of this Intelligence. This higher form of cosmic pantheism has attracted in the past and still continues to attract a good many people.

Others go one step further. They find an irremediable inconsistency in the idea of an Intelligence being at the same time both divine and imperfect, joined to matter and progressively realized in and by it. They say therefore that the *Intelligence* that orders the cosmos transcends it, but they see nothing more in it than a *Demiurge* organizing a pre-existing matter and transforming it from chaos to cosmos. They seem to think that this explains everything as well as could be desired: order is due to the Demiurge, disorder to the resistance offered by matter to the action of the Demiurge. This resistance might even be explained, as in Manicheism, by an evil Principle, cause of matter and antagonistic to the Demiurge or good Principle.

How can it be shown that these systems are radically unsatisfactory? How can we prove apodictically that the source of the order of natures is to be found in an *infinite* and, therefore, *unique creative Intelligence*?

It is easy enough to dispose of the theory of a Demiurge. The *dualism* of Demiurge and matter conceived as two absolute principles is contradicted by the action of the former on the latter. Matter is not, therefore, an absolute reality; it is dependent, being passive and subject to transformation. On the other hand, a *Creator* of natures is alone capable of explaining the finality that stems from their essences. Nothing but the cause that produces being can give it its own peculiar nature, the source of the determined activity by which it realizes its finality. But how are we to prove that this Creator is *unique*, except by proving that he is *infinite*? And is it possible to show that the Creator is infinite without going beyond the finite *as such* by proving that *every* finite being is caused?

We return once again to the "royal road", the *metaphysical proof* of the existence of God by the relativity of finite being and of the whole order of things finite. In place of reasoning solely about *finality* and its connection with intelligence, it will be proved directly that finite natures are *conditioned* or *caused* realities. In place of starting solely from the *material things* that enter into the world of our experience, we shall start from *finite being as such*, no matter what it is, and, passing beyond the whole order of things finite, we shall rightly assert that a non-finite or infinite, and consequently unique, Being exists. As for the problem of evil in all its forms, a problem that plays no small part in dualistic systems, it will have to be examined *in the light* of the theistic doctrine once this is established. Any proof of the existence of God that does not result in the affirmation of an infinite and unique Being, total cause of the order of finite beings, is unsatisfactory and incomplete. This is the case with the *Fifth Way*. On the contrary, every proof that, by rigorous inference, results in that affirmation, is satisfactory. For, from this conclusion it is easy to prove that this infinite and unique Cause is a personal, intelligent, loving and provident Being. This we hope to prove in a later chapter ([18]).

([18]) On the proof by finality, see also F. VAN STEENBERGHEN, *La démonstration de l'existence de Dieu par la finalité d'après les «Quaestiones de veritate" de saint Thomas d'Aquin*, in *Medioevo e Rinascimento. Studi in onore di Bruno Nardi*, Florence, 1955, vol. II, pp. 715-731.

Chapter VIII

THE FIVE WAYS

The problem of God's existence is often treated in-adequately in Thomist writings on the subject. This judgment may seem harsh, but it is in fact the opinion of the majority of those interested in this most important question.

We seem to have made less progress in this domain than in many other sections of philosophy. Two factors are responsible for this paradoxical situation — respect for tradition and intellectual servility; because of the importance of the problem they have unfortunately wielded more influence here than elsewhere.

This has meant, inevitably, that the letter of St. Thomas's writings has been preserved at the expense of the spirit. At all levels of discussion, in works of apologetics, in manuals of philosophy, even in more specialized works of theodicy, we are confronted with the *quinque viae*, isolated from their historical and literary context, badly presented, badly explained and evaluated. In some cases, it is true, the formulas of St. Thomas have been trans-formed and enriched in an interesting fashion (notably in the works of P. Garrigou-Lagrange and P. Sertillanges); ordinarily, however, even when corrected and enlarged, these proofs are not wholly convincing.

The scrupulous fidelity of Thomist writers to the formulas of the *quinque viae* is also partially explained as a reaction against the ill-considered attacks of certain contemporary thinkers who, not content with denouncing the real defects of these medieval proofs, have called into question the most fundamental principles of every realist and intellectualist system of metaphysics: recall, for example, the rightful protest of P. Maréchal against the criticisms of Edouard Le Roy ([1]).

The present state of the Thomist renaissance demands something better, however. Provided we pose the problem correctly and resolutely avoid all out-dated modes of thought, we should now be in a position to offer our contemporaries a well-founded, satisfying solution of the problem of God's existence. This is, we hope, one of the conclusions to be drawn from a reading of this work.

We have already analyzed and discussed each of the five ways in the preceding chapters: the *quarta via* has been classified with the unsuccessful attempts at a solution ([2]), whilst the other four have been branded as incomplete ([3]). If we now return to the subject, it is because the Church and the world of Thomist thought is to-day confronted with a "problem concerning the *Five Ways*", a problem to which, I believe, it is essential to give a clear and convincing solution.

([1]) Cf. J. MARÉCHAL, «*Le problème de Dieu» d'après M. Edouard le Roy*, in *Nouvelle Revue théologique*, March-April 1931.

([2]) Cf. *supra*, pp. 68-70.

([3]) Cf. *supra*, pp. 119-139.

The Problem of the Five Ways

First of all, let us try to understand the attitude of those conservative Thomists "of the strict observance". No disciple of St. Thomas can assist in the struggle of the Church against atheism without wishing to place the resources contained in the writings of his Master at the service of the cause of God. Now the most celebrated passage in St. Thomas dealing with the existence of God is clearly that in which he expounds the *Five Ways*. In view of the fundamental importance of the subject, St. Thomas must have brought all his intellectual ability to bear on the construction of these arguments. To question their definitive value is, in the eyes of these Thomists, to imperil well-founded traditional certitudes; it is virtually equivalent to undermining the whole Thomistic edifice.

Only by keeping this in mind can one understand those very revealing incidents which marked the Third International Thomist Congress, held at Rome in 1950 (⁴). In a paper presented there I set out to examine "whether certain objections put forward against the *Five Ways* by able and well-meaning critics could stand up to a thorough examination (⁵). The meetings of an International Thomist Congress seemed to me an admirable opportunity for provoking a debate on this highly im-

(⁴) Cf. *Acta III Congressus thomistici internationalis* (11-17 Septembris 1950), in *Doctor Communis*, 1950, II-III, Turin, Marietti, 1951.

(⁵) Cf. F. VAN STEENBERGHEN, *Réflexions sur les «quinque viae», ibidem*, pp. 237-241.

portant topic. The admiration felt by disciples of St. Thomas for the holy doctor and their profound conviction concerning his providential role in the life of the Church tends to blunt the edge of their criticism; few realize the harm thus rendered to the cause of Thomism. The author was not informed of any objection or reservation concerning his paper, even though the complete text had been in the hands of the organizing committee for some weeks. But immediately after the public reading of the paper, the Secretary General, speaking in Latin, set about demolishing the lecturer's line of argument: he "refuted" my criticisms and declared in conclusion that the objections formulated against the *Five Ways* were devoid of value. The execution over, the next lecturer was called to the rostrum without further delay. This extraordinary and unpleasant intervention was inspired by the most laudable motives. Roman circles were obsessed by the encyclical *Humani Generis* which had been published some days previously; during the sessions of the Congress it was cited daily and at length. The shadow of the Holy Office hung over the assembly. It was not an opportune moment for criticism of tradition or indeed for liberties with language and the dissolving influence of these "reflections on the *Five Ways*" had to be neutralized with all haste if the fears of the defenders of orthodoxy were to be allayed.

But experience proves that the majority of those, priests and laity, who seek in this venerable text for proofs capable of withstanding all objections, go away dissatisfied and uneasy. We are not concerned here with difficulties encountered by those insufficiently instructed in the thought and terminology of St. Thomas; still less with objections formulated by non-Thomistic philosophers imbued with the ideas of, for example, Kant and Bergson. It is a question simply of difficulties which the text of the *quinque viae* presents to those who have received a sound Thomist formation ([6]).

This fact is even more disconcerting at first sight, since the *Summa theologiae* was written for *incipientes* (beginners) and the text of the *quinque viae* should therefore be within the scope of those whom St. Thomas addresses. To-day, however, the deficiences and imperfections of that celebrated page are recognised, implicitly at least, by all exegetes, who affix explanations and additions which, by any standards, exceed the literal meaning of the text.

It seems opportune, therefore, to outline those principles which should be followed when using texts similar to that of the *quinque viae*.

One should realize, firstly, that it is a *medieval* text, dating from the 13th century. It should be clear, even for those who have little sense of history, that any piece of writing from that distant age needs to be adapted to the usages of the 20th century. An intelligent appraisal of the work of St. Thomas considered in its historical back-

---

([6]) A friend of mine, a brilliant D.D. and a university professor, wrote to me on 2 October 1950 as follows: "I hope you have not been upset by the Muscovite behaviour of some of the Congress organizers. I heard vague rumours of what happened. I was amazed. What you have to say in your *Ontology* on the value of the *Five Ways* literally taken appears to me no more than common sense".

ground reveals to what extent that work carries the imprint of the period in which it was written. If his profound thought has often a supra-temporal, and therefore a permanently actual, value, it is expressed in a literary form and with a logical structure which are as relative and impermanent as any expression of human thought.

This situation in no way condemns us to a pernicious relativism. *Truth* does not change. But thought must necessarily be expressed in the language of its time and be conditioned by the prevailing human outlook. If, *per impossibile*, this did not occur, the writer in question would be unintelligible to his contemporaries. The inspired authors of scripture, despite the assistance of the Holy Spirit, were themselves subject to the cultural contingencies of their age and environment. In the *expression of truth*, then, you will always find something of the relative and the provisional. To recognize this is simply to accept the human condition and the necessity for a ceaseless effort to obtain a better understanding of the eternal truth. St. Thomas is not exempt from this universal law. It is our task, therefore, as his disciples, to strip his thought of its medieval trappings so as to present it in a form which answers to the legitimate demands of our time. Only thus can its permanent value and illuminative power be utilized to the full. Hence this is also the only means of avoiding relativism.

Among certain Thomists one finds a fidelity to the very *words* of St. Thomas, a cult of the *literal*, which betrays a dangerous confusion between thought and its human expression. Sometimes they seem even to attribute to the holy Doctor a kind of infallibility which he himself would have been the first to reject. We must recognize the deficiencies and limitations of St. Thomas; we must recognize above all the typically scholastic imperfections which mark his writings. It is ridiculous, dangerous even, to maintain that St. Thomas speaks always in formal terms (*semper formalissime loquitur*): his thought is much more human, 'historical', shaped by traditions, than many Thomists believe; his arguments are often taken from tradition without having been subjected to sufficiently critical examination.

We must condemn, therefore, the attitude of all those disciples of St. Thomas who regard Thomism as a supratemporal entity. In overlooking the fact that St. Thomas was a child of his age, they overlook likewise the need for adapting his teaching to the pressing necessities of our time. By their loyalty to what is inessential in St. Thomas, they betray their inability to grasp what is of value in contemporary thought, their helplessness in the face of its legitimate demands. Furthermore, by seriously impeding the progress of Thomism they run the risk of renewing in our age the fatal errors of the Thomists of the fourteenth and sixteenth centuries (⁷).

The deficiencies and imperfections of the *quinque viae* need to be explained at both the historical and psychological level. The other texts of the holy Doctor must be used to correct and complete the formulas of the *Five*

(⁷) These considerations are taken from the article *L'avenir du thomisme*, in *Revue philosophique de Louvain*, May 1956, pp. 201-218. Cf. especially pp. 207-209.

Ways. But we cannot deny the limitations of that text or pass over them in silence.

The Group of Five Ways

The first question to be answered is: What should we think of the *group* of five ways? Did St. Thomas conceive them as five elements of one unique proof? Is each of these proofs distinct and independent? Did St. Thomas regard them as exhausting all the possible ways of demonstrating God's existence?

A certain classification can be made immediately. The first three ways appear as three parallel developments, reminiscent of the synoptic Gospels ([8]). The *Fourth Way,* on the contrary, is of an entirely different type; its metaphysical inspiration evokes the gospel of St. John, the herald of the divinity of Christ. Finally, the *Fifth Way* is inspired by a different tradition from the others.

There have been many attempted logical classifications of the *Five Ways* in the course of centuries. But in his reappraisal of the question Fr. Motte has provided an answer which may be taken as definitive ([9]). That there was nothing systematic about this alignment of *Five Ways* is clear from a study of the sources. St. Thomas never claimed that they formed a logical scheme, or that

([8]) The comparison could be carried still further: the *tertia via* differs considerably from the first two, as *Luke* differs from *Matthew* and *Mark.*

([9]) A.-R. MOTTE, *A propos des «cinq voies»*, in *Revue des sciences philosophiques et théologiques*, October 1938, pp. 577-582.

they were the only possible proofs. They seem to be the result of a personal reflection by St. Thomas on the historical sources at his disposal; he gathered together what he considered best in tradition. We may add that, as always, Aristotle had the lion's share in his choice of sources. The prestige of the Philosopher had been growing steadily since the beginning of the thirteenth century and St. Thomas wanted to channel, and at the same time utilize, the rising flood of Aristotelianism.

The unsystematic character of the group of *Five Ways* does not mean that we are not to inquire further into the connections that do, in fact, exist between them. We have already stressed the relationship between the first three ways. These state, under various forms, the *metaphysical condition for becoming in the cosmos*: an unchangeable reality (*First Way*), a self-necessary Being (*Third Way*), a first cause of everything subject to change (*Second Way*). The *Fifth Way* considers change in an inverse perspective: the *end* or purpose of this change rather than its origin, the fact that it realizes an order of purposeful natures. Finally the *Fourth Way*, seeing the world as static rather than dynamic, seeks to establish the existence of an infinite being by considering the degrees of perfection which are present in finite being.

We can propose the following scheme, therefore:
Dynamic Order:
  (1) the being which *changes* is caused (first three ways);
  (2) the being which *tends* towards an end is caused (*Fifth Way*).
Static Order:
  finite being is caused (*Fourth Way*).

The Third Way

We have already stated with regard to the *Third Way* that St. Thomas abandoned the more satisfactory formula of the *Summa contra Gentiles* for one more complicated and, to my mind, less rigorous [10]. The explanation for this 'regression' must be sought in some historical contingencies. We may suppose, first of all, that St. Thomas changed the text so as to render the *Third Way* more original in relation to the second, where causality had been dealt with already. But the fact remains that if he accepted this change of formula, he must have considered the new text as at least as valid as the old. The thing can be understood only on the supposition that the holy Doctor, when formulating the *quinque viae*, regarded an infinite series as impossible. This hypothesis is highly plausible since that is, in fact, the position which he defends in question 7, article 4 of the *Prima Pars*; here he declares that an infinite series in act, that is, one already realized, involves a contradiction; he excludes therefore the idea of a world which had no beginning, since such an idea includes the realization of an infinite series of events. In this perspective the argumentation of the *tertia via* is unassailable: if every being which exists is contingent and the entire collection of beings is finite, then we can arrive, by a process of thought, at a first contingent. We are then compelled to recognize that "aliquando nihil fuit in rebus" [11].

[10] Cf. *supra*, p. 127.
[11] At a certain point in the past, nothing existed.

This is an example of how an examination of the literary and historical context enables us to understand, if not to justify completely, a text which is at first sight disconcerting.

The Fourth Way

In the *Fourth Way* St. Thomas yields to the attractions of the Platonic dialectic. He sees in the degrees of perfection which are present in reality an immediate indication of the existence of an infinite perfection, of an absolute maximum. We have already indicated why this dialectic is not convincing ([12]). Why then does the holy Doctor employ it here? The explanation lies, we believe, in two converging facts of history: the influence of Neoplatonism in the thirteenth century and the scholastic weakness for dialectic.

Thomism has long been presented as the result of St. Thomas's preference for Aristotle over Plato. It is now established, however, that Neoplatonist influence played an essential part in the formation of the Thomist synthesis, principally at the metaphysical level. Nor was this an isolated phenomenon: medieval Aristotelianism is always found combined with Neoplatonist elements. This Platonist contribution has, on the whole, been very beneficial; it enabled the medievals to transcend the limitations of Aristotle and thus led to the formulation of a metaphysics of participation and of creation — both very definite acquisitions for philosophy. But in their initial enthusiasm

([12]) Cf. *supra*, pp. 68-70.

to explain and prove the great themes of this metaphysics, the thirteenth century doctors were led astray: they accepted too easily certain principles and methods of demonstration of a Platonic origin without realizing that these were direct consequences of Platonic idealism.

Here the second factor comes into play — the scholastic weakness for dialectic. Logic occupied a very important place in the philosophical and theological formation of the medieval student. The continued 'juggling' with purely mental entities resulted in some kind of mental deformation, in a tendency to express ontological relations between things indirectly by the logical relations existing between the concepts which represent things.

The influence of Neoplatonism and a weakness for dialectic: the combination of these two factors resulted often enough in a confusion between the real order and the logical — a tendency to reify abstractions, to affirm of the real order what is true only in the order of concepts.

This is, in fact, what has happened in the *Fourth Way*. The degrees of perfection and, more generally, the multiplicity and diversity which are present in the real reveal to us immediately that the perfection of being is *shared* among finite beings and that, as a result, all are *linked* by a fundamental resemblance. So much for the real order. At the conceptual level, there is a parallel situation constituted by the fundamental properties of the idea of being, which is transcendental and analogical, and by the resulting *logical participation*. The idea of being is limited by "differences" which are intrinsic to it and which serve to bring out the inexhaustible riches it contains implicitly. Generic and specific concepts "participate" in the concept of being, therefore, and are diversified in the conceptual order as they recede from this transcendental unity. *In the conceptual order*, therefore, the more and the less are predicated by reference to a maximum, which is the transcendental concept. Is there a unity in the real order corresponding to the unity of the concept of being in the logical order? Platonism, because it reifies the concept of being, answers 'Yes'; it regards being as an Idea, an entity *sui generis* belonging to the intelligible world. Neoplatonism of the type found in the *Fourth Way*, when confronted with the degrees of being, immediately postulates the existence of an infinite Being or of a *Maxime ens*, since "more and less are predicated with reference to a maximum", which "is cause of all its inferiors". But the doctrine of *metaphysical participation* is reached much too quickly and lacks sufficient proof. Being is a perfection shared by finite beings: this is a fact. But can it exist otherwise than in an order of finite beings which are opposed to one another while, at the same time, they resemble one another? Is not "infinite being" a contradiction in terms? The possibility of an infinite being is, in fact, revealed to us only through its actual existence; this must be demonstrated and it cannot be done through the simple dialectic of the degrees of perfection, for it is not evident that "more and less are predicated with reference to a maximum". It must be proved first of all that an infinite being exists: only then will it become evident that finite beings are participations in an infinite being and that, therefore, more and less, when predicated of transcendental perfections, refer to a *real* maximum.

The very structure of the *Fourth Way* needs to be modified, therefore, if it is to become a satisfactory proof. This is suggested to us by St. Thomas in a passage from *De potentia* (III, 5), which was probably written somewhat later than the first pages of the *Summa theologiae*. The following argument represents what he says here: Finite beings, while opposed to each other in so far as they are finite, resemble each other in their being, their unity, their truth, their goodness. The similarity of beings which are diverse and opposed reveals their common dependence on a Being which pre-contains them as cause and is not therefore finite. Hence there exists a principle of all finite beings, a non-finite or infinite Being, the fullness of being (*maxime ens*) in whom all other beings participate in proportion to their essence (*magis et minus*).

We shall soon see that this modified version of the *Fourth Way* coincides with the great metaphysical proof for the existence of God.

Inconvenience of the cosmological proofs

The *Third Way*, as we have already pointed out, can be corrected with the help of a parallel text from the *Summa contra Gentiles* ([13]). Once this has been done, the first three and the fifth ways furnish suitable demonstrations that can still be employed, provided the following observations are kept in mind.

[13] Cf. *supra*, pp. 126-127.

1. These four ways belong to the *cosmological* type of rational method ([14]), that is to say, they *begin* with certain facts derived from our experience of the material world. This is of interest to the natural sciences as well as to cosmology or the metaphysics of the material world. Consequently, these facts must be stated in terms which, far from evoking the pseudo-science of Aristotle, are acceptable to modern scientists. On this point the opinions of Sir Edmund Whittaker are well founded ([15]).

The *Second Way* will serve as an example. It begins by saying that there exists in the sensible world *an order of efficient causes,* i.e. it begins with a fact. In the 13th century this was so evident that St. Thomas did not for an instant dream of proving it or even of explaining it. Every one admitted the existence in the material world of a hierarchy of causes — celestial spheres and terrestrial bodies. But since that time there has been, in the 14th century, the nominalist critique of the idea of cause and of the principle of causality, later the occasionalism of Malebranche, then the phenomenalism of Hume and the Kantian critique, and finally the nominalist and idealist conception of science. A 20th century Thomist who just repeats what St. Thomas said without bothering to justify his starting point can be sure beforehand that he will not convince his contemporaries.

2. None of the four ways as they appear in the *Summa theologiae* constitutes a *complete* proof for the existence of God, the unique, provident Creator of the universe.

([14]) Cf. *supra,* p. 43.
([15]) Cf. *supra,* p. 91.

They have to be supplemented by the later questions of the *Summa* which deal with the deduction of the divine attributes. Consequently, we must be careful not to present these ways isolated from their context as independent demonstrations.

What, in a word, is the immediate conclusion of the four ways? It is that the absolute, the primordial reality, the ultimate explanation of the real must be sought beyond the world of beings which change, which are caused or contingent; beyond those natures which are unconsciously purposeful. There exists, therefore, outside our sensible universe, one or several unchangeable realities, one or several first causes, one or several beings necessary *per se*, one or several intelligences responsible for these purposeful natures. Is it necessary to say that such a conclusion does not constitute an adequate response to the question: Does there exist a provident Creator of the universe?

Assuming that the question can be answered positively, our enquiry must pass through several further stages before it can be completed:

— we must establish that there exists *only one* unchangeable being, *only one* first cause, *only one* being whose existence is necessary *per se*, *only one* intelligence responsible for purposeful natures;

— we must show that the unchangeable Being, the first Cause, the Being whose existence is necessary *per se* and the Supreme Intelligence *are identical*;

— we must prove that the Supreme Being is the *creative* cause of the entire universe;

— finally, we must say precisely in what sense the

creative Intelligence is interested in his creatures and what is the exact signification of divine *providence*.

In his commentary on the *Summa theologiae*, Cajetan acknowledges that the unity of God is not proved at the conclusion of each of the *Five Ways*. But he adds that St. Thomas's intention is realized, since each of the *Five Ways* proves the existence of a being possessing an attribute which belongs to God alone. This is in fact true: of God alone can it be said that he is unchangeable, an uncaused cause, a being whose existence is necessary *per se*, an infinite being, an intelligence who is responsible for the order in nature. But to attain to a knowledge of the true God it is not sufficient to discover an attribute which in fact belongs to God alone; it has to be *known* that this attribute belongs to one being and to one being only and that it is therefore a distinguishing attribute of the divine nature. In other words, *the proof of the unicity of God is an essential part of every complete proof of the existence of God*. This is missing in the *Five Ways*, with the exception of the *Fourth Way*, i.e. with the exception of a demonstration that we had to put aside as being defective and inoperative.

It must be added that the deduction of God's unicity from the conclusion of the *viae* is a rather involved process. This will be clear to anyone who has read the article of the *Summa* (qu. 11, art. 3) where it is developed. None of the three proofs proposed by St. Thomas is a direct deduction from the conclusions of the *Five Ways*. The first deduces God's unicity from His *simplicity* (qu. 3), which is itself deduced from the *First Way*. The second depends upon the divine *perfection* (qu. 4, art. 2), which is first deduced from the *Fourth Way* (16), then from the notion of *esse subsistens*, which is itself the result of considerations attaching to the *secunda via* (First Cause), the *prima via* (Pure Act) and the *quarta via* (First Being). Finally, the third proof infers from the *unicity of the cosmos* that the Principle of universal order is also unique. This Principle, though St. Thomas does not say so explicitly, can be identified with the Intelligence that orders natures and so this third proof can be linked with the *Fifth Way*.

It is however less rigorous than the other two, being more in the nature of a confirmation based on simple probability. "We see that *all* beings form an order", says St. Thomas; and later: "unity of order is *better* brought about by one principle than by several". Now it is clear that the first statement goes beyond the data of experience — the universe is not accessible to us in its entirety — whilst the second expresses expediency rather than necessity. We should not imagine that all St. Thomas's arguments were intended to be rigorous demonstrations.

The involved character of the demonstration of the divine unicity is an unavoidable shortcoming of the

(16) The text might lead one to believe that the divine perfection is deduced in the first instance from the *Second Way*, which proves the existence of a *First Cause*. We have seen, however, that the *Second Way* does not prove that the First Cause is the creative and not only a motor cause (like Aristotle's first cause). Now the first argument of qu. 4, art. 2, rests on the existence of God as "*prima causa effectiva rerum*", this being understood as creative. This argument has to be referred, therefore, to the *Fourth Way*.

cosmological method. Since it is based on selected signs of dependence in *the material world as such*, the cosmological type of argument is not immediately able to do more than transcend the material world. To transcend the entire created order (spiritual beings, on the supposition that they exist, included) and to discover the unique Principle of that order, a new type of reflection becomes necessary: one based on marks of dependence *common to all creatures*, i.e. of *finite beings qua finite*. This alone can lead immediately to the discovery of a non-finite or infinite Being, unique cause of the order of finite beings. This reflection, which we have already called the royal way of the metaphysical proof, will be examined shortly ([17]).

Conclusion

One very clear conclusion results from these remarks on the famous text of the *Five Ways*: in working out a proof for the existence of God the text has to be used with discrimination.

Too many contemporary Thomists are so attached to the letter of St. Thomas that they put forward, in works of apologetics and philosophy, the *Five Ways*, word for word, as complete and rigorous proofs of God's existence. This cannot be too severely condemned; it makes a very bad impression on a great many people. And it has to be condemned not merely in the name of philosophical

([17]) Cf. *supra*, p. 138.

criticism, but also in the name of history and out of respect for the genuine thought of St. Thomas.

Remember, therefore, that none of the *Five Ways*, literally taken, constitutes a complete and satisfactory proof of God's existence: the *First* and *Second Ways* must be developed, the *Third* and the *Fifth* have to be corrected and completed, whilst the *Fourth* is no good. On the other hand, in his deduction of the divine attributes (qu. 3 and following questions of the *Summa theologiae*) and in many other passages from his writings — passages incomparably richer and more penetrating than the text of the *Five Ways* — St. Thomas has provided all the elements of the real metaphysical proof. They contain the necessary complements of the *Ways* and from them we can glean the substance of a complete demonstration inspired by the purest Thomism and worthy to be set before our contemporaries ([18]). When we

---

([18]) Exegetes of the strictest observance acknowledge at least implicitly that the *Five Ways*, in their literal tenour, are unsatisfactory, since they embroider them with commentaries that go well beyond what is authorized by the text itself.

For example, here is how P. Garrigou-Lagrange translates the first minor premiss of the Fourth Way (*Magis et minus dicuntur de diversis secundum quod appropinquant diversimode ad aliquid quod maxime est*): "When a perfection, the notion of which implies no imperfection, is realized in various degrees in different beings, none of those that possess it to an imperfect degree is sufficient to account for it and it must have its cause in a higher being which is this very perfection"*(Dieu. Son existence et sa nature*, 6th ed., p. 282*)*. No historian will admit that the principle enunciated by St. Thomas contains all that P. Garrigou-Lagrange discovers in it. Would it not

isolate the text of the *Five Ways* from its immediate context, we are guilty of unjustifiably mutilating the thought of St. Thomas. We do something wrong when we present as his last word on the subject a summary and incomplete exposé of his ideas on the proofs for God's existence.

This verdict may appear too severe or, in any case, too blunt. I believe it is fully justified. Clear speaking is essential if we are to put an end to a deplorable state of affairs that has lasted only too long ([19]).

be good method to distinguish clearly between the literal exegesis of the *Five Ways* and borrowings made from other passages of the Master to fill their obvious lacunae?

([19]) Concerning the question of the *Five Ways*, see also Th. C. O'BRIEN, O.P., *Metaphysics and the Existence of God*, Washington, 1960, and my critical review of this work in *Philosophical Studies*, XII (1963), pp. 140-151.

CHAPTER IX

THE METAPHYSICAL PROOF

In the passage in the *Deux Sources* in which he examines the problem of the existence of God, Bergson arrives at the conclusion that the problem can and should be tackled *experimentally*. "Indeed we fail to see", he writes, "how philosophy could approach the problem in any other way. Generally speaking, we look upon an object as existing if it is perceived, or might be perceived. Such an object is therefore presented in actual or virtual experience. No doubt you may construct the idea of an object or of a being, as the geometrician does for a geometrical figure, but experience alone will decide whether it actually exists outside the idea thus constructed. Now, you may assert this is just the question, and that the problem precisely is to know whether a certain Being is not distinctive from all other beings in that He stands beyond the reach of our experience, and yet is as real as they are. Granted, for this once; although an assertion of this kind, with its attendant arguments, appears to me to imply a fundamental illusion. But then you must prove that the Being thus defined, thus demonstrated, is indeed God" (¹). Bergson then goes on to criticize the God of

(¹) H. BERGSON, *The two sources of morality and religion.*

Aristotle "adopted with a few modifications by most of his successors", and he remarks that there is an abyss between the God "most men think about" and this philosophical God that "no one ever dreamed of invoking" ([2]).

Let us admit without more ado that the Prime Mover or Pure Act of Aristotle is not the true God we are seeking: from the beginning of this study, in giving a more accurate idea or "nominal definition" of God to help us to present the problem, we took care to meet the current idea men form of God as object of religion and asked whether philosophy could prove the existence of "a provident Creator of the universe". We are discussing then the same God as Bergson and, indeed, as the God discussed in the philosophy of St. Thomas and in that of all the great scholastic doctors. It is by no means correct to say that the God of Aristotle was adopted with only a few modifications by the Christian disciples of the Philosopher, for the abyss that separates the "Prime Mover" of Aristotle and the "infinite and provident creative Cause" of Thomist metaphysics is much greater than that between this Cause and the God of Christian revelation ([3]).

Translated by R. Ashley Audra and Cloudesley Brereton with the assistance of W. Horsfall Carter. London, 1935, p. 206.

([2]) *Ibidem*, p. 207.

([3]) It must be admitted that the scholastics, both ancient and modern, are partly to blame for Bergson's mistake: they adopt the Aristotelian demonstration of a "Prime Mover" to prove the existence of the "true God"; many authors of textbooks publish courses of "Aristotelico-Thomist" philosophy

Our real quarrel with Bergson does not therefore concern the notion of the true God, i.e. the *object* of the problem of God, but the *way* to solve it: Bergson appeals to experience and to the witness of the mystics because he disputes the possibility of rational proof — which is the same as denying the possibility of metaphysics.

Anyone adopting the empirical and agnostic attitude of the French philosopher would have no option but follow him also in his way of seeking God and we have no intention of condemning this method in spite of the reserves it calls for from a strictly scientific point of view[4]. It is reasonable and prudent to trust the converging witness of people like John of the Cross, St. Theresa of Jesus, Francis de Sales and many other great Christian mystics; in order to admit the existence of God as a *fact*, it is reasonable to appeal to the testimony of the Apostles and, above all, to that of Christ himself. Some people, of a positive turn of mind, find this empirical method, this method of finding God as a duly established fact, more satisfactory and more convincing than any metaphysical demonstration. There is nothing to stop us from respecting these preferences.

But there are others who are more exacting in their demands. They want to arrive at *personal evidence* where that evidence is available and they want to know whether or not the existence of God can become the object of a rational certainty that is critically founded. I believe that

as if Thomism were nothing more than some sort of continuation of Aristotelianism.

[4] Cf. below, pp. 229-242.

metaphysics can give an affirmative answer to this question.

Metaphysical Knowledge

Bergson, as we have seen, does not believe in metaphysics for he rejects all conceptual and rational philosophy; in his eyes only a philosophy of intuition can disclose the profound nature of the real.

This is not the place to discuss the nature and value of human knowledge (⁵). Let us remark simply that though he brought out the imperfections of conceptual knowledge and though he rightly condemned the excessive claims of *scientist* rationalism, Bergson allowed his justifiable reaction to carry him too far when he condemned *en bloc* all conceptual metaphysics.

All our basic concepts are empirical concepts, i.e. abstract representations of a reality given in experience. The proposition or judgment that has for subject an empirical datum is an expression of the real; deductive reasoning is explanatory, tending to bring out what is implicit in the propositions from which the deduction starts. In short, the conceptual order refers wholly to the real order and must remain subject to experimental control. Hence, if it can be proved that basic metaphysical

(⁵) The reader who wants to examine these basic questions more closely can start with my treatise *Épistémologie*, 4th ed., Louvain, 1965. English translation by M.J. Flynn (*Epistemology*, New York, 1949). Many pertinent suggestions are also to be found in M. E. JACQUES, *Introduction au problème de la connaissance*, Louvain, 1953.

concepts are genuine representations of the real world of experience, and if the inferences are validly deduced from these concepts, metaphysics does not cease for one moment to be the science of the real, the genuine expression of the real order. Metaphysics starts from the simplest statements embodying unimpeachable knowledge of the real and has no other aim than that of finding all that is implied by these basic assertions. Not only has metaphysics for object whatever is real (and not some ideal world constructed by the mind), but it is *the only human science* that studies the real *qua real*, the existing *as existing*: it is the only science having for object knowledge of what is implied in the fact that something *exists*.

So it is easy to understand why the examination of the problem of the existence of God is reserved, in the last analysis, to metaphysics. As the science of "being *qua* being", ontology alone has for mission to determine the general laws governing the real and, so doing, to throw light on the mystery of existence. Thanks to the transcendental significance, i.e. the unlimited extension, of the idea of being, which expresses the formal object of metaphysics, the latter, alone among the sciences, has really unlimited jurisdiction, extending to all that exists. Metaphysics alone has the right to examine the problem of "ultimate reasons" or "first causes". It is its role to tell us if the transcendent Being, defined as "provident Creator of the universe", has any place in the metaphysical synthesis and if He has to be accepted as the ultimate explanation of reality.

Present day fashion is *existentialism*. Being a philosophy of actual experience or of concrete "subjectivity", a philosophy of man's plight or of tragic and mysterious existence, it shows a deep distrust of and often an open dislike for concepts, reason, discourse; it is anti-rationalist and no doubt to a great extent anti-intellectualist. I am not referring to atheistic existentialism, the philosophy of the absurd and of despair, which is assured of an ephemeral success by the moral and intellectual disorder of the day, which is very often the result of snobbery and bad taste. But there is an existentialism of the "right", there is even a Christian existentialism, which attracts some intelligent people because of its concrete method and acute sense of reality. What are we entitled to expect from this method in the search for God?

The existentialist method has so far proved remarkably successful by its penetrating, often ingenious and occasionally brilliant, exploration of the inexhaustible world of human experience; in this field existentialism makes a very valuable contribution to what we have called "psychological preparations" for the proof of the existence of God: the radical misery and precariousness of man's state, the sense of sin and the sense of death, man's dramatic longing for happiness, justice, immortality, perfect fellowship of persons, etc.; all this is excellent and, moreover, calls to mind many famous passages of people like St. Augustine, Pascal, Ollé-Laprune, Blondel and many others.

As long as existentialism precludes methods other than those of empiricism and phenomenology, we can rest assured that it will not get beyond these "psychological preparations", for God is not an object of human *experi-*

ence, the Infinite is not the *immanent* goal of our desires, but the *transcendent* Principle and Goal of the universal order, the Creator. But if existentialism should be willing to break through the barriers of empiricism and emerge into the field of metaphysics in order to find the metempirical conditions or implications of the facts of experience, it can do so only with the help of conceptual and discursive thought: for this is the only means we have of getting beyond the world of experience and legislating on all reality.

To justify its refusal to accept this conclusion, existentialism should show that beyond conceptual thought we have some sort of intellectual intuition that puts us more directly and concretely in touch with the personal Infinite. But, apart from an appeal to mystical experience (and this takes us away from philosophy), there is nothing that would lead us to believe that an intuition of that kind will ever be discovered: the repeated failures of all efforts in this direction in the course of history, from Plato to Bergson, give little ground for hope to the incurable utopia seekers of an angelic mode of knowing for human beings. The attempts made so far by the best representatives of the new school in their search for God do nothing to lessen our scepticism; all the more so as the analysis of the human consciousness renders extremely improbable the existence in us of this mysterious faculty. Conceptual and discursive thought seems to be the suitable mode of intellection for a mind that assimilates its object, a mind whose activity begins with an experience consisting of sensory perceptions and of a certain consciousness of subjective activity. From this experience conceptual and discursive activity is perfectly capable of leading us to knowledge of the Infinite and it is hard to see why any special intuition should be required for this purpose.

The metaphysical reflection that leads to the existence of God comprises of its nature two stages. In the first we prove the existence of an *absolute* or unconditioned *reality*. In the second we show that this absolute reality must be looked for *beyond finite beings*, that is to say, that the Absolute transcends the finite, or is infinite.

The Absolute

Absolute (*absolutum*, unbound) is opposed to *relative* or *dependent*. An absolute reality is one that is independent, unconditioned, uncaused, not relative to something else; it is therefore one that exists *per se*.

The *first stage* presents little difficulty and held back no great thinker. Radical empiricism alone declines to admit the need for an absolute. But this radical empiricism amounts to a refusal to think, and discussion of it is not worth while. The first stage can be summarized briefly, accurately and, for very many people, convincingly in these words: "Since something exists, something is self-existent". That this is so is evident from the impossibility of its contradictory. To say that nothing exists is not only false since it is a denial of the most evident of all data, but it implies a contradiction *in actu exercito*: to be able to assert that nothing exists, it is necessary to exist. As for the proposition "All that exists, exists in virtue of something else", it is obviously contradictory since what is affirmed as "all" in the subject is denied as "all" in the predicate, as something "else", over and above "all", is postulated.

Of course, from a critical point of view, this is a simplification. If we wish to make a rigorous application of methodic doubt and meet all the demands of criticism, we have to proceed more cautiously. The first step is to prove, against the sceptics, the *validity of judgment* and, against radical phenomenalism, the validity and significance of the *judgment of existence* (something exists).

The next step is to show the *transcendental character of the idea of being*, which enables us to synthesize, not only all the data of experience, but all that could exist beyond our experience — in short, that enables us to grasp in a confused but real way all that exists.

The last step will be to show that the integral object of intellect, grasped in this confused way in an act of thought, comprehends within itself *a value that is absolute*. For, that which is opposed to nothing can be relative to nothing; but the whole of reality is opposed to nothing; therefore, it cannot be relative but is absolute or unconditioned. Consequently, the ultimate explanation of the real must be found in the totality of the existing. As a result, *at least something* in the totality of the existing, must exist *per se* and explain the existence of all the rest. In short, an absolute, unconditioned or uncaused reality exists.

We could put this in slightly different terms. We do not know why something exists. But since something does in fact exist, it is clear that something exists *per se*. The

proposition "everything exists by another" is contradictory, i.e. it destroys itself. There is then *at least one being*
that is self-existent, that is its own *raison d'être*, that is
necessary, that has existence without having received it
from a cause, that must exist, that cannot not exist.
Briefly, there is in the reality a value that is absolute,
unconditioned. The reality contains its own ultimate
reason.

This first stage of the proof of God's existence can be
found in various forms in most of the classical proofs.
Aristotle, for example, rejects the explanation of motion
by an infinite series of "moved movers" as it is absurd to
suppose that all that exists is dependent or conditioned;
without a *First* or *Unmoved* Mover, movement is unintelligible. St. Augustine, too, demands the existence of an
eternal and *self-necessary* reality. The essential attribute
of St. Anselm's "quo maius cogitari non potest" being ([6])
is *necessary existence*. Avicenna ascends from things
composite and contingent to that Being defined by
existence, *whose essence is to exist*. The first three Ways
in the *Summa theologiae* of St. Thomas condemn infinite
regress (*processus in infinitum*) because an *absolute principle* is necessary at the origin of all that exists. The
"maxime ens" of the *Fourth Way* is the *uncaused* or
unconditioned cause of all that partakes of its fullness of
being. To sum up, aseity, the property of existing of
Himself (of being *a se*), is a fundamental attribute of God
according to all thinkers who admit the existence of a
personal God. But Pantheists also conceive the real

([6]) The being than whom no greater can be conceived.

principle of the universe first and foremost as "the Absolute" and often expressly call it that. Spinoza's *Substance*, Fichte's absolute *Ego*, Schelling's *Nature*, Hegel's *Absolute Spirit*, the *Will* of Schopenhauer, the fundamental feature of all these metaphysical entities is necessary and unconditioned existence. Even materialistic pantheism admits that an absolute reality is necessary, for it attributes aseity to Matter or Nature.

It is in the course of the *second stage* of the metaphysical proof of the existence of God that the real differences between philosophers make themselves felt. It is here that the metaphysical poverty of materialistic philosophies becomes manifest. It is at this point, too, that the defects in many famous attempts to prove God's existence are shown up.

Criticism of Materialism

The virulence of Marxist propaganda calls for a brief examination of the postulates of dialectical materialism that are repeated *ad nauseam* in communist anti-religious literature: matter is eternal, it has existed from all eternity and will continue to exist eternally; it extends to infinity in space; everything that happens in the world is but a manifestation of matter in motion. These assertions are both gratuitous and naïve. Besides, they are open to serious objections. But that seems to make no impression on the minds of Marxist philosophers. Let us recall a few of them.

"Matter is eternal in the past". That this postulate is

scientifically unverifiable is but too obvious. It is also philosophically indemonstrable unless it can previously be shown that matter is self-existent and this no materialist has ever succeeded in doing. It is strange to find a postulate of this kind so readily admitted and dogmatically asserted by persons who pride themselves on admitting only scientifically established facts.

In reality, asserting the eternity of matter is an inevitable *consequence* of atheism: all those philosophers who denied the existence of an immaterial creative Cause were forced to admit the eternity of the material world; this was the case with Aristotle and the Stoics. The consequence is the same for all those thinkers who hold that the world is a necessary emanation from the supreme Being: Avicenna and Averroes, for example, hold that the world proceeded eternally from God. On the other hand, Christian theologians have often attacked the eternity of the world with faulty arguments — like St. Bonaventure who confused creation *ex nihilo* with creation *post nihilum* and was led to declare altogether absurd the idea of an eternally created world. It is amusing to remark that Marxist philosophers unknown to themselves have adopted the (so "reactionary"!) position of the Seraphic Doctor: they are of opinion that to say that God is the cause of the world is the same as saying that the world is not eternal but had a beginning in time, seeing that the cause must exist before the effect ([7]). But St. Thomas

([7]) O. KLOHR, *Naturwissenschaft, Religion und Kirche*, p. 48. Let us remark *en passant* how easily the theological phrase *productio ex nihilo* or expressions like the following: "God drew all creatures out of nothing", "without him all would

showed, as early as the thirteenth century, that the problem of creation is entirely independent of that of the *duration* of the created world: granted an eternal creative Cause, there is nothing to prevent (on the part of the cause) the eternity of the effect. And St. Thomas concluded from this that it can be known only by Revelation that the world had a beginning in time ([8]).

On this last point, I think that St. Thomas falls victim to his great regard for Aristotle and to his extreme reaction against conservative theologians. He is perfectly right in dissociating the question of its creation from that of the duration of the corporeal world; he might even have gone further, together with the philosophers, by remarking that, if we take into account only the immediate term of the creative act, i.e. the order of finite substances, the question of a beginning in time has no sense: time is the measure of motion and does not exist apart from beings that become. An order of substances could not then "begin in time" if no temporal being existed prior to

sink back into nothingness", can be misunderstood. It is easy for a Marxist to reply that it is absurd to say that something comes out of or returns to nothing. St. Thomas is better inspired when he speaks of the "emanation of creatures from God": creatures evidently come from their Cause and not from nothing. Of course we are quite aware that the expressions we are criticizing for their dangerous ambiguity have an acceptable sense.

([8]) Read, for example, *Summa theologiae*, I[a], qu. 46, art. 2 and the opusculum *De aeternitate mundi contra murmurantes*, which betrays the author's impatience with the claims of the theologians.

this order. But created corporeal substances are active and their activity is becoming, change, evolution, successive and continuous duration, that is to say, temporal duration. This evolution must have had a beginning; otherwise it would have been indeterminate and, consequently, unthinkable and impossible. With this evolution time began. Strange to say, St. Thomas laid down the principles which irrevocably condemn the idea of an eternal world when he showed that every real, existing series had to be finite; a world eternal in the past is then impossible for it would imply an infinite series of events *already realized* and — the height of absurdity — an infinite series which is not yet complete, since it is for ever being extended by new events. But when he comes to discuss the question of the eternity of the world, he seems to forget his own principles in his anxiety to spare Aristotle and pagan philosophers [9].

An infinite series of past events is, we have remarked, both unthinkable and impossible. What makes a series distinct, determined, measurable, is the number of units it contains. In the real order (we are not talking about conceptual constructions relating to the mathematical infinite) every series of things or events is necessarily finite; there can be no question of anything other than *potential infinity* or the *indefinite* to indicate a series that increases indefinitely. Thus, for example, were the material world to last for ever, it would be eternal in the future and the series of events would increase indefinitely.

[9] Compare *Summa theologiae*, I^a, qu. 7, art. 4 with I^a, qu. 46, art. 2.

But this implies that the real or realized series would *always* be finite.

It would obviously be impossible to disprove directly the hypothesis of an infinite series or of an eternal past: being unthinkable, it does not lend itself to direct refutation. But it is easy to point out what absurd consequences it gives rise to. Here is a very simple illustration. If the past is eternal, the events that have succeeded one another up to the present are infinite in number. Are all these events at a finite distance from the present moment or are some of them infinitely distant? If you answer that *any* past event is at a finite distance from the present, then the past is finite and had a beginning, since even the event furthest removed from the present is at a finite distance and must therefore be called the first event of the series. If, on the contrary, you answer that one or many events are infinitely distant from the present, how do you conceive the transition from infinitely distant events to events that are only at a finite distance? If you answer that you get from the infinite to the finite by subtracting one, you are saying that the finite plus one is equal to the infinite. This is complete nonsense.

In conclusion: the materialist postulate of a world eternal in the past is an over-simplification and implies an internal contradiction, that, namely, of an actual or realized infinite series ([10]).

The idea of a "spatially infinite material world" is

([10]) Cf. F. VAN STEENBERGHEN, *Ontologie*, 3d ed., Louvain, 1961, pp. 248-251. English transl., *Ontology*, New York, 1952, pp. 240-243.

just as gratuitous and just as incoherent. It is gratuitous, for how could science prove that the world is infinite? Clearly, scientific instruments can discover only what is finite. It is incoherent, for all that exists is distinct or determined. All that exists corporeally is corporeally distinct or determined, i.e. has geometrical figure and measurable dimensions. The ensemble of bodies constitutes a determined multitude or a number. Here, once more, the infinite is conceivable only under the form of the indefinite, i.e. of an ever finite quantity though ever capable of increase. To imagine a *real* infinite space is like imagining an object that is undetermined, indistinct, immeasurable, unthinkable and impossible ([11]).

According to Marxist philosophers, eternal matter evolves unceasingly and it is the different movements of matter that produced the universe as we know it. This is another example of a disarming over-simplification that leaves unanswered three questions of capital importance.

1. How could an absolute, uncaused, self-existing reality, that owes all that it is to itself, change, i.e. *become other*? Is it conceivable that it should cease of itself to be itself, to be identical to itself? How explain that an absolute reality, *per se* fully determined, should be perpetually determinable, subject to transformation?

But perhaps all the changes that affect matter are no more than "exchanges" between the elements of the

([11]) Cf. THOMAS AQUINAS, *Summa theologiae*, Iᵃ, qu. 7, art. 3; F. VAN STEENBERGHEN, *Ontologie*, 3d ed., 1961, pp. 189-190. *Ontology*, pp. 175-176.

universe, without progress, without addition of new perfection, without, therefore, any change in the total perfection? Let us suppose for a moment that this is really the case. How are these "exchanges" to be explained? Why does the absolute, the autosufficient, want to transform itself by these exchanges? If these exchanges lead to no improvement, what do they mean? And if they bring about an improvement, how can the absolute be improved, become more perfect?

But it is false to say that the evolution of matter involves nothing more than "exchanges". Science does not confront us with an eternally perfect revolving material universe as Aristotle thought. No: the universe has a history and has been evolving through thousands of millions of years towards increasingly perfect forms. The Earth, for example, was gradually formed in the course of countless millions of years; life on it became possible only at a relatively late date and assumed increasingly complex forms, developing from unicellular organisms to the most perfect mammals and to man, the inexhaustible resources of whose genius form a radical contrast to the stagnation of even the most marvellous animal instincts. How are we to explain this enormous advance, these new perfections, this multiform "added" being, if we start off with nothing but eternal and uncaused matter? Very briefly, how can the greater come from the less?

2. How are we to conceive, in a world that has supposedly always existed, evolution from the imperfect to the perfect? If the past is eternal, this evolution had no beginning and the most perfect forms of matter have

always been realized. In other words, one is forced to admit (as were Aristotle and the Stoics) an eternal *cyclic return* in the evolution of the world — including the cyclic return of civilizations and historical events. Dialectical materialism has no solution to this problem.

3. How is one to explain the stupendous *finality* apparent everywhere in nature, but especially in living organisms? Marxist "philosophers", deeply imbued with 'scientism', readily proclaim that science can explain, and will be able to explain better and better, everything that takes place in the material universe. A personal God, creation, providence, finality, are all superfluous. They are myths invented by a capitalist society to ensure more effectively the oppression and subjection of the popular masses.

We have already pointed out the radical ambiguity in this 'scientist' thesis. It is true to say that the aim of positive science is to explain phenomena by their antecedents and that, by virtue of its methods, it remains on the plane of what philosophers call efficient causes of a phenomenal kind ([12]). Let us admit then, for the purpose of discussion, that the present state of the universe can be *adequately* explained as the result of the evolution of the material world by the *natural* unfolding of the virtualities contained in the original matter. But does that mean that the problem of finality has been eliminated? Are we to attribute to chance the wonderful potenti-

([12]) Even the idea of "efficient cause" is foreign to science in the strict sense, and many scientists prefer to speak only in terms of "sequences" and of "relations" between phenomena.

alities of the original matter? Is it not evident that the existence of these potentialities in matter calls for an explanation? How can one fail to acknowledge the presence of an "intelligence" that has conceived the relations of means to ends, i.e. the infinitely complex order that was to issue from primitive matter, the marvels of which not even present-day scientists are able to exhaust? Materialists should at least admit the existence of an immanent mind in eternal and absolute matter; but perhaps they are afraid of being unable to stop at that and of being forced to acknowledge at the end of it all the creative Mind, the Face of the Living God [13].

It is time to conclude. By identifying the Absolute with Matter, materialism betrays a truly lamentable philosophical poverty, an intellectual retrogression that is inexcusable after twenty-five centuries of philosophical reflection to which so many great men dedicated themselves. This materialism rests on gratuitous postulates that not only leave unanswered many important questions, but involve inconsistencies that reason refuses to accept.

The Infinite

We come now to the second stage in the metaphysical proof for God's existence. In its essential structure the demonstration is very simple and can be reduced to this:

An absolute reality is necessary.

But it is not to be found in the order of finite things.

Therefore, the absolute reality is non-finite or infinite.

[13] Cf. *supra*, pp. 128-138.

Still more briefly:

An Absolute exists.

But it is not finite.

Therefore, it is infinite.

The point really is to determine the *nature of the Absolute* (the existence of which is known at the end of the first stage) by means of a disjunctive argument of which the disjuncts are *finite* and *infinite*: what is not finite is non-finite or infinite.

It can easily be seen that the second stage of the metaphysical proof consists in showing that *the order of finite beings is conditioned or caused in its entirety*. Now by a metaphysical critique of finite being as such it is possible to show that every finite being is caused in its very being and that, consequently, the whole order of finite beings depends on a reality which transcends it. We can do this by considering finite being either in its *being* or in its *activity*.

What, in the *being* of the finite, is the sign of fundamental dependence? Contrary to what some Thomists (and occasionally St. Thomas himself) say, it is not *composition* as such. It is indeed possible to demonstrate that every finite being is composed, that it has an inner structure, that it is a synthesis of two essentially correlative, constitutive elements. However, this composition, of which the human mind has but a confused glimpse, remains mysterious and nothing can be directly deduced from it. Neither is it *finitude* as such, for, *a priori*, there is no reason for saying that the Absolute cannot be finite. A finite being is one that is opposed to other beings, i.e., a being whose reality is not that of other beings, which

are also finite in relation to it. This "relation of opposition" considered exclusively in itself does not *of itself*
imply real dependence between these beings but, rather,
separation, isolation, independence. It is not immediately
evident that there cannot be more than one Absolute
being, i.e. many finite Absolute beings. What reveals
the fundamental relativity of finite beings is *their profound
similarity despite their diversity*: this similarity is completely unintelligible if we refuse to go beyond the domain
of things finite.

We have just pointed out that finite beings are opposed
one to another, are different one from another. Consequently one cannot be the adequate cause of another,
i.e., the cause of being or creative cause. If one were the
creative cause of another, it would pre-contain that other
adequately and, as a result, could not be opposed to its
effect in the way that finite is opposed to finite. Yet
finite beings are altogether alike as beings, having a
real deep-seated "kinship", a "family relationship" which
must have a reason unless it is to remain totally unintelligible. This profound ontological family likeness, which
cannot be accounted for by the relations of creative
causality *between* finite beings, can only be explained by
their *common dependence* on one single Cause transcending all finite beings or infinite.

Thus, therefore, every finite being is one that is caused.
An *"absolute finite being"* is a contradiction in terms: as
being it is ontologically related to all other beings by a
fundamental similarity. This similarity is unintelligible if
it is both *finite* and *absolute*, for, as *finite*, it cannot be
the adequate *cause* of the others and, as *absolute*, it cannot

be *caused*; it has therefore no real relationship with other finite beings.

The demonstration can be reduced to a proof *per absurdum* by bringing into relief the incompatibility of the Absolute and the finite: the Absolute can have no real, adequate similarity except with its own effects; but, if it were finite, it could not be the adequate cause of any other being; therefore, it cannot be finite.

In the order of *activity* the proof is still more striking. However, it has to be shown beforehand that every finite being is necessarily a source of activity.

Let us start from our consciousness of our own activity. I breathe, eat, see, think, will, walk, speak. What does all this mean? It means that I am not satisfied to be and remain what I am: I am forever the source of new actions that make me more perfect; I acquire new perfections ceaselessly; I am the principle of an inner development which really enriches me without, however, altering my fundamental identity. This "added being" of which I am the principle is called *activity*. It is, then, a mysterious *power of expansion*, allowing the subject to reach outwards, to surmount the barriers of finitude by entering into relation with surrounding beings; it is the profound *dynamism*, the *natural tendency* which ceaselessly inclines a being towards its perfection by communion with other beings. It is by my activity that I develop and realize myself fully, that in a certain sense I transcend myself.

Whence comes this power of expansion? Certainly not from the surrounding beings. I need them in order to act, no doubt: to breathe I need oxygen, I need food to keep myself alive, objects of visual perception etc. But clearly this indispensable complement of my power of acting is not action, but merely its preliminary condition. Fill a carboy with oxygen: the carboy will not breathe. Pour water into a vase: the vase will not drink. Expose a photographic plate to the light: it does not see the landscape. *Activity proceeds from the active subject*: *I* breathe, *I* eat, *I* see. The mysterious power of assimilating oxygen, food, objects of perception, is mine. Once more, whence this power of self-perfection, of transcending the limits of the self?

I am *being* and I am *such a being*. I share in the common, universal perfection of being. But my being is limited by my nature: I am a man and nothing more. My *own nature*, my concrete human nature, which limits my being and sets me in opposition to all others, can explain the *nature* or the *limits* of my activity. If I perform human acts, it is because I am a man. I cannot do things that are beyond the power of man. But activity proper, my power to expand, the dynamism which carries me beyond myself, can have no source other than my own being: "*agere sequitur esse*", St. Thomas constantly repeats. Activity accompanies, results from and is an essential property of being. Briefly, *in me* no other explanation of activity is possible but being; to have the basic perfection of being is the necessary and sufficient condition of acting. The "added being" that acting is proceeds from being and from it alone. To be is to be able to act.

The case is the same for all finite beings whatsoever: all possess the fundamental perfection of being and all possess it in proportion to their proper nature. Consequently all possess the source of action, the necessary and sufficient condition of the dynamism of activity and in all beings this power of expansion is proportionate to the nature of the being: "*agere sequitur formam*", says St. Thomas. Action is determined by a being's form, i.e. by its nature or essence. Every finite being has its own way of acting; its nature limits its power of expansion without ever suppressing it, as it limits its being without ever suppressing it.

Every finite being is then a principle of activity, i.e. it tends to perfect itself by entering into relation with other finite beings. Now this state of affairs betrays essential indigence and dependence in every direction.

In the first place, active being is dependent because it is *perfectible*. An absolute being cannot be perfectible since perfectibility implies the possibility of being causally influenced. Nothing can perfect itself, nothing can give itself a perfection that it has not got. Since finite being is perfectible *in virtue of its essence* or nature, which is limited, it is dependent also in its very essence.

In the second place, active being is dependent because it *tends positively* towards other beings to perfect itself. An absolute being could not tend towards something else. Since this active tendency is *essential*, it reveals an essential relativity. In other words, its power of expansion directs finite being towards other finite beings in which it finds its complementary perfection. But this power of expansion comes to it *from its very being*, from its innermost constitution and it manifests, therefore, a relativity in being or *fundamental* dependence.

In the third place, the need that active being has of

finding in others the *complement* of its power of acting is a result of its essential limitation: without the help of others it cannot conquer its isolation and realize itself fully. This is a fresh indication of *essential* indigence.

In the fourth place, activity that is really exercised reveals a *pre-established harmony between the active beings* or finite natures since, on account of their very nature, these beings complete one another mutually and are therefore orientated one towards another. This, too, is a sign of *fundamental* or *essential* relativity.

Finally, the active being that *produces its actus secundus* is truly its immediate principle or source. But it perfects itself by the activity that emanates from its innermost being. How could this be the case if it was not constantly, *in its very being*, under the influence of a cause which, in giving it being, gives it by that very fact, this power to expand and transcend itself.

It can be seen that the activity of finite being everywhere betrays radical or essential dependence: in its constitutive reality finite being is relative, dependent being. *An "absolute finite being" is a contradiction in terms*, for, *qua finite*, it includes the power of acting that it excludes *qua absolute being*.

Thus whether considered in its being or in its activity, finite being appears as an entirely relative, conditioned or dependent being.

But is it not conceivable that every finite being is relative *to the other finite beings*, that it is conditioned by the *order of finite beings* conceived as the absolute reality and the ultimate explanation of everything?

This final attempt to explain the finite by the finite is altogether illusory and owes to imagination whatever semblance of consistency it seems to have. For the order of things finite has no reality other than that of the finite things themselves. A collection of beings each of which is dependent in its very being and none of which can account for the being of any of the others is totally dependent. A new global effect can be obtained by a synthesis of several elements provided that each is partly efficacious. With a number of stones you can build an arch, for each contributes its cohesiveness, geometrical form and weight; several horses can move a chariot that one alone could not set in motion as each one contributes to the global effect by its muscular exertion. But you can never obtain an absolute being from the multiplication of completely relative beings, any more than you can set a chariot in motion by harnessing it to wooden horses. Keep for ever multiplying beings that are dependent in their very being and you multiply imperfection infinitely.

Moreover, let us consider the matter more closely and ask ourselves how the order of finite beings could account for either their ontogical *similarity* or their *activity*.

Their fundamental similarity has no ground in the order as such; on the contrary, it is the ground of the order, i.e. of the unity of the many. Because all these beings are finite i.e. opposed, different, isolated, none of them can pre-contain any other as its total cause and, consequently, the fundamental similarity uniting them remains unintelligible.

As regards their activity, it adds a new perfection to

the whole order. Each of the finite beings receives increase, really develops by its activity. The activities of finite beings are not to be taken as mere "exchanges", with no effect on the global perfection of the universe. An acting being is really a source of new perfection, which increases the perfection of the universe. In a word, the order of finite beings is perfectible. But if this is the case it is obvious that it cannot be an absolute reality, for all change involves dependence. No being can give itself a perfection it did not possess.

This brings us to the end of the second stage of our demonstration and we can state as follows the conclusion to be drawn: every finite being considered separately, and the whole order of finite beings, manifest an indigence, a dependence or a total relativity towards a reality that transcends the finite, i.e. a reality that is non-finite or infinite.

Features of the Metaphysical Proof

Here we have, in broad outline, the reasoning leading from that most elementary assertion, "something exists", to the summit of human thinking and culminating point of metaphysics — the assertion of the existence of an infinite Being, creative cause of all finite beings or of the order of finite beings.

In order to bring out the full force of this reasoning or demonstration a few supplementary remarks are indispensable.

It is easy to see that the *strength of the proof* lies in the radical antinomy of *absolute* and *finite*, which forces us logically to admit the existence of a being that transcends the finite. But in order to perceive the consequences of this antinomy we have to bring the principle of causality into play in its most general and, also, most evident form: "that which is not self-existent, depends on a cause"; or again "that which is not self-explanatory has to be explained by a cause". This is precisely the case with finite being: neither its fundamental similarity with other finite beings nor its activity are intelligible by themselves; these two essential features of finite being show its essential dependence on an infinite Cause.

Let us return for a moment to the *method* used in the outline of the proof just given and endeavour to see why every really satisfactory proof is reducible to it. The problem is to find the "Creator of the universe", i.e. the sole adequate Cause of all that is distinct from it. This is possible only on condition that, having first proved the necessity of an Absolute, we then *transcend the finite as such*. For if we are content merely to transcend *certain categories* of finite being (material things, for example), we do not show the relativity of *other* finite beings that may exist outside these categories and consequently we are not entitled to say that the Absolute is *infinite*. To prove, however, that he is *one*, it is necessary to prove that the First Cause is infinite. In consequence, by relying on only one category of finite beings, you cannot affirm that there is only one Absolute nor that there is only one Creator of all.

There are then two things indispensable in every

rigorous proof of the existence of God: the knowledge that *an Absolute is necessary* and the knowledge that *the finite as such is relative*. Knowledge of these two things is essentially of a metaphysical nature and that is sufficient to rule out as inadequate every proof that remains below the level of metaphysics. On the other hand, knowledge of the relativity of the finite as such can be acquired only by the metaphysical critique of its *being* and of its *activity*, for these are the only two aspects of any finite being which are accessible to us.

In the light of these considerations it would not be difficult to show in detail the weak points in many proofs that we have rejected. Some fail to show the necessity for an Absolute. Others do no more than prove that certain categories of finite being are contingent. Others endeavour to prove the relativity of finite being by proofs that are defective: by the real composition of essence and existence, by the fact that existence does not enter into the definition of finite being, by the very notion of finite being which, it is claimed, immediately reveals the existence of the Infinite, and finally, by the hierarchy of finite beings implying, it is said, at its summit an absolute maximum. Others aspire to knowledge of the infinite Being without any appeal to the relativity of the finite as such, relying, for example, on the dynamism of the intelligence. We have pointed out the defects in these different proofs.

The proof just outlined is an *a posteriori* proof, i.e. one which proceeds from effects (finite beings) to cause (infinite Being). It never departs from the real plane, the plane of existence: we see that finite beings exist, the whole order of finite beings is synthesized by the mind and we make the discovery of the infinite Being as the cause of all existing finite beings.

It is also a *metaphysical* proof. Metaphysics alone, we have already insisted, has jurisdiction over all that exists. Alone among the sciences it can lay down the general laws governing reality and discover the secret of the universal order. When it has shown that an absolute reality exists, it goes on to the metaphysical analysis of finite being and shows how radically imperfect it is. The proof of the existence of the infinite Being coincides in fact with the essential stages of metaphysical reflection. Infinite Being is affirmed as being *metaphysically implied* by the order of finite beings, that is to say that, by an inference or regressive deduction, going from the conditioned to its condition, we show that the existence of the infinite Being is *implicitly* affirmed whenever the existence of the finite is affirmed. We have no experience of the infinite Being: He belongs not at all to the world of "phenomena", He is not an object of sensory perception nor of internal experience. He is not discovered even as a hidden phenomenon, with the help of scientific instruments that enable us to penetrate beyond the field of natural experience. His existence must be *demonstrated* by a reflection on the nature of reality as such and on the conditions of existence of finite being as such.

The affirmation of the infinite Being is then the natural result of metaphysical research, illuminating all its stages and solving all outstanding antinomies.

It is its metaphysical character that gives the proof of the existence of God its *absolute rigour*, a critical value surpassed only by the evidence of an object apprehended immediately in itself without recourse to reasoning. Thus, like all the theses of ontology, the affirmation of the infinite Being carries with it the highest intellectual certainty, metaphysical certainty, the exclusive property of absolutely necessary truths.

But the mind must be open to this kind of demonstration; it must be capable of grasping its nature and value. However, it is clear that there are many who are not properly disposed to understand even the mere statement of a metaphysical problem: engrossed whether in business or other material concerns, or in the pursuit of pleasure and distraction, or in scientific research or technical endeavour, they can never spare time to stop and reflect on essentials. The human mind, too, is never fully open to metaphysical truths: when forced to go beyond the domain of day-to-day experience and venture into the unknown regions of metaphysical realities, it feels a kind of dizziness. Aristotle remarked that when face to face with highest truths the human intellect was like the owl who is dazzled by the bright sunlight. Finally, sensibility gets no pleasure out of the austere asceticism of abstract reflection and reasoning.

All this explains the feeling of insecurity and dissatisfaction that some experience at the end of even the most rigorous metaphysical demonstration.

But the wise man is aware that the impotence of the mind's regard in metaphysics marks the summit of the life of the spirit and he does not fall into the empiricist trap which would almost inevitably imprison him in an agnostic frame of mind. A man must love the truth with his whole soul and make the effort that is necessary to seek and find it. When the issue is a vital one like the existence of the Creator, no effort that leads to the light can be spared. The principal metaphysical problems are profoundly human ones, for they concern the meaning of existence and the destiny of the person. Every intelligent being wants to solve the riddle of the universe; in every human mind there sleeps a metaphysician. He must be aroused, the slumbering sense of wonder must be stimulated, man's love of truth must be awakened and he must be made alive to the incomparable nobility of thought. He can then be asked to make the necessary effort to reflect and grasp the essential stages of the itinerary to be followed by the human intellect if it is to reach the knowledge of the Infinite. The man in whom the love of truth has enkindled the flame of an insatiable desire renounces willingly the rewards of a merely worldly curiosity so as to enjoy were it even but a faint ray of the eternal Truth.

Progress in Metaphysics

The problem of the existence of God is not only of its nature *a* metaphysical problem; it is *the* metaphysical problem *par excellence*. All other problems converge towards this one as brooks and streams towards the river.

However, despite the deep underlying agreement that can be found among the greatest thinkers, the discord of metaphysicians, the multiplicity of metaphysical systems, the diversity of arguments put forward in proof of the existence of God, are a subject of scandal ([14]) to many people. Is it possible to get over this? Is there reason to hope that agreement among metaphysicians will spread and become firmer, not unlike the growth and consolidation of a universal society of men in spite of the many set-backs?

It would be a great mistake to think that metaphysical knowledge had reached perfection centuries ago and that progress in this field was now just a matter of detail and nuance. Here, on the contrary, are the main lines of the history of metaphysical thought. It was born and grew up in Greece and developed in two opposite directions: Platonic idealism and Aristotelian realism. Each made remarkable discoveries: Platonic participation, developed by Greek and Arabic Neoplatonism, and the principal Aristotelian themes: potency and act, analogy of being, substance and accident, Pure Act etc. The first great philosophical synthesis of Western thought appeared only in the thirteenth century, made by St. Thomas Aquinas — a synthesis which combines harmoniously for the first time in a rigorous metaphysics the best insights of Platonism and Aristotelianism. The keystone of the system is the creative cause. Nevertheless, St. Thomas uses very imperfect and very disconcerting expressions. His literary output was immense and his thought has to be followed through writings of very different kinds, most often theological. Centuries of discussion will be necessary to

([14]) Cf. *supra*, pp. 80-81.

correct these expressions and bring out clearly the metaphysical synthesis of the *Doctor Communis*: the criticisms
of Scotus and Ockham, the more or less compromising
commentaries of Cajetan, John of Saint-Thomas, Suarez
and of contemporary Thomists. Since the sixteenth century, side by side with the philosophy of the School, the various currents of modern thought have made their appearance: many of them (empiricism, Kantism, positivism,
Bergsonism) reject metaphysics; others (cartesianism, ontologism, rationalism, transcendental idealism) leave room
for metempirical knowledge and, especially, for the
problem of the Absolute; but their approach has all the
more or less serious drawbacks of their systems. Since
the beginning of the twentieth century there has been a
notable revival of metaphysics, not only within Thomism,
but even in circles that had lost the habit of that kind
of speculative thinking. Men like Blondel, Lavelle and
Le Senne in France, Hartmann and Husserl in Germany,
have adopted metaphysical insights that are often very
traditional and sometimes quite close to Thomism.

The proof of the existence of God necessarily gained
by this advance and it is perhaps reserved to our century
to reach at last a really satisfactory formulation of the
proof. There is nothing surprising about this, once it is
admitted that metaphysical knowledge has reached in our
day for the first time the term of its historical genesis;
a relative term indeed, as progress is always possible and
necessary here as in every other science. Those whose
task it is today to bring up to date the scientific demonstration of the existence of the Creator reap where others
have sown before them, or, to use another well-known

metaphor, they stand on the shoulders of giants and, notwithstanding their miserable stature, their gaze penetrates beyond that of the masters from whom they derive inspiration: so true is it that science is the fruit of the collective effort of the human race.

CHAPTER X

THE GOD OF THE PHILOSOPHERS

Does the infinite Being whose existence was revealed at the close of our reflections on the order of finite beings *correspond to the description of God* that we gave at the start of our inquiry when we suggested the following nominal definition: "the provident Creator of the universe"? In other words, does the infinite Being answer to the idea of God proposed by the great monotheistic religions as the solution of the human problem of the ultimate explanation of the universe? [1]

The infinite Being is *creator*, as he is the cause of being for the whole order of finite beings.

He is the *sole* creator of the universe: unicity is an immediate corollary of infinity. We observe that the beings we experience are opposed one to the other, limit one another mutually; the reality of one is not that of another. This is what we mean when we say that these beings are *finite*. We next show that these beings, all radically dependent, are caused by a Being not possessing the characters of the finite, *not finite* or *infinite*. The exact meaning of ontological infinity is thus brought out: the

[1] Cf. *sup.* pp. 24-38.

infinite Being is that being who *is opposed to nothing*, who is *limited by no other*. There is evidently only one such being for, if there were many infinite beings, they would be opposed to one another and consequently finite. The expression "many infinite beings" is a contradiction in terms (²).

The Infinite Being is one, exhausting all ontological perfection. He is the fullness of being. Whatever else exists can come to be only by him and can only be a finite participation of his infinite perfection (³).

But is the infinite Being a *provident* creator? Is he a personal being, who knows and loves his creatures and is concerned about their destiny? Demonstrating his existence does not prove this explicitly. We may ask, however, if it is not implicit in the conclusion of the demonstration. This is the same as asking to what extent

(²) In the brochure he published under the title *Dieu* (Collection *Appels*, 3ᵉ série, 1, Liège, 1951), Canon J. Leclerq writes: "there can be only one Absolute, for Absolute and One are the same thing. Many and Absolute are contradictory terms" (p. 9). — It does not seem to me that the human mind can immediately grasp the necessary connexion between Absolute and One; the idea of Infinite must serve as a middle term. It is not immediately evident that there could not be many Absolutes: they would all be finite, the reality of one being opposed that of another. Cf. *sup.* p. 196.

(³) The infinite Being is not *opposed* to finite beings for, as their creative cause, he precontains them adequately. He is however *distinct* from finite beings as the cause is distinct from its effects.

We are speaking, needless to say, of *ontological* and not of *mathematical* infinity.

a deduction of the attributes of the infinite Being is possible and if it can be deduced that he is a personal and provident being.

Fundamental Attributes

It is easy to see that, once we have demonstrated the existence of the infinite Being, we know him by means of *four concepts*. This was the conclusion of the demonstration: "the absolute is an infinite Being, cause of finite beings". We know therefore that this transcendent being is *being*, *absolute*, *infinite* and *cause* of the finite. Two of these concepts are positive (*being* and *cause*) and two are negative (*absolute* and *infinite*, i.e. *not relative* and *not finite*).

The two positive concepts by which we represent the supreme Being are *common* to the finite and infinite as the finite is also *being* and can also be a *cause*. The two negative concepts, on the contrary, provide us with a *distinctive* knowledge of the supreme Being as he alone is *absolute* and he alone is *infinite*. But we have no concept, to designate this Being, that is *both distinctive and positive*. No concept of ours represents the first Cause positively as he is in himself; we do not know positively what he is (4). This is the logical consequence of our way of getting to know the supreme Being in metaphysics: we

(4) This is what St. Thomas means when he writes: "*de Deo non possumus scire quid sit, sed solum quid non est*" (we cannot know what God is, but only what he is not). Cf. *Summa theologiae*, I^a, q. 2, art. 2, *obiectio* 2.

discover him starting from the finite and in opposition to the finite.

A fuller knowledge of the attributes of the infinite Being is possible in as far as we are able by deduction to bring out *explicitly* what is implicit in the fundamental attributes. We shall soon see what results may be hoped for from the use of this method. But before we put it to the test, it is important to note that the situation facing us at the beginning will remain unchanged throughout the whole process of deduction. Those *positive* attributes deduced from the two basic positive attributes will be common to finite and infinite. It is clear nevertheless that they are not predicated of finite and infinite in the same way, but proportionately or (to use the technical language of the scholastics) analogically. We shall therefore have to correct the positive attributes in each case if we are to avoid lapsing into dangerous anthropomorphisms. Now the *negative* attributes, as we have seen, provide us with a distinctive knowledge of the first Being and so make it possible for us to respect his transcendence. The dangers of anthropomorphism are averted therefore by the negative attributes which are used to correct the positive attributes. Consequently, deduction of the negative attributes must come first so that they may be used in the deduction of the positive attributes.

Negative Attributes

The two fundamental negative attributes of the supreme Being appear in the conclusion of the proof of his existence: the *absolute* is an *infinite* Being. The *absolute* is the not relative, the not conditioned, the not dependent, the not caused; that is absolute which is self-existent and, therefore, necessarily existent. The *infinite* is the not finite, the being opposed to no other, limited by no other.

The principal negative attributes derived from the two first are the following:

Immutability: this is an immediate consequence of aseity ([5]): every being that changes depends on an outside cause ([6]); but the absolute cannot depend on an outside cause; therefore the absolute cannot change.

It is important to stress very carefully the exact significance of this attribute if we are to avoid becoming involved in inextricable difficulties. The attribute is a purely negative one and it denies only that the absolute Being can *become other*, that he can become more or less perfect, that he can gain or lose any perfection whatever.

Simplicity: "Simple" signifies *not composed*, not made up of complementary parts. It is proved in metaphysics that a composite being is necessarily finite ([7]). Hence,

---

([5]) Aseity (latin: *aseitas*): property of that which is *a se* or self-existent, of that which is absolute.

([6]) This is the Aristotelian form of the principle of causality: *quidquid movetur ab alio movetur*. It is an analytical principle, i.e. it is the result of a simple analysis of the terms: to change is to become other, to cease to be the same; no being can, of itself, cease to be itself whether by losing what it has or acquiring what it has not.

([7]) Cf. F. VAN STEENBERGHEN, *Ontologie*, 3d ed., Louvain, 1961, pp. 186-187. *Ontology*, pp. 172-173.

the infinite Being must be free from all composition.

Once again, this attribute must be taken in its strict sense which is purely negative. It denies merely that the Infinite can be composed of parts which are mutually opposed and complementary.

Spirituality: "Spiritual" signifies *incorporeal*. A corporeal being is an extended reality, subject to spatial extension. The Infinite is not a body but a spirit; he is incorporeal or unextended. Firstly, because he is *simple* and extension is a form of composition: a body is made up of quantitative parts external one to another. Secondly, because he is *infinite* and extension implies finitude: unless a body is to be altogether undetermined and formless, it must have "shape", geometrical form and, consequently, spatial boundaries: within its own bounds every body is opposed to the other bodies that are or could possibly be around it [8].

Eternity: Time is the duration peculiar to corporeal beings which are subject to continuous change; it is therefore *successive and continuous duration*. When there are limits to the existence of a corporeal being — as in the case of living beings, for example — its duration is comprised between two extremes, the beginning and the end. Temporal duration in its strictest sense has therefore three characters: beginning, succession and end: man is a temporal being and his life is measured by time because

[8] The spiritual nature of the infinite Being can be shown also in other ways, but they are not as easy to grasp by those who have had no training in metaphysics. Cf. F. Van Steenberghen, *Ontologie*, pp. 188-190. *Ontology*, pp. 174-176.

it begins at a moment of time, it flows in an uninterrupted succession of events and it comes to an end in another moment of time.

It is easy to see that the duration of the Infinite is free from all the marks of time: the Infinite, necessary and immutable, has neither beginning, succession, nor end. This is what we mean when we say that he is eternal. The duration of the Infinite is an unchangeable present, an unalterable permanence: *immobile nunc*, says St. Thomas [9].

The negative attributes play an essential role in our knowledge of the infinite Being, keeping it free from anthropomorphism and purifying our conceptual representation from all that is incompatible with the absolute transcendence of the Infinite in regard to the finite. These attributes alone, once more, give a *distinct* knowledge of the Infinite.

We must be on our guard against possible distortion due to the imagination which receives little consolation from the idea of a simple, immutable and incorporeal being. It conjures up a picture of a being devoid of richness, variety, movement, grace and life, that risks being considered a symbol for something poor, inert

[9] It is well to note that the term *eternity* is also used less strictly to indicate duration which partially excludes the characters of time. In expressions like the following, for example: "According to Aristotle, the world is eternal in the past" (i.e. it always existed, *without beginning*); "hell is eternal" (i.e. it is *never-ending*); "according to Averroes, the intellect of the human race is eternal" (*in the past and in the future*).

and uninteresting. There is little food for the imagination in such a representation.

This unfavourable impression is radically false. To form a correct idea, it is necessary to keep in mind that these attributes are purely *negative*; they remove from the Infinite whatever might imply privation, imperfection, dependence. We shall see shortly that, as creative cause, the Infinite possesses eminently all that makes creatures estimable and attractive. He possesses all that is good in one simple never-ending act. In contrast to this fulness, the attraction that variety and change have to offer vanishes like the flicker of the candle in the dazzling brilliance of the sun ([10]).

Positive Attributes

Purely negative knowledge would not be knowledge at all; negative attributes would be of no interest if they did not apply to a being known and expressed somehow positively. This is so in the case of the infinite Being: before we deny that he is finite and relative, we assert that he is *being* and *cause*. But he is being and cause *in his own manner*, in accordance with his nature, i.e. in an infinite and absolute way. This means that the positive attributes have to be corrected by the negative attributes, as has been said above.

([10]) We shall see in a later chapter how strikingly Christian revelation confirms the purely negative character of the attributes so far considered.

Let us apply this principle to the fundamental positive attributes:

The Infinite is truly *being* i.e., truly *real*, truly *existent*; he has the fundamental perfection common to all beings. But he does not exist in the same way as the finite. He is *infinitely*, i.e. unopposed to anything whatever. He is *absolutely*, i.e. without depending on anything whatever. He is *immutably*, i.e. he cannot change or become other in his being; he is imperfectible and indefectible. He is *simply*, without any composition of parts or constitutive elements.

The Infinite is the *cause* of the finite, the order of finite beings owes its existence to his *action*. Consequently, finite beings exist only as depending on the Infinite, who is their total cause. The Infinite has therefore a nature such that he has the *power* or *capacity* to bring finite beings into existence. But the Infinite is not a cause in the same way as the finite. Being an *infinite* Cause, i.e. without opposition, his causal influx encounters no obstacle, no resistance. Being an *unconditioned* or *absolute* Cause, he depends on nothing in the exercise of his causality. Being an *immutable* Cause, his power knows neither growth nor decay; his effects do not "react" on it. Being a *simple* Cause, he exercises his causality by his very being and not through any accidental activity.

Infinite causality is rightly called *omnipotence* because there is no obstacle that can resist it. It determines the bounds of "possibility": whatever can be an effect of the infinite Cause, a "participation" in his perfection, is possible.

Infinite causality is also called *creative* causality or

creation (in the active sense of the word) to distinguish it from the causality of finite being that can only *transform* some previously existing thing. The Infinite is the cause of being (*causa essendi*), the finite is the cause of change (*causa movendi*). To create is to give existence to that which is not self-existing and therefore to be the *total cause*, for he who gives being gives everything. Hence, the creative cause must *fully precontain* his effect and this a finite being cannot do, since it is completely opposed to every other finite being. Only the Infinite can create, for, since he is the fulness of being, he pre-contains all that can exist and nothing can be outside him.

It is easy to deduce the attributes implied in the first positive attribute of the Infinite: being. They are the *transcendental* properties, i.e. properties that belong to all beings without exception, because they result necessarily from the basic perfection, namely, being.

Ontology proves that every being is *distinct, undivided, similar, intelligible* and *appetible* [11]. Finite being possesses these attributes imperfectly, proportionately to its nature, but the Infinite possesses them fully. Let us try to explain what this means.

Like every being the Infinite is *distinct*, i.e. he is confused with no other. But whereas finite being is distinct *by opposition*, the Infinite is distinct from the finite *by transcendence*, i.e. as the creative cause is distinct from its created effects. The Infinite pre-contains creatures in his power, but he brings them to be as finite beings

[11] Cf. F. Van Steenberghen, *Ontologie*, 3d ed., pp. 57-79. *Ontology*, pp. 46-69.

completely distinct from himself. This supreme distinction, peculiar to the Infinite, is called *transcendence* because it is a distinction by "excess" or "superiority", and not by "limitation" and "opposition".

Transcendence is a very important attribute in that it enables us to avoid *subsistential monism*, the most radical form of *pantheism*. It is an error that has cropped up often enough in the course of history and was championed by vigorous metaphysicians, like Spinoza. The Infinite is represented as a quantitatively unlimited whole outside which there is nothing. Consequently it seems as if there is no room for finite beings; there exists one single being, the Infinite (*monism*), and finite beings exist in this one being as "modes" or constitutive elements. Everything is divine (*pantheism*), since finite beings do not subsist in themselves and are not distinct from the Infinite, the Absolute, the Divine. These views arise from a mathematical representation of the Infinite and are incompatible with the transcendence of the supreme Being: finite beings are *effects* of the infinite and not *constitutive elements* of his being, which is completely distinct from the world of finite beings. The Infinite is distinct from the finite not only as every cause is distinct from its effect but also *supremely* distinct as the absolute from the relative, the unchangeable from the changing, the simple from the compound. The finite however adds no new perfection to the infinite; it is a "participation", an imperfect imitation of the Infinite and nothing more.

In fine, pantheism, under the pretext of not diminishing the Infinite, but, on the contrary, reserving for it a monopoly of being as it were, irremediably compromises its supreme perfection: it reduces it to a being composed of finite modes in which it is subject to becoming, marked in its very being by finitude, with the whole cortege of its imperfections. This doctrine will not stand up to metaphysical criticism.

Like every being the Infinite is *undivided*. In himself he is perfectly one for he excludes all manner of composition and multiplicity of constitutive parts. In contrast, the unity of finite being is imperfect for, as is proved in ontology, it is composed in the order of subsistence and in that of activity. Among finite beings, corporeal things have a still more complex structure: not only are they subject to quantitative composition, but it can be shown that their essence is composite. Thus, the farther removed a thing is from the perfection of the supreme Being, the farther removed it is from his supreme simplicity.

The Infinite *resembles* every being distinct from him. This is a new attribute — similarity —, common to all beings. But, once again, the Infinite possesses it in an eminent manner. He resembles finite beings because he is their total cause: he pre-contains them adequately in his creative power and the order of finite beings can be no more than an imperfect copy of the infinite model. In short, the Infinite is similar in that he is the *exemplary cause* of the finite.

The Infinite is *intelligible* as is all being, i.e. he is capable of being known by intelligence, which is — by nature — the faculty of being, the power to comprehend reality with all its structures, the universal order. The Infinite is eminently intelligible because he is so *of himself* (since he is the Absolute) and has no need of being explained by something else. Moreover, he is *source* of all intelligibility (for he is the creative cause and, consequently, the ultimate explanation of the order of finite beings). Nothing is fully intelligible except by the Infinite. He is the supreme intelligible in whom all outstanding antinomies are resolved. The mystery of him raises no problem to which he doesn't hold in himself the adequate solution.

It follows immediately that knowledge of the Infinite is essential to the perfection of every finite intelligence, not only in that every intelligence has an unlimited (or transcendental) capacity as a faculty of being, but because perfect knowledge of the universal order is impossible without knowledge of the Cause which is its principle.

The Infinite is supremely *good* or *lovable*. Every being can be an object of intellectual appetite or will, for the capacity of will, as of intelligence, is boundless. But the Infinite is eminently lovable, in the first place, because he is lovable *per se*, since he is the absolute value; and, secondly, because he is the *source* of all lovableness, since he is the cause of all finite beings and of all their values; therefore the ultimate reason of the lovableness of all creatures is to be found in him.

That is why no created will can attain perfection nor find the happiness it aspires to, unless it enjoys the Infinite known by intelligence: not only because will is an unlimited appetite intent on enjoying the goodness of all things, but also because its deepest aspiration is towards the Infinite, supreme good and source of every finite good.

The deductions made so far have doubtless added to our knowledge of the infinite Being. Yet they are but preliminary considerations when compared to the important demonstrations that follow. These make explicit what is implied in the second fundamental positive attribute: the Infinite is the *Cause* of the order of finite beings. We already know what this attribute signifies [12]. Further reflection will open up extremely interesting considerations that will wonderfully enrich our knowledge of the supreme Being.

We have shown that the fundamental similarity of all finite beings in one of the signs of their fundamental dependence: this similarity is intelligible only if all finite beings, opposed in virtue of their finitude, are nevertheless connected because they derive from a common non-finite cause, who pre-contains them all in his creative power. Finite beings resemble one another, not only as do sons of a common father, but as would sons who owed all that they are to their father [13]. In fine, the ontological resemblance between finite beings is based on their common *participation* in the Infinite who is their total cause.

It is clear that the analogy existing between every finite being and its infinite Cause pertains to the very nature of causality. The cause necessarily precontains

[12] Cf. *sup*. 204-205.
[13] Cf. *sup*. 180-182.

its effect. In the case of a total or creative cause, the effect is wholly pre-contained in its cause. There is nothing in the effect that is "outside" the cause, nothing that is not "imitation of" and "participation in" the cause.

In these circumstances, a new path, full of promise, seems to open out before us in our effort to acquire knowledge of the perfections of the supreme Being. It seems that all perfections found in creatures reveal the perfection of the Creator, since he is their adequate source and must, therefore, pre-contain them all in his power, which is identically his being. Up to this we have been using the *imperfections* and *shortcomings* of finite beings as a springboard to reach the Infinite and to describe him by contrasting him with finite beings; from now on we shall rely on the *perfections* of creatures to help us to penetrate the secret of infinite perfection.

This is undeniable and extremely valuable. But it is still necessary to determine exactly what "to pre-contain" means here and to be able to make the distinctions that are called for if we are not to fall into a crass anthropomorphism.

When we say that *the perfection of an effect pre-exists eminently in its cause*, we do not mean that causality ought to be conceived as a simple "transfer" of a perfection from the cause to the effect. This naive representation in no way conveys the nature of the causal influx. What we mean is that, in order to have the *capacity* or *power* to produce some effect, the cause itself must possess a *degree of perfection* at least equal to that of the effect: to deny this is to render causality unintelligible, for it is the same as trying to explain the more by the less, the more perfect by the less perfect and, in final analysis, being (the perfection produced) by not being (the absence of equivalent perfection in the cause).

It goes without saying that the principle applies only to the relation between a cause *as cause* and the effect *as effect*. If A is only the partial cause of B (as always happens in the case of created causes, which merely *transform* a pre-existing subject), then A pre-contains B in proportion to the causal influx it exerts on B.

Applying this general principle which we have just explained, we can say that the whole reality of finite beings is eminently pre-contained in the Infinite, the creative Cause. This means at least and in any case that the Infinite has power to create, to bring into existence, the immense and wonderfully varied universe certain sectors of which we experience. Consequently, a close study of this created universe — its vertiginous dimensions and awe-inspiring energies, the marvellous structure of atom and molecule, of crystal and cell, of the most complex living organisms, the unfathomable wealth of human thought and love —, a careful study of this universe gives us a glimpse of the *power*, *greatness* and *wisdom* of the Infinite, the sole, adequate cause of this universal order.

Is it possible to go further and discover, by analogy with the perfections of creatures, perfections that can be predicated *formally* of the Infinite?

We have to make a very important distinction at this point. It is clear that all that is genuine perfection, pure quality, real worth in creatures pre-exists in an incomparably more intense and purer way in the creative Cause. But we need only glance at the things around us to see that most of their perfections are not and cannot be unmixed perfections, qualities in their pure state: they are "mixed perfections", i.e. perfections that are *essentially* finite and often even corporeal. "Colour", for example, is a mixed perfection since it cannot be conceived without extension and, therefore, can affect only bodies. Try to purify the notion of colour from all connexion with matter and it will lose its formal or specific nature and lose consistency: a "spiritual colour" or a "coloured spirit" are expressions without meaning. "Activity", too, is a mixed perfection as it is becoming, growth, increase in being, production of new acts. Therefore it presupposes perfectibility and, consequently, finitude and relativity. Try to purge it of all reference to the finite, and it will lose its specific connotation ([14]). These mixed perfections cannot be predicated *formally* of the Infinite since this would imply attributing to him finitude or even corporeity. The Infinite possesses them *virtually*, that is to say, in his power (*virtus*): He has power to create them. If they are sometimes attributed to the Infinite (especially in religious literature and in poetry), it can only be in a purely *metaphorical* sense. This recourse to metaphor, in spite of its disadvantages, is of considerable psychological value as it portrays the eminent perfection of the Infinite, inaccurately no doubt,

([14]) Some authors use the term "activity" in a wider sense, either as synonymous with "causality" or as a synonym for "immanent act". Understood in this wider sense it is no longer a mixed perfection.

yet with a greater power of suggestion than do metaphysical concepts: descriptions such as "the uncreated Light" or "the Sun of minds" are more evocative than "supreme Intelligible "or "first Truth".

Are there to be found in the world of our experience perfections that are unmixed? With this question we reach the culminating point of our inquiry, for it brings us to that attribute of the Infinite that is the condition and justification of religion: the Infinite is a *personal* being.

Our experience is twofold: it comprises external experience or the perception of the corporeal world and internal experience or knowledge of self. In the corporeal world all we can perceive is mixed perfections, since sense intuition apprehends only what is corporeal or extended, and all aspects of the real given in sense intuition are aspects of extension. Internal experience, on the contrary, puts us in presence of a kind of reality different from extension: a *conscious* subject or *person*, i.e. a subject capable of *thinking* and *willing*, a centre of *knowledge* and *love*. To be conscious of one's self, to know that one exists and that the world exists, to be able to enjoy all that reality has to offer, to be able to love the things that satisfy the aspirations of the conscious self, freely to determine the course of one's actions, in short, to be a person — this is surely the highest of our prerogatives, the source of our dignity, the condition of all values. In us, personality is imperfect: it is a finite, dependent, changing reality. In us, thinking and willing are limited, autonomy is relative, happiness precarious. But, in contrast to "mixed perfections", the perfection of personality (with all that it comprises) is not essentially bound up with finitude. You by no means destroy the ideas of person, consciousness, thought, love, joy, freedom, by freeing them from their finite wrapping. On the contrary, you purify them, you set them free from all that threatens or endangers their essence. In short, they are "simple perfections", perfections that are not necessarily mixed with imperfection.

Now, the Infinite Being, total cause of these perfections, pre-contains them in an eminent way. And since we are talking about simple perfections, that are in no way bound up with finitude, it is not enough to say that the Infinite pre-contains them virtually or in his power; we have to say that he pre-contains them *formally*, i.e. in their own form. *He is really a personal and conscious Being, able to think and will, to love and enjoy, supremely free in all that he wills.* As a lowly human being, I enjoy the excellent privileges of being a person; it would be absurd to imagine that the infinitely perfect Being on whom I depend for my very being is deprived of these privileges. It is evident, on the contrary, that he enjoys them in all fullness.

This is indeed a wonderful conclusion, marking the summit of human thought and opening up overwhelming insights into our relations with the infinite Being.

We see here the ground for the traditional distinction between *vestigium Dei* and *imago Dei*. The mixed perfections of corporeal beings, "vestiges" of God, are incapable of portraying his infinite perfection. Person, on the contrary, a simple perfection, is created in God's "image"; knowledge of the human person can give us some idea of the Infinite as a personal Being, though we must be careful to use the method of negation to correct this idea accordingly to the principles that have been already laid down.

We shall now try to determine what can be known about the personality of the Infinite.

The fundamental attribute of person is *thought* or *intellectual knowledge*, i.e. knowledge of being in itself, of the real in itself. It involves both self-knowledge or *consciousness* and knowledge of things distinct from the self, things with which the self happens to be in relation. Knowledge of the non-ego we shall call *science* to distinguish it from consciousness. Intellectual knowledge or thought is a modality of being that we find in ourselves, a primitive, irreducible datum that can be described as a kind of "possession" of the real, a most mysterious manner of possessing self and other beings; but only a thinking being can know what thinking means. This mode of being that we call "thinking" is obviously an excellent perfection; Plato and Aristotle, St. Augustine and St. Thomas, Averroes, Descartes, Pascal, Bergson and many others among the greatest considered it to be the noblest gift of man and the condition of all other values. As it implies no essential imperfection or limitation it must be attributed formally to the infinite, who must, consequently, be conceived as a thinking, conscious, intelligent being, in short, a *mind*.

But the Infinite is not a limited, dependent, perfectible mind whose thought is accidental and progressive. He is subsisting Thought, simple, immutable, imperfectible. Non-finite or Infinite Mind is perfect self-knowledge. He is unlimited ontological perfection, perfectly "self-trans-parent".

The Infinite is not only perfect consciousness of self; in him there is necessarily knowledge of the created world, or perfect *science*. Because in him thought and power are identical with being, it is evident that his power is fully conscious. In other words, the Infinite knows that he can create a world, knows that he creates it and knows perfectly what it is he creates.

This knowledge has none of the imperfections of our finite knowledge: it is not *limited*, baffled by the mysterious or the impenetrable, painstakingly gaining possession of its object by extracting it from the domain of the unknown; it is not *conditioned* by its object or by any factor beyond the knower; it is not *perfectible*. On the contrary, it is *infinite* science: knowing his power, which contains its effects adequately, the Infinite knows the nature and properties of these effects. It is an *unconditioned* science, since the Infinite knows the world in knowing his own power; he knows it by and in himself. He does not know the world because it exists and is there for him to know, as it were: the world exists because the Infinite knows it and creates it. Finally, his science is *immutable* and *eternal* ([15]).

In our human consciousness, thought is but a partial factor of our whole activity and is intimately bound up with *will* or *intellectual appetite*. The capacity of knowing

([15]) The problem has to be stated in entirely different terms when the question of our free actions arises. We cannot deal with it here.

is correlative to the capacity of *loving* or of *willing what is good*. Love first takes the form of *desire*, i.e. of tendency towards a good not yet in one's possession; when desire is satisfied, when the good is possessed, love becomes *complacence* or *delight*. Delight in the good is therefore the perfect act of the will, the perfect form of love; in this act, as in its goal, the dynamism of the human conscience attains full realization.

It is clear that love of complacence or delight in the good is a perfection. It can only be said that thought is man's noblest perfection on condition that it is not cut off from its natural goal, which is love. If cognitive activity were to fail to develop into affective activity, if cold contemplation of the true did not lead to love of the good and to union of persons through reciprocal love, human personality would be seriously diminished. But is love a simple perfection? Doubtlessly, as it is not essentially bound up with finitude. On the contrary, the further removed delight in the good is from all condition and limitation, the deeper and the more intense it is. The Infinite must be conceived as a being who *delights* in his supreme lovableness, who possesses in the highest degree *joy of spirit* or *beatitude*, who *loves* his own goodness and *delights* in it. Far from being "egoistic" and, to that extent, immoderate, this *complacence* is essential to the Infinite and demanded by his nature, for it is impossible that the infinite goodness should go unloved.

We cannot conceive the will of the supreme Being as we would a *finite* will, i.e. one opposed to its object and capable of being thwarted by obstacles; nor as one that is *dependent* and *perfectible*; nor as an *accidental* power from which emanate multiple and conflicting acts; nor as a will liable to *moral failing*, capable of becoming attached to apparent goods. The Infinite is *subsisting Beatitude*, without limits, free from extrinsic conditions. His is a Will that excludes all imperfect acts of will (desire, hope, sadness, etc.). He is a *Love of complacence* whose essential object is the infinite lovableness of the supreme Being.

Are creatures also objects of this infinite love? The creative act, identical as it is with infinite being, thought and love, is evidently a *voluntary* act or act of *love*, just as much as a conscious act. If the Infinite creates a universe, the reason is that he delights in his infinite goodness and knows it as imitable by finite creatures. To will to create is, then, to will to communicate his goodness to finite beings, to will that creatures exist and be good or lovable in imitation of his infinite lovableness. The will to create is an act of *benevolence*, fruit of that delight the Infinite takes in himself. Infinite benevolence is infinite enjoyment in so far as it is *efficacious*, i.e. manifested in the will to create a world that would share in the infinite goodness.

Infinite benevolence has not the attributes of the benevolent love that is to be found in the finite will. Creative will is *limited by nothing*, suffers from no opposition or resistance, since it is this will that calls all finite beings into existence. It cannot even be said that the creative will comes into conflict with the free will of created persons, who exist and are free only by the will of the Creator. Consequently, if creatures abuse their freedom by willing what is evil, their disorderly acts by no means frustrate the creative will; they belong to the order of things created and in no way affect the transcendent Cause. Creative will is also *unconditioned*: it is not "attracted" or "solicited" by its object; it is not the result of any "inclination" or "tendency" towards creatures. It results from the Creator's complacence in his own goodness; in himself he delights in his work because it is his participated goodness. There is nothing lovable in the Creator's work that is not received, that does not come from him. That is why creatures are good *because* the Creator loves them; the goodness of creatures is not the cause, but the effect, of the love the Creator has for them. Creative benevolence is therefore supremely *disinterested*: the Creator does not create *for pleasure*, to increase his happiness or to reap some advantage from creation; he is imperfectible and, furthermore, creation is no more than a limited participation of his own perfection. He creates *because he takes delight* in his own goodness and wills to communicate it to creatures.

Here we must be on our guard against all anthropomorphism. There are two pitfalls to be avoided. The first is to picture the Creator as an *egoistic potentate*, interested only in being served and worshipped by his subjects. The second is to imagine him *at his creatures' service*, a means as it were towards an end — the end being the perfection and happiness of created things. The truth lies in the happy medium between these errors: the creative act is both supremely *disinterested* (the Creator reaps no profit from it) and necessarily *theocentric* (the created order cannot possibly not have for end to know and love the Creator, the proclamation of his sovereign goodness by personal creatures). In short, the created universe can have no end other than the "glory" of the Creator, which in fact coincides with the happiness of created persons, provided they respect the natural order of creation.

These remarks regarding the nature of the creative act bring to light important new aspects of the causality of the infinite Being and it is at this point that the key notion of *providence* makes its appearance.

We know already that the creative act must be conceived as both conscious and benevolent: the Infinite knows what he creates and he creates out of love. But new questions immediately spring to mind. Is it essential for him to create the world of finite beings or is the world the fruit of a free initiative of the first Cause? In other words, is the world necessary (a necessary effect of its Cause) or contingent, optional? What, in the supreme Being, is the motive of creation? Has the universe an end, a goal, a meaning? Is the Infinite interested in the end and how? Can metaphysics give any answer to these questions?

The deduction of the attributes of the Infinite provides to some extent an answer to these questions.

It must be said, in the first place, that the creative act is a *free initiative*.

Non-Christian thinkers who have arrived at the notion of a creative Cause generally conceive creation as an eternal and necessary act, the effect of which — the world — exists and evolves inexorably. In this view, the universe is a necessary emanation of the first Cause. It is the result of mistaken ideas concerning the divine simplicity and immutability. Because God is simple it is inferred that the creative act has to be identified with the necessary and immutable being of the first Cause; this act is therefore necessary and immutable and this, evidently, entails the necessity of its effect.

In reality, when we say that the Infinite is *simple*, we exclude only all composition of parts or complementary principles; but we have no idea of the positive riches hidden in the mysterious reality of the Infinite ([16]). And when we say that the Infinite is *immutable*, we deny only that he can acquire or lose any perfection; but free initiatives, made in sovereign independence, imply not at all that the creative Cause is either perfectible or defectible.

The problem is to determine whether the *freedom of choice*, which we experience in our voluntary activity, is a simple or mixed perfection. Though the will's natural dynamism carries it irresistibly towards the good as such, we enjoy freedom of choice in regard to all the particular goods that solicit its adherence: we are not determined to will them, either by the action of material agents, or by our own nature and instinctive tendencies, or by the motives we have for willing them. We determine *ourselves* to will one of these goods rather than another and even to will or not to will them, for none of them appears absolute-

([16]) Thus we do not even suspect that there exists in the infinite Being a real plurality of persons. This truth, known only through revelation, is not incompatible with the divine simplicity: the three Persons are not "parts" or "components" of the divine Being.

ly indispensable. Freedom of choice in our case however has many imperfections: it has its place among means towards the end, in a *tendency* which is not free in regard to the end, its absolute term; it involves the possibility of choosing *evil* that has assumed the appearance of good. But, in its essence, freedom of choice is the expression of the autonomy and worth of the human person, the sign of his superiority over the relative and imperfect goods that come his way. This prerogative of the person is not necessarily inseparable from the imperfections that were pointed out in human freedom: on the contrary, freedom of choice is more perfect when it is independent of any kind of dynamism, i.e. of all appetite in quest of perfection, and when it excludes all possibility of defection. Consequently freedom of choice is a simple perfection and it must be attributed formally to the creative Cause: finite beings are not *necessary means* in regard to the perfection and beatitude of the infinite Being. He can create or not create, create this kind of world or another: the decision rests exclusively with his sovereign liberty.

Moreover, how could it be otherwise? It enters into nobody's head to say that the Infinite is determined to create by an external agent or alien motive: it would be altogether incompatible with his sovereign independence and he would cease to be the Unconditioned. Besides, there is nothing outside the Infinite except what the Infinite creates. The only other hypothesis is that of an inner necessity. Since the creative act, however, is fully conscious, there can be no question of an unconscious natural determinism, of a blind, necessary causality. If the creative act were necessary, it could only be question of "psychological" determinism, i.e. the Infinite would have a *determining motive* for creating. But that is impossible, for his goodness is the sole necessary object of his will, the sole essential term of his complacence. A created universe, because it is no more than a *participation* of this infinite goodness, could not form an essential element of the infinite perfection, an indispensable complement of the Creator's nature, a necessary condition of his beatitude, in short, a determining motive for creating.

The creative act must, therefore, be considered as a free, contingent initiative of the infinite Being. It follows immediately that this act cannot be absolutely identified with the necessary being of the creative Cause. But we have no positive idea of how this free act and this necessary being are distinguished. There is here a mystery just as inaccessible as that of the trinity of persons in the unity of the divine nature. We must not try to make the Infinite fit into the framework of our conceptual categories.

But though the creative act has no *determining* motive, it must, however, have a *sufficient* motive and this must be worthy of the supreme Being. A free act is a conscious act, an act of intelligence as much as of will and, therefore, an act inspired by a reason for acting or a motive. Though creation is *optional* since the infinite Being has no *decisive* reason for creating, it is *possible* on condition that there is a *valid* reason for doing so: otherwise the creative act would be futile, capricious, void of meaning and value. What is this reason? What does creation add that can be worthy of the Creator?

Creation, to have any meaning, must include one or more *persons*, capable of knowing the created order and its transcendent Principle and capable of enjoying this knowledge. It is obvious that a universe without personal beings would have no meaning: it would be of no value to itself as it would be unconscious; it would be of no value to its creative Cause as it would not add to his perfection or happiness. A person, on the contrary, is in himself a value; he has an end of his own because he is conscious and able to enjoy. This value is worthy of the Creator and can be willed by him as it is perfectly subordinated to the infinite Value of which it is but a participation. Consequently, in loving his creatures the Creator loves nothing that is *alien* to him; he does not tend towards a perfection to be acquired. In his creatures he finds himself.

The creative act is, then, a *meaningful* or *motivated* act, i.e. an act of *wisdom*. Creative wisdom is infinite intelligence considered as it directs the created universe to its final end, that is to say to the realization of the values required by the nature of created persons.

The notion of wisdom is very close to that of *providence*. The latin verb *providere* means *to provide*, to see that all the means necessary are disposed with a view to the end to be attained: the father of a family provides for the needs of his wife and children, the legislator provides for the enactment of laws that ensure the common good of the nation. The providence of the Creator is therefore his intelligence considered as it disposes all the elements of the created universe with a view to the realization of the end to be attained. Seeing that the Creator exercises his causality with intelligence, benevolence and wisdom, his work cannot possibly contain lacunae attributable to lack of foresight or to inadvertence. The universe must be such that it afford all created things the possibility of acting in accordance with their natures. The whole universe must contribute to the perfection of created persons, who must find in their surroundings all that is necessary to attain their perfection.

At the end of this deduction of the attributes of the infinite Being it is easy to see that the notion of God given at the beginning of this inquiry in the light of the religious history of mankind is fully realized in him. The infinite Being is "the provident Creator of the universe".

The discovery of the *infinite Being* as the transcendent cause of the order of finite beings produces a reaction of surprise and wonder in the mind of the philosopher, which finds expression in a desire to know the inner nature of the mysterious being whose supreme grandeur he glimpses. The discovery of the infinite *personality* awakens before long sentiments of reverence and joy: the first Cause to whom we owe our existence is a personal being like ourselves. Our thought is but a reflection of his thought, our will but a distant copy of his love and blessedness. Fresh questions occur immediately: can there be personal relations between the Infinite and us? Is he interested in our lot? Or does his transcendence set between him and us an impassable gulf? The deduction of *providence* answers these questions and stirs up in us all the forms of religious sentiment: adoration, gratitude, love of complacence, submission etc. Henceforth the infinite Being possesses the essential traits of the God acknowledged by the great monotheistic religions.

We are now in possession of all the concepts which mark the "God of the philosophers". The metaphysical knowledge of God is assuredly the summit of human thought left to its sole natural resources and is valuable, in spite of its imperfections, for it is very fruitful, not only in the further development of philosophy (especially in ethics), but also in theology and in one's own personal religious life.

However, if this knowledge of God is to be as fruitful as we have a right to expect, various pitfalls have to be avoided.

In the first place, we must never mistake our human *concepts* and the *images* which accompany them for the *reality* they express in a very imperfect manner. Such a grave mistake would entirely destroy the results of metaphysical reflection, for it would lead to the adoration of an idol — the conceptual construct of our minds. The ineffable reality that God is, is infinitely richer, infinitely more worthy of admiration and love than we can conceive by means of human concepts. Think, for example, of the very poor ideas and still poorer images that we spontaneously form when we say that God is simple, immutable, eternal and incorporeal, when we say that he knows his effects "in himself", that the creative act is free, etc.

In the second place, we must never forget that the metaphysical knowledge of God is *indirect* and *incomplete*. It is indirect, because we know him only through the medium of finite beings and by opposition to them. It is incomplete, because we know him only as cause of the finite, that is to say, in so far as he manifests himself in his effects.

Fortunately we are not without protection against these pitfalls. The first way to avoid them is to be fully aware of them by cultivating *humility of intellect*, i.e. a sense of our intellectual limitations, a clear picture of the ridiculously inadequate means at our disposal to rise beyond the world of sense. The second way is to enlarge our horizons *by studying the marvels of the created universe*. All the positive sciences can make a valuable contribution to our knowledge of God since they all manifest — each in its own field — the power, wisdom and providence of the Creator as displayed in his wonderful works. It is evident, for example, that the study of the universe with its inconceivable dimensions, the awesome energies it contains, the unswerving laws that govern its movements, can reveal God's greatness to the human mind much more effectively than the negative concept 'infinite'. Finally, the third remedy against the pitfalls of the metaphysical knowledge of God is recourse to the teaching of *Christian Revelation* and to the witness of the great mystics or of the saints who have illustrated or explained this teaching. This presupposes of course that one has proved beforehand the divine origin of this Revelation. Once this has been shown, it is clear that it surpasses all other channels of knowledge, since it is God speaking about himself and revealing to men the mysteries of his inner life.

The assistance that Revelation can give the philosopher

should not be misunderstood. Metaphysical research must adhere strictly to its own methods and the metaphysician's concern must be to present a rigorous deduction of the attributes of the infinite Being. But this effort is not infallible and it is possible to be led astray. That is why, *psychologically*, it is useful for the philosopher to know the teaching of Revelation. It serves as a valuable *control* and *corrective* of his own conclusions: a control, in that it puts him on his guard against silly statements or inaccurate representations; a corrective, by reminding him of the divine initiatives that constitute the order of grace and that modify profoundly man's relations with God. We shall throw further light on these remarks at a later stage.

Chapter XI

THE WAYS OF RELIGIOUS EXPERIENCE

We have heard Henri Bergson say that, in his opinion, an existing object is one that is perceived or could be perceived. It is one given in actual or possible experience. Bergson concluded that the problem of the existence of God has to be examined *experimentally* ([1]).

The metaphysician is inclined to adopt a diametrically opposite point of view and to hold that the creative Cause, because his nature is transcendent, can form no part of the phenomenal order and can be the object of no human experience.

I believe that Bergson was wrong to reject metaphysical knowledge of God. As for declaring that any experience of God is impossible, it would amount to saying that the creative Cause could in no way manifest or "reveal" himself in the created world; it would amount to an *a priori* rejection of Christian teaching concerning Revelation and the supernatural order, which is characterized precisely by the irruption of the divine into the natural order.

Putting aside prejudice, let us therefore examine,

([1]) See above p. 161.

without preconceived ideas, what religious experience can contribute.

Ordinary religious experience seems unable to provide a solid foundation for affirming that God exists: it is not an experience of the Deity itself, it can be communicated only with difficulty and it is exposed to the danger of illusion (²).

This is not the case in some *exceptional* kinds of religious experience, once it can be shown that they involve a genuine experience of God's presence or of his action. Here we are faced with a real proof of the existence of God by the empirical method. Now there can be no doubt that some people, whose distrust of metaphysical speculation is insurmountable, are more open to a proof of this kind than to the most rigorous rational demonstrations. We heard Sir Edmund Whittaker observe that most people will always be more disposed to believe in God than in a system of metaphysics (³). This is a state of mind that is common enough in scientific circles. An eminent colleague of mine, now called to his reward, of the Faculty of Science, wrote to me in 1948: "For myself, I never entertained any doubts about the existence of God and I have therefore never been worried by being unable to understand any of the demonstrations I read and cannot even remember. May it please God that I may never think that my belief in his existence depends on my appreciation of the validity of an argument, for if that were to happen, I might begin to doubt about it,

(²) See above pp. 56-57.
(³) See above p. 88.

as I have often doubted various propositions, without being able to say where they were wrong".

But the method, we said, can be developed along two different lines, one *historical*, the other *psychological* (⁴). An interesting example of the first is to be found in the *De libero arbitrio* of St. Augustine; the second was thrown into full relief in the famous proof of Bergson based on the experience of the great Christian mystics. We shall examine each of these two examples in turn.

The Proof of Evodius

Book II of this celebrated dialogue contains the fullest statement of the "Augustinian" proof of the existence of God. At the beginning of the book however, when St. Augustine first tackles the problem of God, he asks his friend Evodius how he would set about it, if he had to convert a *bona fide* atheist. — If he is in good faith, replies Evodius substantially, it will not be hard to convince him. For, after he has asked me to believe that he is sincere before beginning to discuss with him, he cannot very well, in turn, refuse to accept the sincerity of the eminent men who wrote the Gospels and to believe in the existence of God on the testimony of those who lived in intimacy with the Son of God. For these witnesses testify that they saw things that could not have taken place unless God existed. And my opponent would be

(⁴) See above p. 47.

very foolish to blame me for believing these witnesses whilst expecting me to take him at his word. Surely he could find no excuse for failing to imitate what he could not rightly blame me for doing. — Augustine does not dispute the validity of the argument, but he asks Evodius why he does not rely on these trustworthy witnesses for the solution of all outstanding questions, instead of tiring himself by trying to find the answers by himself. — We want to know and understand what we believe, replies Evodius, and this answer meets with the approval of his brilliant friend ([5]).

Let us analyze more closely the suggestions made by Evodius.

They comprise, in the first place, a kind of *argumentum ad hominem*. The atheist, Evodius believes, who wants others to accept his sincerity, should, in exchange, accept the sincerity of the Apostles. It is reasonable and prudent to take the word of the Apostles that Jesus Christ is the Son of God and that he has revealed to men the existence of his Father. The argument has some value and can be admitted by any prudent man.

But if such a proof is to withstand criticism, it becomes indispensable *to examine the twofold testimony* appealed to (that of the Apostles and that of Christ). And immediately the problem rebounds and becomes more involved. We can pass over the authority of the Apostles as it is relatively easy to show that they were sincere and that

([5]) *De libero arbitrio, liber secundus*, beginning. In the Thonnard edition (Bibliothèque augustinienne. Œuvres de saint Augustin. Opuscules, VII), pp. 208-218.

they were well-informed about the actions and sayings of Jesus. But how are we to give a critical estimate of Christ's testimony? By saying that his *sincerity* is manifest and that he talks about what he knows from *personal experience*? Granted; but this is not a rigorous proof as it depends, in ultimate analysis, on an appeal to faith in Christ's word before its authority has been established. By appealing to the signs (miracles, prophecies, eminent sanctity) that guarantee the authority of Christ? This is all very well, but then we have to undertake a *critical investigation of these signs* (6). The New Testament shows that the Apostles did this. But, in their case, it rested on the presupposition of God's existence and they saw our Lord's miracles as marks of divine approval. In the case envisaged by Evodius, on the contrary, the existence of God is itself called in question and, as a result, the critical study of the signs must be transformed into a proof of God's existence. It will have to be shown that the miracles (e.g. the healing of the man born blind, the resurrection of Lazarus), because they are absolutely inexplicable by natural causes or by any human means used by Christ, are an evident *sign* of the intervention of a higher Being, Lord of nature, intelligent and good, who approves, by

(6) Evodius suggests the idea of a *critique of signs* when he says of the Apostles:"*quia et ea se vidisse scripserunt, quae nullo modo fieri possent, si non esset Deus*" (for they wrote that they saw things which could nowise take place if God did not exist). This is a manifest allusion to the miracles of Christ, which reveal the presence of a transcendent power and can, on that account, provide a starting point for the search for God.

these signs, the mission and teaching of Jesus Christ. In this manner we reach the existence of a transcendent, personal Being, whose providence manifests itself in a very special way in the work of Christ. All that remains then is to learn from Christ himself more about the nature and attributes of this higher Being whom he calls his Father and Creator of the universe.

Reflecting on the nature and constitution of this demonstration, three parts can be distinguished: an appeal to *testimony* (of the Apostles and then of Christ), an appeal to *religious experience* (that of the Apostles who lived with a divine Person manifesting himself in the sensible actions of his human nature; that of Christ himself who lives in permanent communion with the Person of the Father), an appeal to *rational reflection* (critique of testimony, critique of signs). It will be observed that the final stage (critique of signs) comprises at least an embryonic metaphysical proof. Starting from the observation of some extraordinary event (the healing of the man born blind, for example), the principle of causality is invoked ("what is not of itself intelligible, must be explained by some outside cause") and the conclusion drawn that there exists a transcendent Being who is Lord of nature and who, by his merciful intervention, manifests his benevolence towards Jesus Christ and towards those who hear him. Briefly, we find ourselves in the presence of a variant of the *Fifth Way*, the proof from finality. But, instead of relying on metaphysical reasoning for the complete elaboration of the proof, especially for the demonstration of the unicity and universal providence of God, we appeal to Christ, God's envoy, for this additional information on the attributes of God.

In the *De libero arbitrio* of St. Augustine, the argument from authority put forward by Evodius is no more than an introduction to the subject. In accordance with the method dear to the convert rhetorician, the search for God begins with an act of faith (not of divine faith, but of faith in the veracity of the Apostles, witnesses of the living God). But this is only the beginning: *credo ut intelligam*; faith does no more than stimulate our desire to know and to understand. It gives rise to a long, purely rational, demonstration of the existence of God [7].

The historical method employed by Evodius suffers from the drawbacks of all apologetical demonstrations that depend on the life of Christ or on other facts going back to the beginning of Christianity. It presupposes that all the difficulties concerning the authenticity and historicity of the New Testament documents have been solved. It is true that their value as evidence of the transcendent mission of Jesus has emerged victorious, in all essentials, from the attacks of rationalist criticism. Nevertheless, there are many who have an almost instinctive distrust and who are incurably sceptical of any affirmation resting on evidence two thousand years old.

Cardinal Deschamps, in the nineteenth century, advocated a method of apologetics the object of which was to side-step this obstacle by starting with the Catholic Church today, with contemporary religious facts, and by trying to find in them signs of God's presence and action. This method can also be applied in the search for God.

[7] See above pp. 59-63.

Instead of beginning with Christ's doings, we could begin with Lourdes, for example, or from the concrete lives of great contemporary miracle-workers (the Curé of Ars, St. John Bosco, or other saints), whose activities are not open to serious questions. The critique of signs will operate here as in the case of the Gospel miracles.

Bergson's Proof

This proof, which appeals to the evidence of the mystics, was developed by Bergson in a famous work that cannot be too highly praised ([8]).

Scientism and Positivism had for long been describing religion as a survival of the instinctive credulity of primitive man. The "law of the three states" of Auguste Comte said that the theological age gives way to the metaphysical and the latter, in turn, to the positive age, marked by the triumph of experimental science. Even still, Marxists, neo-Positivists and a good many scientists believe that scientific progress results in the decay of metaphysics and of religious "superstitions": when science reaches the final term of its development, metaphysics and religion will be completely eliminated. These naive claims of Scientism we have already dealt with ([9]), but it has to be admitted that a superficial survey of the history of civilization seems to confirm these opinions; the triumph

([8]) H. BERGSON, *The two sources of morality and religion*, Engl. trans., pp. 181-205.

([9]) See above p. 115.

of science, the scientific explanation of phenomena, have often resulted in pushing back the frontiers of metaphysical and supernatural explanation.

Now, Bergson's work marks a categorical reaction against this state of mind. His learning and genius lent exceptional authority to his exposure of the ambiguity that vitiated the Positivist thesis: confusion between "the two sources of morals and religion", between "static religion" and "dynamic religion".

The former is developed in closed societies (tribal or national) and has for its object to ensure order and stability by putting a curb on egoism and fear. It is the product of the creative imagination, which gives rise to *myths*, and of intelligence (in the Bergsonian sense of the word), which helps to organize them. Static religion elaborates a system of sanctions against the egoism of individuals and a system of defence against fear, either by impersonal means (such as *magic* and *sorcery*) or by personal means (such as *ancestor* worship, worship of *spirits* and *gods*, and occasionally even of the supreme God). It is clear that scientific advances are made at the expense of this static religion as they tend to eliminate myths, magic, sorcery, and all beliefs that cannot stand up to scientific criticism.

But dynamic religion is something entirely different. Reaching out towards the Source of all life, it rises above earthly contingencies and issues forth in love over all things. That is why it must have a suitable cultural environment, an open society, transcending, in its human perspectives, the frontiers of the clan and of the nation. Dynamic religion is developed on a plane higher than that of scientific explanation and aspires after values that transcend science. Consequently, it is not affected by the progress of science ([10]).

It is at the very heart of dynamic religion that we come accross mystical experience, which reaches its peak in the case of the great Christian mystics. We cannot subscribe to the explanation put forward by psychologists like Pierre Janet, who see nothing in mystical phenomena but pathological states and, in mystics, people who are unbalanced. The intellectual health of the mystics, on the contrary, is shown in many aspects of their behaviour and in their extraordinary achievements in practical affairs.

"When we grasp that such is the culminating point of the inner evolution of the great mystics, we can but wonder how they could ever have been classed with the mentally diseased" ([11]), though they might "provide us with the very definition of intellectual vigour" ([12]). It is true to say that the mystical state is an abnormal state and that it is difficult to distinguish between the abnormal and the morbid. It is also true that the phenomena of genuine mystical life can be associated with certain morbid states. But "we must not be surprised if nervous

([10]) In the concrete history of human societies, static and dynamic religion, closed and open morality, are often mixed together. A ceaseless effort of purification and elevation is necessary to get away from inferior forms of morality and religious life.

([11]) *The two sources...*, pp. 194-195.

([12]) *The two sources...*, p. 195.

disturbances and mysticism sometimes go together; we find the same disturbances in other forms of genius, notably in musicians. They have to be regarded as merely accidental. The former have no more to do with mystical inspiration than the latter with musical" (13).

The great Christian mystics are, then, men of superior standing and worthy of credence. But what scientific value has their evidence? "For it is alleged that the experiences of the great mystics are individual and exceptional, that they cannot be verified by the ordinary man, that they cannot therefore be compared to a scientific experiment and cannot possibly solve problems" (14). Bergson replies that science accepts a single experience if there are adequate guarantees of honesty and competence. Others can follow the journey undertaken by the mystics and verify, to some extent at least, the accuracy of their descriptions. The deep-seated agreement of the mystics among themselves when they describe the object of their intuitions and, more generally, the successive phases of the mystical life, confirms what they have to say. Finally and above all, the analysis of mystical experience leads to the same result as the analysis of biological experience: both lead to the discovery of creative Love, living Source of the vital impetus.

"The mystics unanimously bear witness that God needs us, just as we need God. Why should He need us unless it be to love us? And it is to this very conclusion that the philosopher who holds to mystical experience

(13) *The two sources...*, p. 196.
(14) *The two sources...*, p. 210.

must come. Creation will appear to him as God undertaking to create creators, that he may have, besides himself, beings worthy of his love" (15).

The mystics are, therefore, authentic witnesses of God for other men.

The steps in the demonstration propounded by Bergson correspond to those we distinguished in the argument of Evodius: appeal to the *testimony* of the great Christian mystics, appeal to their *religious experience*, appeal to *reflection* (critique of testimony and critique of the signs which guarantee that the mystical experience is genuine). The value of the demonstration obviously depends on the result of this critical reflection.

It will be readily granted that the *testimony* of the great Christian mystics is *sincere*: a close study of the lives of people like St. Theresa of Jesus, John of the Cross, Francis of Sales, John Bosco, the Curé of Ars, Bernadette Soubirous, will leave no doubt about their trustworthiness.

Could they not have been the victims of illusion? Is it possible to establish scientifically that the *experience of the divine* which they claim to enjoy is genuine? It may be perfectly adequate for its beneficiaries, for it seems to be able to provide them with objective evidence of the existence of God. But the experience and the evidence are strictly incommunicable and, consequently, the proof of God's existence based on them does not hold for those who do not share the experience and the evidence. It seems therefore to have no scientific value.

(15) *The two sources...*, p. 218.

We have seen how Bergson endeavours to overcome these difficulties and we have no hesitation in following him. His suggestions appear capable of development and amplification in several directions: the critical examination of the *content* of mystical experience ([16]), the critical examination of the *signs* manifesting the intervention of a personal Providence in the lives and extraordinary influence of the great mystics in the field of apostolical action ([17]).

In fine, we return to the conclusions we reached at the end of our examination of Evodius's argument in St. Augustine's *De libero arbitrio*: every proof of God's existence by the empirical method must finish with a reflection of a metaphysical nature if it is to carry us beyond the stage of pure and simple assent to the testimony of those who claim to have experience of God. There is nothing wrong in believing what people like Christ or St. Paul, or St. Theresa, or. St. John Bosco tell us. But we are not forbidden to look for supplementary guarantees — it is even praiseworthy to do so — by looking for the internal evidence in the motives for affirming God's existence. This intrinsic evidence can only be obtained by a critique of a metaphysical nature:

([16]) And especially the extraordinary *convergence* of these experiences despite the widely different subjective situations.

([17]) The reader will find interesting developments on the Bergsonian proof and on the complements it calls for in G. RABEAU, *Dieu, son existence et sa providence*, Paris, 1933, pp. 84-91 (*L'expérience mystique et l'existence de Dieu*) and pp. 94-99 (*L'expérience mystique, sa valeur objective, son objet*).

bringing the principle of causality into play once again, we can show that the existence of a personal, powerful and benevolent Being is the *conditio sine qua non* of the "signs" that accompany the mystical experience. This is a fresh variant of the proof of the existence of God by way of finality — with its advantages and drawbacks ([18]).

([18]) See above, pp. 128-139.

Chapter XII

THE PROBLEM OF EVIL

St. Thomas mentions two fundamental objections to the existence of God: He is *useless* since everything that takes place in the world can be explained without Him; He is *improbable*, for, if He existed, evil could not dominate the world as it does ([1]).

The first difficulty — it is that of a number of scientists who expect that Science will solve all problems — has been solved. Briefly, it is easy enough to show how groundless their hope is: positive science, by virtue of its methods, leaves more problems unsolved than it succeeds in solving. It leaves unsolved, especially, the problem of the Absolute: there must evidently be an absolute reality at the origin of things and science is competent neither to raise the question nor to answer it.

This is the task of metaphysics. Metaphysics provides a rigorous demonstration that the Absolute is to be looked for, not only beyond the corporeal world, but beyond the order of finite beings; the Absolute is an infinite Being, creative cause of finite beings. This sovereignly perfect Being is a personal Being, who knows and

([1]) See above p. 12.

loves what He has made and who provides all that created persons need for their perfection and happiness.

Religious experience, critically examined, provides valuable *confirmation* of the conclusions of metaphysics. It can also, if God so wills, impart to men fuller knowledge of the intimate nature of the Creator and of His providential designs. We shall point out at a later stage that the Christian religion claims to be the depositary of a divine Revelation that is the expression of the Creator's merciful love for man.

The Problem

It is at this point that we come up against the second objection mentioned by St. Thomas. Metaphysical deduction has to take into account our daily experience of evil under all its forms. How can we reconcile it with an omnipotent and infinitely benevolent Providence? If God is love, how can we explain that so many disorders and so much suffering make the human situation apparently so unenviable? This problem has never ceased to puzzle men and it remains the principal weapon of the atheist. It would be easy to illustrate this from the blasphemous or pessimist publications inspired by Marxist materialism or by atheistic existentialism [2].

[2] M.J. COTEREAU, secretary of the Federation of French Free-thinkers, said again quite recently in the course of a discussion on secular versus religious morality held in Brussels: "I do not believe in God because if he existed, he would be Evil. I had rather deny him than make him responsible for evil" (February, 1960).

In fact there is no general agreement on the preponderance of evil in the world, on the proportion of good and evil, of pleasure and of suffering, that is to be found in any human life. There are pessimists who see evil in everything and who dramatize every situation. One day's sickness is enough to make them forget six months' good health, one reverse of fortune enough to make them forget long years of ease and prosperity. Married people, who have to put up with one another's shortcomings, can lose sight of the good points and thus cease to appreciate the happiness to be found in the home. The honest citizen, disturbed by the stories of accidents and crimes he reads in his daily newspaper, loses sight of the hundreds of millions of human beings who passed the day peacefully. Optimists, on the contrary, look on the bright side of things — every cloud has a silver lining. They quickly forget suffering and prefer to look for a way round obstacles rather than risk knocking their heads against a stone wall. When they are tried, they console themselves with the thought that there are others who have to bear heavier crosses. Instead of exaggerating their suffering, they immediately think of the good it will eventually do them.

But all this does not essentially modify the problem. It still remains true that the ravages of evil are terrifying and that the history of the human race presents us with the sorrowful spectacle of a veritable stream of tears and blood.

The history of ideas contains many different accounts of the nature, origin and significance of evil. Let us recall a few typical attitudes. In ancient times, the Stoics professed *fatalism*: man is caught up in the necessary evolution of the cosmos, as are all beings, and he must learn to accept his destiny with serenity. Manichaean *dualism* postulates the existence of two absolute principles — Good and Evil; all the disorders we suffer from are due to the Evil Principle. Leibniz was an *optimist*: he taught that ours was the best possible world. Opposed to Leibniz is Schopenhauer, who was a *pessimist*: Will, an eternal principle immanent in the world, is a source of aspirations that, in human consciousness, take the form of ever-insatiable desires, i.e. of suffering, and the more intense the desire, the greater the suffering, so that man's natural state, and the inescapable fulfilment of nature's dynamism, is suffering; we must, therefore, destroy in us the will to live, firstly, by artistic escape, and secondly, by renouncing all personal consciousness, rather like the Buddhist *Nirvâna*.

These different interpretations of the nature of evil are corollaries of more fundamental metaphysical doctrines. Therefore, it is at the metaphysical level that they have to be confronted, discussed and refuted.

On the contrary, the acute pessimism resulting from contemporary *atheistic existentialism* is based on a penetrating analysis of the human condition as it appears in the contemporary world. Existentialism calls to its aid all the resources of psychology, phenomenology and sociology, depicting human suffering in all its forms with brutal realism and, even more so, the egoistic instincts, at times savage, that inspire human behaviour and that are, because of man's inhumanity to man, the source of innumerable evils. The final conclusion of the analysis is that human existence is absurd, that the world is meaningless and that everything, for the individual man, is consummated in the crowning absurdity of death.

We shall try in this chapter to ascertain the nature of evil, to discern its principal forms and to indicate to what extent philosophical reflection is able to explain and justify it.

The Nature of Evil

Traditional metaphysics distinguishes in every finite being the *subject* which exists (the substance) from the *activity*, i.e. everything the subject does in the course of its existence to develop its virtualities and reach its perfection. Plants breathe, feed themselves, grow and reproduce their kind. Animals, in addition, see, hear, move from one place to another, attack their prey, are attracted to the opposite sex, protect their young. Man thinks, expresses himself by words and signs, desires, enjoys, suffers.

What is evil and where does it reside?

It is defined in contrast to good. Firstly, it is the *privation* of a good, i.e. the absence of some good that *ought* to be there if a thing were what it ought to be in virtue of its nature. Famine is an evil as it is the privation of the food that people must have if they are to live and work. Poverty is the privation of the material necessaries of life. Ignorance is the privation of the knowledge necessary if a man is to earn his living and enjoy the benefits of intellectual culture. Blindness is the privation of sight. Paralysis is the privation of movement. Evil, however, is often more than privation: frequently it is a *positive disorder*. Cancer is not merely the privation of harmonious cellular development; it is the aggressive presence of disorderly cellular proliferation attacking the organism and upsetting the vital functions to an ever-increasing extent. Blasphemy is not merely the privation of the praise due to God; it is a positive disorder of judgment and will in one who deliberately thinks evil about God or deliberately wishes him evil.

Where does this privation and this disorder reside?

Evil is not "a being": all finite beings come from God and are necessarily good as being. It is a privation or disorder that affects a being. It cannot affect a being in its *substance*: no finite being, since it is the immediate term of divine action, can be *substantially* evil. There are no evil *substances*, i.e. substances deprived of what is their due by virtue of their nature, or disordered in their essential constitution. Where there is question of imperfection, it concerns a being's *activity* and only its activity, and it takes the form of privation or deviation or disorder in so far as this activity is not performed as the nature, whence it emanates, demands.

This being the nature of evil, it is immediately apparent that its significance changes radically according as it affects the activity of bodies or that of spirits.

Activity of bodies is determined by their nature, but it comes up against the activity of other bodies. These concurrent activities are not always in harmony and, as bodies are passive as well as active, they are affected more or less by the activities of surrounding bodies. When activities clash, the result is a more or less serious *disorder* that we call *physical evil*: it could lead even to the destruction of the body it affects. Here are a few examples from the many that spring to mind. A hurricane uproots trees and strips the roofs off houses. Storms cause shipwrecks. Fire destroys forests, dwellings etc. Locusts devour crops. Bacteria attack living tissue. Earthquakes devastate entire cities. The antelope is the lion's prey; rabbits eat cabbages and lettuces. A pedestrian is knocked down by a motor car, an old man asphyxiated by gas seeping from his heater or cooker. The absence of harmony between the activities of bodies often results in *privation* which can have serious consequences: a plant may wither through lack of sunlight, moisture, fertiliser; an animal can die of thirst or hunger, of cold, of lack of oxygen. In all these cases, the being that suffered failed to find in its environment what was necessary for its sustenance and growth.

The spiritual activity of man is of a different category — at least for those who believe in free will. When we act freely (less frequently doubtless than we imagine), our action is determined neither by outside compulsion, nor by our nature, nor by the motives present to our minds; we determine ourselves to act in a particular way and we decide what motive shall prevail over the others. This is the formidable mystery of our personal autonomy. Now this free activity — we are but too often aware of the fact — is subject to disorder and liable to deviate. Our autonomy is such that we can choose motives for acting knowing that they do not conform to the prescriptions of the moral law. *Moral evil* is a conscious and deliberate disorder of free activity. Here are a few examples. The thief takes what belongs to others for his own immediate profit even though he knows this manner of acting is contrary to the moral order and, consequently, contrary to his own true interest. The same applies to infidelity in marriage. The liar and the calumniator know that they are violating the moral law. They all deliberately sacrifice their real good for some apparent, relative and illusory advantage. It often happens that the morally bad action is due to some extent to blindness or frailty, and this diminishes the "responsibility" of the agent. The extreme, moral evil in its pure state, is what theologians call the *sin of pure malice*. In this case a created person uses his freedom to defy God and to refuse, out of pride, to submit, in order to assert his independence; it is the "*non serviam*" of Lucifer.

Explanation of Evil

How can evil have any place in the Creator's work? Can its presence be justified?

Physical evil appears to be the natural and inevitable consequence of the passivity of bodies. Several philosophies, from Plato to Bergson, set matter at the bottom of the hierarchy of beings. According to St. Thomas, it is the most distant and most imperfect participation of the divine perfection. The fundamental property of matter is quantity and its concomitant, extension in space. A body is virtually divided: it is extended, dispersed, and, as a result, exposed to the action of other bodies.

Physical evil, as long as we confine our attention to

the *material world*, raises no problems. Corporeal beings, as a matter of fact, are not a value for themselves nor are they their own end, as they are deprived of consciousness; they exist only for the sake of human beings who make use of them. On the other hand, physical evil is an integral and even indispensable part of the order of material beings. The conflict of corporeal forces contributes to the normal evolution of the universe by the ceaseless physico-chemical transformations that are necessary for the activity of human beings and by regularly reducing the number of living beings — their increase would render the earth uninhabitable if it was not checked in the struggle for existence.

Here however there arises a first difficulty and one which seriously preoccupies some people: we are referring to the question of animal "suffering". There can be no doubt that animals do, at times, behave like suffering human beings: they cry, they tremble, they try to escape etc. when they are in pain, just as human beings do. This is spontaneously interpreted as an expression of mental states analogous to those experienced by human beings when they are in the grip of pain. Consequently we are moved to pity and compassion. But, if we reflect a little, it may occur to us to doubt the interpretation put on animal behaviour in terms of human psychology and to ask ourselves if we are not being the victims of a serious illusion.

The main question is to decide whether animals are or are not *conscious*, i.e. beings who know themselves, who are conscious of existing and aware of what is going on inside them. With the entire body of traditional philosophers, I believe that being conscious implies being *spiritual*, having a spiritual vital principle that is the source of spiritual activities. It implies, therefore, being a *person*, having rights and duties, having a personal destiny in the hereafter. Is this so in the case of animals?

A scientific answer to this question can only be given by psychology — first on the plane of positive science and then on the plane of philosophical criticism. It appears to me that an examination of instinctive animal behaviour reveals a very interesting and, indeed, very mysterious, psychism, but one that is *devoid of consciousness of any kind* and, for that reason, of free will. If this is indeed the case, the problem of animal "suffering" is an empty one, as "unconscious suffering" is a contradiction in terms. To suffer and not to be aware of the fact, to suffer and not to be conscious of suffering, is the same as not suffering at all. Because their organic constitution is similar to ours, animals are subject to all the physiological phenomena, and appear to have all the nervous reactions, that accompany suffering in human beings. Because they possess a genuine psychism, they can experience strange reactions that we interpret anthropomorphically as states of "fear", "sadness", "anger" etc. But these reactions are not conscious and affect beings that are not persons and that have neither rights nor duties. They pose no problem, therefore, about the meaning and value of "suffering".

Those who refuse to admit this interpretation of animal life and who claim that animals are genuinely conscious beings must be prepared to put up with the consequences of their opinion. It means that animals are persons, having rights and duties, that they are inviolable and cannot be killed and eaten, that they have to be treated in all things with the respect due to persons! As for the problem of animal suffering, it would be the same as the problem of human suffering with which we shall now deal.

Physical evil poses a problem in so far as it *affects persons* and manifests itself under the form of *suffering*, physical or moral.

Physical evil (privation or disorder) that attacks a man in his body, in his material possessions or in the person of those dear to him, is a real evil and no normal man pursues it for its own sake. It jeopardizes a man's natural activity: sickness, for example, prevents a man from working and, in some cases, even from thinking or praying; poverty can prevent a man from providing himself with food or clothing or a roof over his head, from educating himself etc. Neither does anybody claim that suffering is something good, desirable for its own sake. In itself, it is an evil: firstly, because it is the result of disorder or privation, i.e. the result of evil, and secondly, because it disturbs the conscious activity of the person and more or less completely imperils his happiness, which consists in the enjoyment of good.

This being the situation, how are we to *explain* and *justify* the existence of physical evil and of suffering as they affect the human person?

In regard to its *origin*, we have already pointed out that physical evil is the natural and inevitable consequence of the passivity of bodies, which, in turn, is an essential property of matter. Scientists and philosophers are unanimously agreed on this point. But, when it comes to the question of *reconciling* evil and suffering with divine Providence, serious difficulties arise. Why has God, who is love and who creates out of love, created human beings, i.e. embodied consciences, and exposed, as a result, to all the evils and all the suffering that spring from matter? Besides, admitting that passivity, essential to matter, inevitably entails collisions, conflicts and disorders, is a corporeal world without the horrors we experience in ours inconceivable? Are the bacilli of cholera, of the plague, of leprosy, of tetanus, of sleeping sickness, of tuberculosis, of polio, indispensable to the material order? Must cancer necessarily form part of it? Why do alcohol, opium and other drugs exercise such tyrannical power over the human organism? Could not sexual anomalies, the source of so many terrible tragedies, have been avoided? The uses of pain have often been pointed out: it is a sign that serves to warn the organism of impending danger, it elevates man by turning him away from sensible pleasure and the satisfaction of his lower appetites, it fortifies and inures him to hardships, it tempers his character to meet life's challenges. Very well; but why that exquisite sensibility which exposes a man, without defence, to atrocious suffering, driving him to delirium, despair or madness? Can extreme suffering produce any good effects on a person? Briefly, not to prolong the list of examples unduly, could not the Creator in his infinite wisdom, goodness and mercy have created a world more propitious, more hospitable, kinder to man? These are the difficulties that preoccupy many people.

As regards man's condition as a conscience obliged to develop and realize its potentialities in a mysterious union with a corporeal organism, it is easy to see that it is a situation that opens up a host of *values* that would find no place in the life of a pure spirit. To describe these specifically human values would take a complete volume. Mention would have to be made of conjugal and parental love; all stages and all forms of human growth would have to be analyzed (physical, intellectual and moral; esthetic, social, professional formation); corresponding to this, the prodigious achievement of educators in all sectors; scientific research, too, the progressive conquest of the material world by scientists, engineers, technicians; medicine — the devotion shown in the service of the sick, the infirm, the orphan, and the aged; the toil of the labourer, the manager's talents, the mission of judge and statesman, the artist's genius — these, together with many others not expressly mentioned, are values associated with the human situation and cannot be realized apart from it. Consequently, even supposing that God had created a world of spiritual beings (it is a theory that was held by some great philosophers and it has been adopted by catholic theologians as an interpretation, commonly held nowadays, of biblical teaching concerning angels), it is evident that the world of pure spirits is far from exhausting the possibilities of creation. By creating man, a link between the spiritual and material worlds, God brought into being an ensemble of magnificent values.

As regards knowing whether the material universe could not be kindlier, whether we might not have been spared the more unbearable kinds of suffering, this is a much more difficult problem. The first thing to do would be to carry out a scientific study of the nature and role of micro-organisms (bacteria, virus, etc.), of the origin and nature of malignant tumours, of the use of drugs, of the causes of sexual aberrations. Then it would be necessary to inquire whether extreme sensibility to suffering is not the *inevitable* price we pay for the extraordinary delicacy of our nervous system and sensory apparatus, especially since this delicacy is the source of many psychological aptitudes and, consequently, of many values. No doubt many human situations remain obscure and perplexing. But it is likely that even now there are many things whose meaning we do not grasp. While we await further enlightenment on the enigmas of the material universe, is it not wiser to put our trust in the loving Providence of the Creator? In any case, it is all philosophy has to offer to him who wishes to unravel these problems.

Moral evil, we have said, affects a man's will and is the consequence of freedom. To be able to shape one's own destiny, to respond to the Creator's love with complete freedom, is the prerogative of persons and it entails, as inevitable consequence, the possibility of refusal. The consequence of refusal is moral disorder. For, even though persons enjoy the prerogative of *psychological* liberty, i.e. the power of self-determination, they do not enjoy *moral* liberty, i.e. the right to act at will with no regard for the natural order established by the Creator. Persons are, on the contrary, bound to regulate their conduct according to the prescriptions of the moral order to the best of their knowledge. They are responsible for their actions and must shoulder the consequences.

What are these consequences? What happens if a man abuses his freedom, if his will chooses disorder? This raises very serious problems, problems of capital importance for every human being, and they are not easy to solve. We are confronted with another paradox of the human situation: left to himself, with only the natural light of reason to guide him, man can only hazard conjectures of varying degrees of probability regarding the vital problem of his destiny. Is there a sanction attached by *nature* to evil action? Does it affect the sinner *in this life* or *in the next*? What does it consist in?

The philosopher, reflecting on the wisdom and benevolence of God, may offer a few suggestions. Because he created the world in order that created persons should partake in the divine perfection and blessedness, God established an order in which they are able to reach their perfection and happiness. Without respect for the moral order this perfection and happiness becomes impossible, for the moral law merely lays down what is required for the harmonious development of human activity. Respect for the moral law ensures the realization of essential human values and, consequently, the essential happiness of the human person. Moral disorder, on the contrary, deprives the person of these essential values and of the happiness that results from them. In this life, however, since moral action forms only one part of human activity, an upright or a perverse will does not automatically entail rectitude or disorder in other sectors. The profligate may be physically sound, he may be a good business man or he may display great professional competence; the upright man may suffer from bad health, he may be a failure in business or he may be married to a shrew. Briefly, it is evident that in this life there is no sanction for good or evil and, if there were no future life, we should be forced to admit the ruin of the moral order and the complete absence of divine justice. That explains why the implications of the moral law correspond to man's deepest aspirations and the indications of his nature in affirming the immortality of the soul, the immaterial principle that confers on man his specific nature and personal dignity. Retribution for good and evil will, therefore, be made in the life to come.

Can we make any conjectures about this future life? We know that every human person has a *value for his own sake*, an end that is his own, a personal destiny. Divine wisdom and benevolence would seem to demand that created persons should be able to reach a state of stable perfection and permanent happiness. This state is not compatible with the precarious condition of a being who would continue to be exposed to the vicissitudes of an existence lacking stable moral orientation and enjoying merely transient happiness. Likewise, divine justice seems to demand that deliberate moral evil, obstinately persevered in during this life, should receive a permanent sanction in the life to come. Without a sanction of this kind, the absolute value of the moral order would be endangered and respect for moral values gravely compromised here below. In short, it is reasonable to believe that, at death, man is confirmed in the moral state that is his at the end of his period of trial on earth. The sanction for good and evil ought to be applied at that moment and it ought to be everlasting.

Does this view not endanger the end of creation? Can we admit that a human will could be irremediably fixed in disorder?

The drama of the destiny of the created person lies entirely in the response made to the Creator's love. This response is free; it would have no value if it were not. Therefore, it is possible to refuse: this is the inevitable counterpart of liberty. The everlasting failure of a human destiny doubtlessly affects the order of creation, but it in no way affects the Creator, as the creation does not increase his perfection or happiness. Responsibility for moral evil falls entirely on the creature who is compelled to confess, even in the depths of his misery, the wisdom, benevolence and justice of God.

Conclusion

These are the perspectives that philosophical wisdom can lay open concerning the problem of evil confronted with the metaphysical thesis of divine Providence. They convey a global impression that can be called *moderate optimism*. *Optimism*, since, in the case of every created person who responds to the Creator's love by acceptance and fidelity, the effects of evil in this life are temporary and always appear as a momentary trial; man's destiny will be fulfilled in a state of permanent perfection and happiness. *Moderate* optimism, because physical and moral evil are redoubtable realities, inherent in the situation of finite beings, and especially because created persons can, by rebelling, become irretrievably fixed in moral disorder and misfortune.

We cannot however claim to have solved all difficulties. There are two reasons for this. The first is that some doubts and uncertainties regarding man's destiny and the meaning of suffering defy rational investigation. The second is that the lot of some people appears to us so cruel, the suffering that oppresses the human race, afflicting the innocent no less than the guilty, is sometimes so terrible that we find it difficult to detect behind it the hand of a loving Providence. No matter how great the achievements his present situation makes possible, they seem to us a poor reward for all the tears and all the blood.

This is the pessimistic view reached by many of our contemporaries. Their rebellion finds expression in the atheistic and blasphemous literature with which we are familiar (³).

Nobody with any sympathy will deny that there are tragedies, apparently with no relieving feature, that explain (though they do not excuse) a gesture of despair. The suffering of some people seems to be more than a human being can bear. There are cases of intense grief when we feel helpless and when any expression of consolation or attempted justification would distress the sufferer still more.

(³) In this connexion reference has already been made to A. CAMUS, *L'homme révolté*, Paris, 1951 (above, p. 17). Reference might also be made to J.-P. SARTRE and many others.

Do we have to stop at this point and give up all hope of understanding some features of the human situation? Before accepting this confession of impotence, we shall turn to the Church of Christ and ask her what answer she can make to our question.

CHAPTER XIII

THE GOD OF JESUS CHRIST

Is there a difference between the "God of Jesus Christ" and the "God of the philosophers"?

There is no *antinomy* between the two pictures of the Supreme Being. Not alone does the Christian Church admit all the attributes metaphysics predicates of the First Cause, but she insists also on the competence of reason in this sphere and teaches that by the light of reason alone man can arrive at knowledge of the Creator and of his essential attributes.

But, on the other hand, Christianity claims to be of divine origin. It teaches that the patriarchs, the prophets, and, above all, Christ, were bearers of a divine message to men, a divine revelation, new insights into the inner life of the Creator and into his designs in regard to man. Let us call to mind briefly the broad outlines of this revelation.

The Fundamental Mystery

Concerning the nature of God, the "fundamental mystery", the central doctrine of Christianity, is obviously the mystery of the Trinity: the Infinite Being subsists in three Persons who share the same unique divine nature. The Father eternally begets the Son or Word, the perfect subsisting expression of his mind. The Father and the Son are, from all eternity also, the one principle of the Holy Ghost, the perfect and subsisting expression of the mutual love of the Father and of the Son. God is, therefore, one and infinite, but he is not alone. Person thrice over, he constitutes necessarily a "family", a "society" of Persons.

Without going any deeper into theological study of the Trinity, we have to point out that the dogma in no way conflicts with the conclusions reached by metaphysics, but, on the contrary, sheds fresh light on the negative attributes of God and helps us to grasp their exact significance. Metaphysics proves that the infinite Being excludes all *composition* and all *plurality*: he is *simple* and *unique*. Now the dogma of the Trinity implies neither composition nor plurality of beings in God. But it teaches us something undreamt of in philosophy — the existence of a plurality *without composition* and *without mutual exclusion*. The Divine Persons are consubstantial and they are not "many Infinite Beings" nor are they "parts" or "components" of the Infinite Being. It is indeed a mysterious and ineffable plurality, quite beyond conceptual categories that are adapted to a world of finite beings, where all inner plurality means composition of different parts and in which all external plurality is plurality of beings opposed each to the other.

Emmanuel

The mystery of the Incarnation is no less distinctive a feature of Christianity than the mystery of the Trinity. "Emmanuel": God with us. "The Word was made flesh and dwelt amongst us" (¹). Jesus of Nazareth claimed to be the Son of God made man. The Catholic Church, on the basis of the Scriptures, defined the meaning of the mystery by the doctrine of the *hypostatic union*: in Jesus Christ the divine and human natures are united so closely that they form only one Person, the divine Person of the eternal Word.

The Incarnation of the Word corresponds to a grandiose design, revealed through all the Scriptures, but brought out with exceptional power by St. Paul: to make of Jesus, the God-man, the centre and end of all creation, to reduce all things to the unity of one Lord, Jesus Christ (²), and to ensure in and by him, provided they accept the divine plan, the return to the Father of all created persons. To bring about this "deification", Christ gave to man the gift of divine life itself, for sanctifying grace, the source of faith, hope and charity, is a genuine participation in the thought and love of the three Persons.

By the entry into the world of the Word and his divine gifts, a new form of *providence* begins to operate. The metaphysical notion of providence (³) must give way to perspectives that are incomparably more elevating, and we have henceforth to speak of the providence of the

(¹) *Jn*, I, 14.
(²) *Eph*, I, 10.
(³) See above p. 224.

Father, which is supernatural. In the order of creation, providence is exercised by the play of *natural laws*, while in that of the Incarnation and grace it is manifested by multiform interventions *superimposed on the natural laws*: revelations, prophecies, inspirations, motions of the will, miracles etc. To this special providence of the Father that is constantly being mentioned in the Gospels there correspond new attitudes on the part of the creature, especially prayer of petition, which would be meaningless in the order of creation.

Evil and Suffering

Christianity claims to be able to give a satisfactory solution to the problem of evil and to that of suffering. Far from wishing to side-track these problems, it places them at the heart of its doctrine of Redemption. Christians are asked to worship, not only the Divine Person of Christ, but the human nature of Jesus crucified. The beatitudes proclaim that the poor, the persecuted, those who weep and suffer, are blessed. Christians are commanded to deny themselves, to make voluntary sacrifices — even the supreme sacrifice of life itself, as conditions of gaining the Kingdom of God.

It is still more remarkable that Christianity has never ceased, from the very beginning, to put this bold pro-gramme *into practice* by putting to the test of experience its paradoxical recipe for happiness. It stands up to the test in exact proportion to man's submission to Christ and compliance with his commands. Paul "cannot contain himself for happiness in the midst of all his trials" (*II Cor.*, VII, 4); Ignatius of Antioch was condemned to the lions and rejoiced at the thought of his approaching martyrdom; Francis of Assisi found perfect joy in poverty and humiliation; Theresa of Avila reached the point when she could no longer live without suffering; Poor Clare convents, where women of all ages lead lives of great austerity, are homes of joy and peace; the blind, paralytics, incurables, succeed in reaching a state of radiant happiness, thanks to the Christian transformation of their suffering; St. Theresa of the Child Jesus died in great suffering at the age of twenty-four in the Carmel of Lisieux, chanting the praises of God's merciful love; in the islands of Hawaï, Fr. Damian De Veuster transformed "the hell of Molokai" into an oasis of resignation and hope; in Turin, the "Piccola Casa" founded in the nineteenth century by St. Joseph Cottolengo, still provides shelter for many thousand human waifs of all kinds, and there continues to reign there an atmosphere of confidence and serenity. The list of examples could be prolonged indefinitely.

Looked at from a purely human point of view, these facts are worth considering. It is worth our while to ask Christianity what answer it can make to the problems we are dealing with. The examples we mentioned above are to be found within the Catholic Church; we shall ask her therefore what answer she can make. We shall make an honest effort to grasp her teaching regarding evil and suffering in its entirety.

To do this profitably, it is not, to start with, indispensable to admit the divine origin of Christianity or of the

Church. All that is required is to put aside prejudice and consider the answer with the open mind of one who is interested only in finding out the truth.

The Cross

Let us transport ourselves in spirit to Calvary, where Christ hangs in agony, crucified between two robbers. Condemned by Pilate to the death of the cross, exhausted by a night of suffering (the mortal agony in the garden, the arrest, the trial, the insults and injuries), he was scourged (the *horrendum flagellum* of the Romans) and crowned with thorns. He was compelled to carry his cross on his shoulders up to the moment when, afraid that he might die on the way, the centurion forced Simon, the Cyrenian, to help him carry it.

Arrived at Calvary, he was stripped of his garments, even of the tunic that stuck to the wounds caused by the scourging. He *refused the drink* offered by the compassionate women to those condemned in order to reduce to some extent the appalling sufferings of crucifixion. He was then nailed to the cross by four large nails and the cross was raised erect. Nothing remains but to wait for death, which alone could put an end to his ineffable agonies. To his physical sufferings were added the deepest mental suffering. Disfigured, covered with wounds, with dust and blood, stripped of his clothes, the sign of human dignity, he suffered the fate of slave and criminal. Two common law criminals hung one on either side of him. The people of Jerusalem and the pilgrims who had arrived for the celebration of the Pasch, egged on and led by the priests and doctors of the Law, overwhelm him with hatred, curses and ridicule. His disciples fled and left him. One of them sold him and then, haunted by remorse, committed suicide. His mother with a few friends stood at the foot of the cross — her presence was both very sweet and very cruel.

What were the thoughts and sentiments that passed through his mind during the interminable hours of his terrible agony? The words recorded by witnesses enable us to catch a glimpse of this profound mystery. Words of *mercy*: "Father, forgive them, for they know not what they do." "Amen, I say to you, this day thou shalt be with me in Paradise". Words of *suffering*: "I thirst". "My God, my God, why hast thou forsaken me" (these are the opening words of Ps. 21). Words of *filial piety*: "Woman, behold thy son; son, behold thy mother". "It is consummated". "Father into thy hands I commend my spirit".

Jesus crucified evidently reaches the highest point in human suffering: He personifies suffering, is in a way a synthesis of all suffering.

Now what has the Church to tell us about the meaning and value of this suffering and tragic death?

Relying on the explicit teaching of the New Testament and, in particular, of the epistles of St. Paul, the Church propounds a doctrine of redemption. It is important to grasp it clearly in all its essential aspects.

Redemption

In the first place, *the destiny of man* is being prepared here on earth, but *is fulfilled in the hereafter*. That is the fundamental characteristic of the human situation and the key to many enigmas. According to the Scriptures there exist personal creatures higher than man: Christian tradition and theology see in them purely spiritual beings who have opted once for all, from the beginning of their existence, for God or against God. By their option, their destiny was for ever fixed, making them either good angels or demons. Man, on the contrary, is a conscience that awakens and develops in a body, in the course of a temporal existence. The body is ambivalent: it ought to help, but it can become an obstacle in man's journey towards his personal end — an end that he reaches, permanently and fully, at the end of a life of probation leading through death to the beyond.

This eschatological perspective is evidently essential to Christianity, which would, therefore, consider vain any attempt to explain evil or suffering without taking it into account. Everything in this life is preparation, trial, learning. Consequently, everything is provisional, shifting, perishable. Time is valued in terms of eternity. Nothing is permanent save that which is a foretaste of eternal life i.e. charity, which is a participation of the divine life in the interior life of the Christian or of every man living in God's friendship.

One of the most dangerous aberrations of our day is the attitude of those Christians, perhaps even of some priests, who believe it opportune to leave the eschatological teaching of the Church in the background, if not to omit it altogether. We know that according to Marx "religion is the opium of the people": because it promises happiness in an after life, it deceives the masses exploited by capitalism, it retards the revolution by preaching that patience and resignation enable us to merit heaven. Nobody has more reason than the disciples of Jesus to protest against the exploitation of the weak, no matter who they are. The law of love, even more than that of justice, makes it a strict duty to fight against every form of human exploitation or enslavement of man by man, and the real disciples of Christ have never failed to do so in the course of history. But it is foolish to put forward an earthly messianism, a Christianity bounded by the horizons of this world, under the vain pretext of escaping the objections of the Marxists — as if it could ever be opportune to disguise an essential truth or to falsify the Christian ideal radically.

In reality, as we have said, the Christian has no need to forget his eternal destiny in order *to assume his terrestrial responsibilities generously and effectively*. This is the second important aspect of the doctrine of Redemption.

It can be said in a certain sense that man's task here on earth is to prepare himself for the happy and blessed life to which he is called by the merciful love of the Father. But this preparation is by no means limited to actions directed immediately towards the hereafter. True, there are some whose vocation it is to remind men of the one thing alone neccessary. Contemplatives try to lead on earth the life of the blessed in heaven by the completest possible detachment from created things (poverty, virginity, fast and abstinence, humility, obedience) and by a life devoted primarily to prayer. But that is not the vocation of the average Christian, nor even of the priest nor of the religious generally. All men contribute, according to their means and their profession, either to the construction and progress of the earthly city, or the organization and development of the Church. Of course, even in those activities directed towards procuring for men the best possible living conditions, the Christian must be animated by a supernatural interior life, i.e. a life centred on God and eternal realities by faith, hope and charity. We see here the essential constituents of a Christian humanism, which, while cultivating human values that are transitory and relative (health, science, technology, fine arts, literature, law, political and social organizations etc.), subordinates them to permanent and absolute values (God, eternal life, charity).

The obstacle that is constantly obstructing man's path is sin. Consequently, during man's life on earth there is no escaping *the struggle against sin*. This is the third aspect of the doctrine of Redemption.

Sin or moral evil is an abuse of liberty. It is the wilful transgression of the moral order. It is the act of a man who chooses some particular good, some immediate satisfaction though he knows that his choice turns him away from his true good and from the final end of his existence. Since the Creator is the principle of the moral order, all sin is a revolt of the creature against the Creator, it is seeking egoistic satisfaction in contempt of God's law. If we pass from these general and theoretical considerations to the concrete reality of human history, we are at once struck and disturbed by the spectacle of the accumulated ruin and devastation due to sin in the course of the ages.

At this point we see the grandiose significance of the Cross. The Son of God assumed human nature to destroy the empire of sin. The culminating point of his life, his "hour", the highest expression of his love for God and man, was the giving of himself on Calvary. By carrying out perfectly his Father's will, his suffering and death became an act of religion, became the sole, enduring, sacrifice of Christian worship — *a sacrifice of reparation and expiation* in which the egoism and rebellion of sinful men find a heroic response in the perfect obedience of the Son of God who willed to endure the most extreme humiliation and suffering in order to manifest his filial submission to the will of the Father.

It is important to form a clear idea of the exact nature and significance of the sacrifice of Redemption. It is not the suffering as such that gives it its value and makes it pleasing to God. The Father derives no pleasure from the torments of the Son. The deicide of Calvary remains history's most heinous crime. The Agony in the Garden shows that Jesus himself was horror-stricken at the thought of his passion. But the grandeur of the sacrifice of the Cross lies in the heroic loyalty of the Saviour in his filial love, despite humiliation and torture.

Why was it God's will that his incarnate Son should suffer such a tragic fate? Why all the horror of the passion? We have to confess that the hyper-civilized man of the twentieth century is no less upset and put off at the thought of professing to be a follower of a crucified God than were Christ's Jewish and Greek contemporaries. Yet a little observation and reflection will enable us to see how God's wisdom appears in the mystery of the Cross — "to the Jews a stumbling block, to the Gentiles, folly" (⁴). The cruel and bloody death of the Incarnate Word seems to be the only adequate remedy for the river of suffering and filth fed, right from the beginning of the race, by human cupidity, debauchery, pride, and countless other vices. Nothing less than the overpowering example of Christ's total giving of himself could bring about the profound conversion of the human will and lead it along the road of renunciation and charity. Besides, Christ's passion enables us to see suffering in a new light. Henceforward all who suffer, whatever the sorrow and no matter what its origin, can find consolation in their suffering from the mystery of the Cross. Henceforward all human suffering, but especially that of the innocent, of those who are the victims of sin, of children, receives a sublime value in the mystery of participation in the redemptive suffering of the Son of God. A striking example of this is given by the Church on the feast of the Holy Innocents, who, the liturgy tells us, "*non loquendo sed moriendo confessi sunt*" (⁵). Herod's massacre plunged

---

(⁴) *I Cor*, I, 23.

(⁵) "They proclaimed Christ, not in speech, but by death"

the mothers of the children into the greatest anguish. The innocents died unaware of what was happening and with no personal merit. Nevertheless, the Lord, in his goodness, associates them with his victory over sin and death and receives them into the Kingdom of heaven. Is that not a wonderful victory over evil? And what comparison is there between the tragic episode at Bethlehem and the eternal happiness of these privileged children?

For — and this is another essential aspect of the doctrine of Redemption — all men are called by the infinite Love to an eternal destiny, a *genuine participation in the intimate life of God*, who is Father, Son and Holy Spirit. All who die in God's friendship will be forever associated with Christ, Mediator and Saviour, and will enter with him into the joy of the Father and of the Spirit with all the elect. Then will begin a life of perfect happiness, of which we can form no idea here below, for man's deification is carried as far as divine transcendence and respect for the human person will permit. Finally, the dogma of the resurrection of the body teaches us that on the last day, when Christ will return in power and glory to judge all men, our natures will be integrally restored and the body will share in the happy or unhappy lot of the soul to which it was united in working good and evil in the course of this earthly pilgrimage. St. Paul, who was carried up to heaven

(Collect of the Mass of the Holy Innocents (Dec. 28) in the Roman liturgy).

during an ecstasy to which he refers in *II Corinthians* (XII, 1-4), could write: "Eye hath not seen, nor ear heard, nor hath it entered into the heart of man to conceive the things that God has prepared for those who love him" ([6]); and consequently, "the sufferings of the present time are not comparable to the glory which shall be revealed in us" ([7]). Anyone who wants to form a correct impression of the solution Christianity has to offer for the problem of suffering must meditate on these things very attentively: it is evident that the most protracted and cruel trials that can befall a human being here below form no serious difficulty once they are the price of everlasting happiness akin to the divine blessedness itself.

Some readers may be surprised to find that no mention has been made of *original sin* in this account of Catholic teaching regarding the Redemption. I have not lost sight of this aspect of Christian dogma, but I think that it does not play an important part in the solution of the problem of evil which is our principal concern. For, though original sin can *explain* the present state of the race, subject to suffering, sinful attraction ([8]) and death, it cannot, taken alone, *justify* it. At the beginning of the Christian era, standards were such that it appeared normal to make slaves of the wife and children of a criminal and even of the whole population of a conquered city. In such a social and cultural context, it was

([6]) *I Cor*, II, 9.
([7]) *Rom*, VIII, 18.
([8]) What theologians refer to as "concupiscence".

alright for St. Paul to represent human solidarity in original sin in terms which did not offend his contemporaries. This is no longer the case. The feeling of personal dignity and responsibility has been so well developed by Christianity itself that it now seems an intolerable injustice to punish Adam's descendants for something for which they were in no way responsible. In these circumstances, to bring in original sin to *justify* the sad state of humanity would be to aggravate the problem instead of solving it.

And indeed it is not the Church's real teaching. This must be looked for in the "*mirabilius reformasti*" and the "*felix culpa*" of the liturgy.

It is true that social solidarity plays an important part in the plans of Providence: the Church teaches that man first existed on earth in a privileged state which theologians call "*status naturae elevatae*" (⁹). As a result of Adam's sin, he lost the free gifts he had received and found himself in a fallen state, "*status naturae lapsae*" (¹⁰). Since his redemption by Christ, he finds himself in a third state, "*status naturae reparatae*" (¹¹). But when he

(⁹) The state of nature *elevated* to the *supernatural* order of divine life and endowed besides with *preternatural* gifts (immunity from suffering and death, from ignorance and concupiscence).

(¹⁰) The state of *fallen* nature: it comprises, over and above the loss of the supernatural and preternatural gifts, a wound in human nature itself, which retains the marks left by Adam's sin and by those of his posterity.

(¹¹) The state of *redeemed* nature: the supernatural gifts are restored to us but not the preternatural privileges of the "lost paradise".

laid down this law of solidarity for man, the Creator was merely respecting the nature of things and making social life possible: the very thought of the contrary hypothesis is enough to show what ludicrous and inextricable situations it would create. Can you imagine a human society in which the just would enjoy preternatural gifts while sinners would be deprived of them, only to have them restored at the instant of their conversion? Can you imagine a husband who is a sinner, subject to ignorance, suffering and death, while his virtuous wife and innocent children enjoy the immunities due to the possession of preternatural gifts? These gifts would become a bonus for virtue and the whole economy of the moral order would be upset. It must be acknowledged therefore that solidarity in the human situation is inevitable and is not the result of any arbitrary decision of the Creator.

Nevertheless, justice forbids that the innocent should pay for the guilty and that the sin of the parent should be imputed to the child.

And now we see God's wisdom and mercy. Despite the loss of the preternatural privileges, despite the sad consequences of sin, the human condition will be more wonderful in its restoration by the Saviour than it was in its first creation: "*dignitatem humanae naturae mirabiliter condidisti et mirabilius reformasti*" ([12]). That is why the Church sings in the liturgy of the Easter Vigil: "*O felix culpa, quae talem ac tantum meruit habere*

([12]) The dignity of human nature was wondrously established and yet more wondrously restored". From the Offertory of the Mass (Roman rite).

Redemptorem'' ([13]). We must repeat insistently: there is
no need to weep for the "lost paradise". The condition
of humanity restored by the Son of God is more beautiful
than that of Adam before the Fall. The gifts we are
offered excel incomparably those possessed by Adam
before he sinned. Nor is this mere theorizing; the story
of Christian holiness proves in a striking manner the
sublime radiation of the mystery of the Cross and the
splendid possibilities offered by the new order established
by Christ.

A whole volume would be required to recall the
victories of the Cross in the acts of the martyrs of all
centuries, in the heroic lives of the apostles, pontiffs,
confessors, virgins and holy women who have made the
history of the Church illustrious and enriched the litany
of the saints; in the generous lives of all the disciples of
Christ who have tried to live the Gospel ideal and,
especially, the Beatitudes. These countless examples
would show the wonderful realization of the *"mirabilius
reformasti"* and the adequate solution of the problem
of suffering in the life of the Christian.

The Mystery of Iniquity

Have all the objections that can be urged against
divine Providence because of the presence of evil in the
world now been answered? I do not think so, for there

([13]) "O happy fault, that merited such and so great a Re-
deemer". The *Exsultet*, the triumphal hymn of the Risen
Christ.

are some particularly difficult aspects of the problem which, at first sight, do not seem to be solved by what we have said above.

In a spirit of complete sincerity and honesty we shall state these objections and endeavour to answer them.

The difficulty that sums up all the others boils down to this. Of course, for one who understands the mystery of the Cross and who, with the assistance of grace, is capable of fully associating himself with it, victory over evil is always secure; the greater the trial, the more wonderful the triumph of patience and love. But such understanding of the mystery of the Cross appears to be reserved for a very select few. The overwhelming majority — primitive peoples from the very earliest times, pagans, including even the most highly civilized, and even the mass of so-called Christians — is incapable of rising to these heights of moral and religious life. The impression remains that the wonderful victories of the saints are gained at the expense of an enormous "wastage" of misunderstood, useless and often harmful sufferings.

This sad impression seems to be confirmed by what we see happening all over the universe. The Creator has distributed energy and life with untold generosity and profusion, so much so that, if the idea had any meaning when applied to a Power that is infinite, whose creative action brings with it no "fatigue", no "exhaustion" or "impoverishment" of its "resources" or of its "reserves", we might be tempted to speak of "extravagance". God cast into space thousands of millions of stars, the thought of whose energies and dimensions makes us giddy, for no other purpose apparently than to provide men, the inhabitants of a tiny planet, with some idea of his grandeur and power. Thousands of millions of living germs and seeds of every species are wasted every instant, whilst a relatively small number of these cells effectively secure the propagation of life. In the case of the material world, this superabundance so characteristic of the divine action, gives rise to no problem as it harms nobody; on the contrary, it shows forth the infinite liberality and inexhaustible wealth of the Creator. But it is different when the destiny of thousands of millions of persons appears threatened by the laws of cosmic evolution and, in particular, those of the slow development of man from his first emergence from the animal state to the highest summits of supernatural life.

To bring the difficulty home to our readers, we shall mention some of its more disturbing features.

Sufferings that are *useless* because they are not understood are countless: those of children, those of the insane, and also those of the great mass of human beings who are unable to reach a spiritual and religious view of life and who, in consequence, are unable to perceive the meaning of their trials.

The problem becomes much more thorny when it refers to *harmful* sufferings, and there are very many of them: prolonged illness that affects the nervous system and, as a result, the mental equilibrium of the patient; illnesses that result in complexes; injustice that provokes rebellion, resentment and bitterness; nervous depression that results in despair and suicide; trials so unbearable that a man loses his reason; unfortunate situations that expose their victims to all manners of vice: think of the moral effects of extreme poverty, of bad housing, of wartime deportation, of the slave trade, of psychological anomalies (homosexuality, sadism, etc.), of children abandoned by their parents; in all these cases and in very many others that it would be easy to mention, far from doing good, suffering seems to be the source of the worst moral downfalls or, at least, a serious obstacle to the moral development of the person.

Here is a final aspect of the difficulty, the gravest, to be sure, for the reason that it concerns moral evil and evil that risks becoming permanent. I am referring to the stranglehold of *sin* on the human race, to the distressing contrast between the uprightness or even the sanctity of the few and the moral corruption of the mass.

From the religious point of view in the first place, twenty centuries after the sacrifice of the Cross, the situation is not heartening: to about 700 million Christians there are approximately 2000 million pagans, who do not confess Christ, the Saviour of the world. Christians are themselves divided into a multitude of Churches and sects. Agnosticism and religious indifferentism are on the increase. Even in catholic countries, religion is often superficial and formalistic, when it is not shot through with superstitions and practices inherited from paganism. Distrust of and hostility towards the Church, anticlericalism, occasionally virulent, fostered by secret societies and by Marxists, find plenty of ammunition in past and present failures of Christians. There are the abuses of the hierarchy and clergy over long periods of history, simony, venality, the abuses of the Inquisition, the mistakes made by the Holy Office, the excesses of the Crusaders and, at a later period, of colonialism, the reactionary obscurantism of some Catholic circles, the egoism of the bourgeoisie and the social injustices of the nineteenth century. How can we be surprised if the light of Christ's true followers has often gone unperceived in this welter of faults and weaknesses?

Of course, the decline of religion is due also to causes other than the imperfection of the Church and its ministers and faithful. Very often it is the outcome of the materialist, pleasure-seeking, worldly atmosphere of a great part of the world we live in. Here we come up against the hideous spectre of all the moral corruption affecting the human race: violence and cruelty of every sort, unjust invasions, conquests and wars of extermination, bloody tyranny, slavery, oppression and exploitation of the weak, unjust accumulation of fortunes, commercial organization of debauchery in all its forms, drug-traffic, conjugal infidelity, sexual perversions, robbery, pillage, assassination, suicide, crimes of every description. At the sight of so many disorders affecting morals, it is inevitable that questions should arise in the minds of thoughtful people: to what extent are freedom and responsibility engaged in all this? Are not these disorders, in very great part, the bitter fruit of instincts, drives, complexes, character, atavism, environment, education? In fine, are they not the inevitable result of the human situation as it has been decreed by the Creator himself? And, if that is so, what possibility is there in reality, for the vast majority of men, to realize their vocation to the supernatural life and gain their last end? Are we not forced to admit the lamentable failure of creation and, what is more, of the Redemption? How are we to detect in all this, traces of divine wisdom, goodness and providence?

We have arrived at the heart of the matter and, consequently, we have to come to a definite choice.

It seems undeniable that some aspects of the human situation and, especially, some aspects of the problem of evil are shrouded in mystery and will, perhaps, always remain so. This seems to be due to the complexity of things and to the weakness of our knowing powers. Many parts of the universal order are hidden from us and the dimensions of God's providential designs are infinitely beyond us ([14]).

What are we to do then?

Two attitudes are possible: rebellion or faith.

Rebellion. The world, we are told, is absurd. Human life is meaningless. Man is condemned to despair, for he is the victim of injustice, suffering and death. There is no Providence. Everything that happens is the inevitable

([14]) Canon J. Vieujean writes in this connexion: "I do not believe that the human intelligence can ever solve the problem of evil. But here is an example that may help you. Suppose you go into a well-built, well-furnished house, but in which everything is topsy-turvy, the doors wrenched from the hinges, chairs upturned, linen scattered all over. You would ask yourself what had happened and your mind would not be at rest as long as the matter had not been cleared up. But one thing that will never enter your head is that there had been no builder, no carpenter, no weaver". (*L'acte de foi et son mystère*, Collection *Appels*, 2nd series, 5, Liège, 1955, p. 7.)

result of the laws governing the cosmos. It is a far better thing to deny God, to refuse to admit the existence of a personal God than to have to hold him responsible for the evil rampant in the world.

It is easy to recognize in this description the stand taken by many of our contemporaries.

Faith. This is the logical attitude of the Christian. What is it and what is there to be said in its favour?

The Christian knows that God is love ([15]) and that He so loved men that He gave his only begotten Son for them ([16]). The Christian knows that the Word was made flesh ([17]), that he lived, suffered and died for men, his brothers — after proclaiming: "Greater love than this no man hath, that he give his life for his friends" ([18]). The Christian knows that God wills all to be saved ([19]). Besides, he is not surprised to learn that God's designs are impenetrable, that his ways are not our ways and that there are things that we find mysterious and disconcerting. In these circumstances he sees clearly that one attitude alone is prudent: *to have faith in Infinite Love.* This attitude is prudent and becomes a man, for we know him in whom we put our trust ([20]) and we have wonderful proofs of his goodness. But it is also a very

([15]) *I Jn*, IV, 8.

([16]) *Jn*, III, 16.

([17]) *Jn*, I, 14.

([18]) *Jn*, XV, 13.

([19]) *I Tim*, II, 4.

([20]) "*Scio cui credidi et certus sum*", says St. Paul: "He, to whom I have given my confidence, is no stranger to me, and I am fully persuaded" *(II Tim, I, 12)*.

meritorious attitude since it is a confession of filial submission to Divine Providence and implies the humble renunciation of the claim to understand and judge everything himself.

A fresh justification of this filial submission to the guidance of Providence is to be found in the lives of the saints. A Paul, a Francis of Assisi, a Philip Neri, an Ignatius of Loyola, a Vincent de Paul, a John Bosco and so many others were well acquainted with evil in all its forms and were overwhelmed with grief at the spectacle of human sufferings and sin. Now, not only did this experience not turn them against God, but we find that they were inflamed by God's love. They proclaim unceasingly the infinite mercy of the Lord and deplore man's ingratitude. It is obvious that their close friendship with God, and, in many cases, their mystical experiences, gained for them a clearer insight into the designs and ways of Providence.

This fundamental attitude of confidence in God's fatherly benevolence towards his creatures does not prevent us from seeking to understand things and solve the riddles of the universal order. Here we shall do no more than point out the lines along which these reflections could be made.

God's purpose in creating man was to realize, around Christ, *all values capable of being realized in a society of persons existing in the material universe*. These values are manifold and extremely various. For a better understanding of the human situation, we have to set ourselves to discover all these values and bring them into relief.

So that this purpose be realized in the history of the

human race, *the Creator normally* ([21]) *respects the play of natural laws*, allowing the beings that go to form the material universe free play, not only when their activities produce effects that are harmonious and beneficent (which is most often the case), but also when the conflict of material energies or the activity of persons results in disorder and ruin. Man is living in a world menaced by typhoons, cyclones, tempests, earthquakes, storms, avalanches, floods, droughts, forest fires. He has to protect himself against wild beasts, poisonous snakes, microbes and insects. He is exposed to sickness and accidents, to the rigours of sun and cold. He has to live in society with his fellowmen and enjoys all the advantages this offers, but he must also put up with aggressiveness, injustice, and, generally speaking, with all the deleterious influences which can flow from his fellows.

Having to live in a hostile world places man in difficult and even cruel circumstances. We have the impression of being delivered up defencelessly to the blind play of natural forces and to the wickedness of men. No paternal Providence seems to be interested in our lot. This feeling assumes tragic proportions and is changed to terror when some deadly plague strikes some region and in a few hours or even minutes brings about the death of thousands of people. History has preserved the tragic record of events like this: epidemics of plague or cholera have swept away three fourths of the population of certain towns. The 1923 earthquake in Tokyo resulted in the death of nearly 150,000 victims; most of them were

([21]) The force of this reservation will appear later on.

burned alive in their wooden homes. The aerial bombard-
ment of the Japanese capital (on March 9, 1945) killed
almost 200,000 people. These examples could, needless
to say, be multiplied.

But we must be on our guard at this point not to judge
under the influence of what are doubtless very human
and very praiseworthy sentiments, but which give a wrong
picture. Death is a strictly personal ordeal. In the designs
of God it brings this life of trial here below to an end
and marks the beginning of the definitive life. A more or
less protracted, more or less painful agony leads to the
final suffering and separation. The problem of death is
no different and no more serious when large numbers of
people are involved. It makes no difference whether
50,000 people scattered over the surface of the globe die
in very different circumstances on the same day or that
50,000 perish in the same place as the result of a volcanic
eruption; the problem of the meaning of death remains
unaffected. In the same way, whether a human being die
in a fire after a few minutes of excruciating suffering or
is consumed by some lingering disease after years of
suffering, in no way affects the data of the problem.

On the other hand, we should not be too quick in
speaking of *useless suffering*. Recollect the example of
the Holy Innocents (22) and, in the light of this striking
manifestation of divine benevolence, let us not hesitate to
believe that the suffering of children and of all innocent
victims of evil is a sharing in the passion of the Saviour
and that this unconscious participation in Christ's Cross

(22) See above, p. 273.

entails participation in his triumph and glory. Then
again, suffering, though of no benefit to the patient, can
be a source of value for others. Think, for example, of
the devotion of parents, nuns, brothers, nurses — who take
care of abnormal children and the mentally afflicted.
For all of us the spectacle of suffering is a constant
reminder of the meaning of life — that it is a trial and
not an end in itself. How essential this reminder is can
be seen from the foolish attachment of people to money,
pleasure and all the vanities of this world. What would
it be like if the absence of suffering gave the illusion of
a terrestrial paradise [23] ?

The problem of *harmful suffering* is without any doubt
the most difficult and most mysterious of all. Yet, even
in this case, we should not be too quick to judge by
appearances. The immediate effects of suffering may be
harmful — discouragement, bitterness, rebellion, clouding
the mind and making prayer impossible. It has nonetheless
a deep salutary effect, but in the long run: it purifies a
man, makes him wiser, weans him from the world and
from false pleasures; it teaches him patience, humility,
compassion, enkindles in him a desire for real goods,
which are everlasting. Besides, when distress is greatest,
it calls forth the most wonderful generosity, the purest
heroism, charity in its most touching forms. The hell of
Molokai was responsible for the heroic life of Fr. Damian,
and his example, for the splendid endeavour made in the

[23] It is well known that wealth, comfort, health, pleasures
constitute for individuals, families, and even for nations,
powerful incentives to practical materialism, egoism, religious
indifference and moral decadence.

struggle against leprosy. The fruits of this endeavour have been the many consoling triumphs over this terrible scourge.

But if suffering were to lead to despair, madness or suicide? The answer in this case is clear: suffering that lessens responsibility or takes it away altogether, lessens proportionately or takes away the moral problem of acceptance. Be sure that we shall find in great numbers in the joy of the Lord, those poor suicides driven by unbearable misfortune to an act of despair over which they had no control.

However, in this reflection on the human situation, we have not yet reached the essential. Though the Creator allows free rein to the laws of nature and these often cause great suffering, man is, we have said, called to a *supernatural destiny*, that is to say, to a genuine participation in the divine life. This uplifting vocation, which makes men adoptive sons of the Father and brothers of Jesus Christ, the only begotten Son, is the beginning of a *special providence* of God towards men. In virtue of this providence man receives constant assistance, though mysterious and normally imperceptible, that Scripture and tradition call *grace*. Revelation teaches that man, in the pursuit of his destiny and especially in facing up to the ordeals of this life, is never left to himself; at every step he is assured of the merciful assistance of the Father. The effects of the multiform action of grace make themselves felt all the more clearly the more a man leaves himself open to this divine influence: they become dazzling in the heroic strength of the martyrs and, generally speaking, in the heroic virtues of the saints. They take the form of sensible and exceptional signs in miracles, which are always either a confirmation of the words of God's legates or an answer to prayer.

For the order of grace is also that of *prayer*: it would be difficult to see what possible sense prayer of petition could have in a purely natural order with God operating only as Creator. But in the light of the special providence that presides over the supernatural order and that is the source of grace, it is easy to see that this prayer has its place: in that context, it is normal that man, now God's accepted son, should ask for rain or sun, deliverance from pest, peace and freedom, or even more striking favours such as being healed of an incurable disease, or other tangible forms of divine assistance. These providential interventions are almost always a divine answer to the confidence of the Lord's really faithful disciple. Those who, like priests, share the confidence of good Christians, know that the marks of God's paternal benevolence are to be found, not only in the lives of the saints, but also in those of very humble Christians, provided that a truly childlike trust lays them open to the merciful action of the Lord.

Conclusions

We have come to the end of these considerations bearing on the Cross of Jesus Christ and we shall summarize in a few words the conclusions to which they have led us.

We live in a world in which the power of evil is formidable. Those who know the world well, know that the ravages of moral disorders are terrifying and that the "mystery of iniquity" ([24]) is no less perplexing today than it was in the days of St. Paul. Besides moral evil there is physical evil, and the suffering it entails is closely bound up with sin. Sin it was that brought suffering into the world and suffering continues to be in many instances the wages of sin. But it is also its reparation and cure. Evil in all its forms makes man's life on earth one of trial, and in its course each one is asked to respond, according to his capabilities, to the call of divine love. Neither ignorance, nor weakness, nor the determinism of instinct, nor social pressures, nor the powers of darkness ([25]), are able to thwart the eternal destiny of the human person. Only a conscious and stubborn refusal to accept the loving will of the Father can bring about man's damnation. On the contrary, "everything helps to secure the good of those who love God" ([26]); everything, including sin atoned for and forgiven, for this excites humility, prudence and gratitude towards the infinite Mercy; everything, but above all suffering, because it detaches and purifies, because through it we are conformed to Jesus crucified.

([24]) *II Thess*, II, 7.

([25]) The existence and the influence of fallen angels are incontestable data of Revelation and it is certain that the activity of him whom Christ called "the Prince of this world" (*Jn*, XII, 31) explains many things in the "mystery of iniquity" mentioned above. Nevertheless, the powers of hell cannot imperil the salvation of anyone unless he freely consents.

([26]) *Rom*, VIII, 28.

Finally, the history of man is the ceaselessly renewed encounter between infinite Love and human liberty. On God's side, all is benevolence, justice, mercy. On man's side, all through the slow evolution taking him from confines of animality to the peak of civilization, from the first glimmer of intelligence to full radiance of mind, from the groping of the moral sense to the heroism of the saints, the only thing that matters is good will in responding to the divine overtures. The sway of evil here below is mighty. Sin is ubiquitous and suffering weighs heavily on the human race. But in the centre of all things stands the Cross of Jesus Christ, Son of God and Saviour: in him is evil vanquished, sin repaired, suffering and death transformed. "Salvation is not to be found elsewhere" [27].

"It is impossible to understand Jesus Christ and disregard the mystery of the Cross. Suffering would immediately become an enigma and a scandal, the human situation would appear meaningless and unjust. In one word, he who seeks Christ without the cross will find the cross without Christ, that is to say, pessimism and despair" [28].

That is the reason why, in the midst of the widespread unrest and disarray, with the apostle Peter we turn to Jesus crucified and we say to him with resolute confidence: "Lord, to whom shall we go? You have the words of eternal life" [29].

[27] *Ac*, IV, 12.

[28] Cardinal E. SUHARD, *Le sens de Dieu* (Collection *Appels*, 3rd series, 2, Liège, 1948), p. 30.

[29] *Jn*, VI, 69.

CHAPTER XIV

CONCLUSIONS

Two conclusions seem inescapable at the end of this inquiry and they can be compressed into very simple formulas: *the living God, the hidden God.*

The Living God

In the study of the great variety of ways leading to God, explored by the human mind in the whole course of history, there is eloquent confirmation of the words of St. Augustine: *"Fecisti nos ad Te, et irrequietum est cor nostrum donec requiescat in Te"* [1]. Men hunger and thirst for God. No matter how far back history pushes its investigations, it finds man in quest of his Creator. It is as if the human mind, in all its proceedings, had the feeling of some ineffable Presence, that is at the same time an End to be pursued. Man endeavours spontaneously to find everywhere in the world traces of God, vestiges of his power and of his providence. In his

[1] "Thou hast made us for Thyself, and our heart will not find rest until it rest in Thee" (*Confessiones*, bk. 1, c. 1).

deepest self, his aspirations after happiness, justice and immortality, all betray his need of God. And once he begins to reflect, once he tries to interpret the riddles of nature and of his own existence, his reason leads him once more, by the most various paths, to God. So deep is his conviction and so inborn his sense of the divine that they appear at all times and in all places in man's religious behaviour, both personal and social, as is testified by the history of the religious sense and by the history of religions ([2]).

In an age of luniks, sputniks and other sensational scientific discoveries, as men of good will try, not without anxiety, to establish here on earth the bases of real universal peace, the supreme reality of the Creator appears more indispensable than ever to thinking minds. "God is dead", proclaimed Nietzsche, the "superman". God is not dead; he has never ceased to be *the living God*.

Science, far from rendering God superfluous, brings to light daily fresh evidence of his infinite wisdom and power in the conception and marvellous organization of the universe.

Metaphysical reflection sees, in the affirmation of the infinite Being, creative cause of the order of finite beings, the keystone of its whole synthesis. Wise and benevolent, supremely free, the creative Cause of the universe cease-

---

([2]) Here is just one of the many references that could be quoted. In *La guérison psychologique*, (French translation, Geneva, 1953), p. 182, C. G. JUNG, the famous Swiss psychologist, writes: "Of all the patients who had reached middle age,... there was not one whose deepest problem did not have to do with the question of his religious attitude".

lessly exercises his providence by the natural play of second causes.

The *religious experience* of mankind, often spurious or, to say the least, uncontrollable, often distorted and corrupt in its expressions and manifestations, reaches, in Christianity, heights where the encounter with God is indubitable, because it is accompanied by signs which guarantee its authenticity.

Knowledge of Jesus Christ and of the mystery of Redemption helps us to get over the great difficulty presented by evil and its terrible hold over the human race. In the light shed by the Cross of Christ on the world, the enigma of human suffering assumes meaning. All who suffer are called to join their sufferings to those of Christ, to become saviours with him and to share one day in the triumph of his resurrection.

God or nothing: this is the title the late Fr. Sertillanges gave to one of his books. He commented on it as follows: "Without God, nothing in our experience holds any more, nothing in all that helps us to live according to the spirit, nothing in all we prize in thought or conscience, nothing in all we expect from life and sometimes claim we find" ([3]).

This is indeed what follows from our inquiry. The existence of the Creator is not a matter of guesswork, not a more or less probable opinion, not a hypothesis open to question. It is a firm certainty — to which the convergent paths of science (in the limited role we have

([3]) A.-D. SERTILLANGES, *Dieu ou rien?* 2 vols., Paris, 1933. Cf. vol. I, p. 6.

defined), metaphysics and religious experience, lead. Without God all is meaningless and absurd — the world, life and death are void of meaning.

The Hidden God

Nevertheless, there are many who do not know God or who know him badly. The number of those who admit his existence and yet rebel against him is no doubt very small. The number of those who doubt, who hesitate to admit his existence, who are disturbed or embittered by the spectacle of evil, is much more considerable. And the scandal of so many agnostics, so many sceptics, so many materialists, shakes the religious convictions of simple people. It can easily lead them to feel some disquiet, to regret that God is not a more "tangible" reality, to regret that his existence is not incontestable and indubitable.

It is important to dispel this uneasiness by calling to mind that the living God is necessarily a *hidden God*.

He is, of his very nature, the Inaccessible, the Invisible, the Impalpable, for he is *Spirit* (he is on that account outside the range of all sense experience), and he is *Infinite*, i.e. he transcends the entire order of finite beings of which we form part. Hence it cannot be thought strange that his sovereign reality should be for us the ineffable Mystery, that the sovereign designs of his Providence should appear impenetrable and disconcerting, that "his ways" should not be our ways. He would not be the true God if he appeared to us with the clarity of a proposition deduced in some geometrical theorem, or with the kind of evidence we associate with an experiment carried out in a laboratory. No matter how knowledge of God is gained — whether through religious experience or metaphysical reflection — it is always after an effort of detachment, recollection, attention, which elevates man above earthly appetites and egoistic desires.

The living God is a hidden God also because *his providential action is necessarily mysterious*, considering the limits of our faculties of knowing. The order of created *natures* is so admirably constituted that the universe evolves by the action of natural causes without the slightest direct and perceptible intervention of the First Cause. That is why positive science, which studies the natural order in as far as human experience can discover it, can never meet God along its way. The marvellous finality which appears in all sectors of the universe turns men's thoughts towards the creative Intelligence which conceived this wonderful order; but the spectacle of evil in all its forms, at times very cruel and revolting, causes people to become worried and disturbed, awakens doubts about the perfection of God's work and ends up by neutralizing the beneficial effects produced by the discovery of finality in nature. As for the *supernatural* interventions of Providence (revelation, prophecies, miracles, apparitions, mystical phenomena and, a fortiori, the ordinary interventions of grace under all its forms), these always take place with that dignity and discretion that become the divine action. In fine, to be perceived through the complex play of natural events, the action of divine Providence presupposes, on man's part, an effort of attention and reflection that many refuse to make because their minds and hearts are too full of the things of earth.

We may be permitted to underline here for the last time the danger awaiting scientists in the field of religion. They almost always suffer from a "professional deformation" which blinds them to values higher than those of science. "What keeps many of our contemporaries away from God is the exclusive attention they pay to scientific and technical values" (⁴). In a remarkable study of the reasons for unbelief, P. Charles wrote: "unbelief is always due to a certain narrowness of mind; and this, unless we are careful, is the natural result of scientific discipline itself" (⁵).

Lastly, the living God is a hidden God because, in the religious history of humanity, "*static religion*", with its fables, its magic rites, its superstitions, its unrefined cult, its manner of exploiting the fear and credulity of the masses, the tyranny of its sorcerers, diviners and priests, *constitute a danger for "dynamic religion*" in the eyes of those who are critically alert: "dynamic religion", the religion that adores the true God "in spirit and in truth" and establishes between God and man relations animated by love. Bergson developed the nature and social manifestations of those two essentially different forms of

(⁴) J. Vieujean, *L'acte de foi et son mystère*, Collection *Appels*, 2nd series, 5, Liège, 1955, p. 9.

(⁵) P. Charles, *Les raisons de l'incroyance*, in *Nouvelle revue théologique*, 1946, pp. 129-144. Cf. p. 139. This article was reprinted in the collection *Appels*, 2nd series, 3, Liège, 1955.

religion in a remarkable way (⁶). Marxists constantly confuse real religion with its many counterparts, the religious bearing of the real man of God and the abuses of all kinds perpetrated by some who hold religious office. This is apparent to anyone who takes trouble to examine the anti-religious propaganda of the Marxists. The confusion is made all the easier (as we pointed out following Bergson) by the fact that the two forms of religion almost always co-exist in human societies. Because men are weak, some elements of static religion infiltrate into even the most perfect religious institutions and may be seen even in religions that we believe to be of divine origin — in Judaism and in Christianity. Here, too, great attention and judgment are necessary to unravel the tangled skein of these human situations where good is mixed with evil. Christians, convinced of the divine origin of the Church, ought to be the first to denounce and deplore whatever — either in the past or in the present — sullies the purity of the Christian religion. They ought to be the first to manifest their disapproval of the weaknesses and shortcomings of some of the popes, of the corruption of the clergy at certain periods, of the abuses of the Inquisition, of Galileo's condemnation, of untimely interventions of the Holy Office or of the Biblical Commission, of crimes committed by Catholic rulers, and of all other faults, failings, or abuses that compromise God's Church in the eyes of men. Too often, alas! God is betrayed by those whose special duty it is to be his witnesses before men.

(⁶) See above pp. 237-238.

Those who should manifest to men the hidden Face of the Lord contribute instead to veil it still more or to cause his Holy Name to be blasphemed.

From all this it follows that the knowledge of God, of the hidden God, is always the fruit and the reward of good will. God shows himself only to those who seek him. His light enlightens only the humble, the poor in spirit, those who hunger and thirst after truth, justice and love. It could not be within the reach of those whose lives are filled by business affairs or money matters, by political ambitions or pleasures of the senses. There is nothing surprising or disturbing in the religious indifference of these people, for they leave no room in their lives for higher things. Rather ought we admire and find some consolation in observing that, even in the case of those who are completely absorbed in earthly cares, when some event or other shocks them out of their usual routine (a bereavement, an illness, the reading of some book, a meeting with some holy person), the sense of the divine is reawakened in them.

"Blessed are the clean of heart; they shall see God" (7).

Popular Presentation

Though the discovery of *the living God*, who is also *the hidden God*, is promised to the good will, it still remains to help this good will to turn towards the light, to open to the intelligence of men the ways leading to knowledge

(7) "Beati mundo corde, quoniam ipsi Deum videbunt" *(Mt, V, 8)*.

of the Creator. The whole purpose of this essay was to ascertain the roads that were best and surest and to close the entry to defective routes and blind alleys. And because the problem of God is not only one of high science, of concern only to specialists, but one of essential human interest, we have good reason to ask how knowledge of God can be brought within the reach of all.

This new problem is complex and delicate since, to reach a satisfactory solution, we would have to take into account the great differences in the psychological dispositions of those we are addressing. To do this would require a whole volume. Here we shall do no more than sketch a plan of exposition that seems suited to the majority of cases and that can be adapted and modified as circumstances require.

The plan will be followed by a brief commentary and references will be given to the sections of this essay where the more or less pertinent developments are to be found. These are, however, no more than an introduction. There is a vast body of religious literature that can be used to supplement the exposition, taking into account the demands of the listener or reader.

I. *The universe in the light of the positive sciences.*
  1. Wonders of the cosmic order.
  2. Limits of scientific explanation and problems unsolved by science.

II. *Man and his destiny.*
  1. The greatness of man.
  2. Man's insignificance and problems arising out of the human situation.

III. *The Creator and his Providence.*

   1. Necessity of the absolute.
   2. Characters of the absolute.
   3. The absolute is transcendent to the finite.
   4. The infinite Being is a personal Being and is interested in his work.

IV. *The witness of men of God.*

In the *first two sections* we make use of the "psychological preparations" which dispose the mind to search for God ([8]). Popular presentation is certainly possible and desirable in this vast domain. We must be on our guard, however, not to attribute to these prolegomena a significance they do not have.

A synthesis of the discoveries of science provides us with a firm starting point and one of general interest. When the marvels of the cosmic order have been thrown into relief, we can deal with the limits of scientific explanation and the problems left outstanding by science: the ontological nature and the origin of matter, finality in nature, perfectibility of corporeal things etc. ([9]).

Another solid starting point, and one of absorbing interest for all, is human destiny. The disconcerting contrast existing between man's greatness and his insignificance can be underlined. His greatness: the eminent value of the human person, the subject of rights and duties; aspirations after knowledge, justice, happiness, immortality. His insignificance: exposed to all manner of suffering, to

([8]) See above, pp. 45-55.
([9]) See above, pp. 53-54, 82-118, 128-139.

injustice, moral evil, sentenced to death. Confined within the bounds of this world, his life loses all meaning. The human situation, then, raises some very acute problems: What is man's destiny? Has human existence any sense? On what do the moral order and moral obligation rest? In particular, what is the ultimate foundation of the social order ([10])?

In the light of these two preliminary inquiries, we discern, at the origin of the universal order (the order of nature and the order of persons, in their individual moral activity and in social life), the existence of an Intelligence that is exceedingly powerful and exceedingly wise, in whose absence the order would be altogether unintelligible. To determine the nature of this Intelligence we must, however, engage in metaphysical reflection ([11]).

Once the ground has been prepared in this manner, the *third section* has for object to make "the God of the philosophers" known. Can we arouse the interest of ordinary folk in these topics? To the extent that their interest in metaphysics can be aroused, yes. We have to be on our guard, however, neither to exaggerate nor to minimize the difficulty of metaphysical reflection. On condition that we keep to the essentials and that we use the clearest possible terminology, philosophical knowledge of God appears to be within the reach of anyone accustomed to reflection on abstract matters. Those desiring to go deeper into the subject can legitimately be asked to make some

([10]) See above, pp. 51-53, 243-261.
([11]) See above, pp. 128-139.

additional effort and to make themselves more familiar with metaphysical problems.

What are the essential stages in this third section? The first step is to prove that it is necessary to admit the existence of an absolute reality ([12]). Then comes the deduction of the *a priori* necessary characters of this reality: the absolute i.e., independent, unconditioned or uncaused, is of itself all that it is and is so, therefore, necessarily and eternally; it can neither begin to be nor cease to be; it can lose none of its perfections nor tend to acquire any new perfection; its similarity to other beings can imply no relativity ([13]). These being the essential attributes of the absolute, it is easy to show that the absolute is to be looked for beyond the material world (which is passive, changing, perfectible) and indeed beyond the order of finite beings (for every finite being, even a pure spirit, tends to perfect itself by its activity; finite being, basically similar to every other, yet not able to pre-contain it adequately as its cause since it is opposed to every other, cannot explain this similarity) ([14]). Lastly, when we have proved that the infinite Being is the creative cause of finite beings, we can show that the infinite Being is a personal being, who knows and loves the persons he has created, who wills them to share in his perfection and happiness. He is the author of the order of nature, the ultimate foundation of the moral as well as of the social order, the last end of every created person.

When dealing with simple people and, more generally,

([12]) See above, pp. 168-171.
([13]) See above, pp. 179-187.
([14]) See above, *ibidem.*

with those who are put off by metaphysical reflection, we can appeal to religious experience. This forms the object of the *fourth section*. It provides even the philosopher himself with a very precious confirmation and with indispensable additional information, for it concerns the encounter with "the God of Jesus Christ".

Appeal will be made above all to the religious experience of the Apostles (15), of the saints and, especially, of the great mystics (16). But appeal to the less exalted, though occasionally very suggestive, experience of good Christians, is not ruled out; they experience frequently in the course of their daily lives that paternal Providence to which we refered previously (17). Divine interventions of this kind are frequent in reply to the confident prayer of those who endeavour to live fully according to the spirit of the Gospel, in filial resignation to the Father's goodness.

The witness of men of God leads in the ordinary course to the God of Jesus Christ. In this new perspective, dominated by the Incarnation and Redemption, the human situation assumes grandiose significance: men are called to divine sonship; saved by Christ, one with him in the Church, his mystical Body, they share in his death, in his resurrection and in his eternal triumph (18).

---

(15) See above, pp. 231-236.
(16) See above, pp. 236-242.
(17) See above, pp. 289-290.
(18) See above, pp. 262-292.

The Outstretched Hand

This is a gesture that is often referred to when communist leaders appeal to Christians to collaborate in building a better world. But, at the end of this essay, the words of the psalmist ring true: "Vain is the builder's toil, if the house is not of the Lord's building" [19]. The worshippers of the living God must, therefore, in their turn, stretch out their hands to all men of good will (and there are many in the ranks of the Marxists) and beg them instantly to revise their attitude towards religious values.

It is "closed religion" that is "the opium of the people". "Open religion", on the contrary, is the only solid foundation of social justice and of love between men, the only solid rampart of peace between nations, because "open religion" teaches the universal fatherhood of God, the universal brotherhood of man, the duty of each man to respect and love all his brothers, to build with them the terrestrial city so that men can prepare themselves there, in the best conditions, to enter one day into the heavenly city, the kingdom of the elect, the Father's home.

Would that this appeal — the appeal of all believers the world over — were heard by a vast number of people! Only on this condition can the human race escape perhaps from the untold catastrophes that grow daily more menacing.

[19] "Nisi Dominus aedificaverit domum, in vanum laborant qui aedificant eam" *(Ps*, 126, 1*)*.

If someone objects that, in spite of this attempt to reveal to him the "hidden God", he is still hesitant about meeting and adoring God, I ask him to say the *Pater of the unbeliever*:

"Our Father, if you exist, I dare turn to you. If you exist, your name is holy: hallowed be it. If you exist, your kingdom is order, and also its splendour: thy kingdom come. If you exist, your will is the law of worlds and the law of souls: thy will be done in all of us and in all things on earth as it is in heaven. Give us, if you exist, our daily bread, the bread of truth, the bread of wisdom, the bread of joy, the supersubstantial bread promised to those capable of knowing it. If you exist, I owe you a great deal: vouchsafe to remit my debts to you, as I myself willingly remit others' debts to me. Henceforth do not desert me in temptation, but deliver me from all evil" [20].

[20] A.-D. SERTILLANGES, *Catéchisme des incroyants*, Paris, 1930, vol. I, p. 6.

SELECT READING LIST

This is not a "bibliography" in the technical sense of the word. A bibliography of this kind would be disproportionate to the scope of this essay. We mention a few works that illustrate or complete what has been said here.

On atheism:

H. DE LUBAC, *The Drama of Atheistic Humanism*, translated by E. M. RILEY. London, Sheed and Ward, 1949. (Meridian Books, 1963.) — This work treats of Feuerbach, Nietzsche, and Comte.

E. BORNE, *Modern Atheism*, translated by S. J. TESTER. London, Burns & Oates, 1961 (Faith and Fact Books, 90).

On the existence of God:

God, Man and the Universe. A Christian Answer to Modern Materialism, edited, with an introduction, by Jacques DE BIVORT DE LA SAUDÉE. London, Burns & Oates, 1954.

H. S. BOX, *God and the Modern Mind*. London, S.P.C.K., 1937. *The World and God: the Scholastic Approach to Theism*. London, S.P.C.K., 1934.

W. J. Brosnan, S.J., *God and Reason. Some Theses from Natural Theology*. New York, Fordham U.P., 1924 (reprint 1943). *God Infinite and Reason. Concerning the Attributes of God*. New York, The America Press, 1943.

H. de Lubac, *The Discovery of God*, translated by Alexander Dru. London, Darton, Longman and Todd, 1960.

R. Jolivet, *The God of Reason*, translated by Mark Pontifex. London, Burns & Oates, 1958 (Faith and Fact Books, 15).

E. L. Mascall, *He Who Is*. London, Longmans, 1943. *Existence and Analogy: A Sequel to «He Who Is»*. London, Longmans, 1949.

M. Pontifex, O.S.B., *The Existence of God: A Thomist Essay*. London, Longmans, 1946.

E. Sillem, *Ways of Thinking about God. Thomas Aquinas and some recent Problems*. London, Darton, Longman and Todd, 1961.

On the problem of evil:

C. S. Lewis, *The Problem of Pain*. London, Bles, 1940.

M. C. D'Arcy, S.J., *The Pain of this World and the Providence of God*. London and New York, Longmans, 1953.

P. Siwek, *The Philosophy of Evil*. New York, Ronald Press, 1951.

H. S. Box, *The Problem of Evil*. London, Faith Press, 1934.

INDEX

Persons

Subjects

Imprimé en Belgique   (620)
par l'Imprimerie Nauwelaerts. Louvain